Four Girls in Europe

Four Girls in Europe

My Tour of England and the Continent, October, 1900 - September, 1901

Clarissa Sands Arnold

Edited by

Deborah Stewart Weber

Deborah Stewart Weber

iUniverse, Inc.
New York   Bloomington

Four Girls in Europe
My Tour of England and the Continent,
October, 1900 - September, 1901

iUniverse books may be ordered through booksellers or by contacting:

iUniverse
1663 Liberty Drive
Bloomington, IN 47403
www.iuniverse.com
1-800-Authors (1-800-288-4677)

ISBN: 978-1-4401-8658-5 (pbk)
ISBN: 978-1-4401-8659-2 (ebk)

Printed in the United States of America

iUniverse rev. date: 1/14/2010

"To think we are really across the Atlantic and have but to look around to find ourselves hurrying to be off the Steamer onto the tug to be brought into Liverpool!"

Clarissa Sands Arnold, October 27, 1900.

Great Britain

Table of Contents

Preface ix

An Introduction..xi

A Map of the Tour xvi

The Itinerary: October 20, 1900 - September 16, 1901............. xix

PART I   * England   1

PART II   * Paris, France   23

PART III * Italy   37

PART IV   * Germany, The Netherlands, Belgium & The Rhine   113

PART V   * Switzerland   176

PART VI   * Return to Paris & Home   204

An Afterword… 217

A Brief Biography * Clarissa Sands Arnold 219

The Endnotes...229

Works Cited..235

Preface

Almost a decade ago, while living in Southern Germany with my husband, I received a notice from the local Customs Office in Freiburg that they were holding a package mailed to me from the United States. The package was determined to be of some value, and I would most likely have to pay a duty to gain its possession. I knew what it was. I had been awaiting the arrival by post of two volumes, written by my great-grandmother, Clarissa Sands Arnold Stewart, while on a tour of Europe when she was a young woman, 1900 to 1901. My parents had recently asked me if I would be interested in trying to decipher her writing in the two journals, and transcribe them for the family.

When I went to collect the books in Freiburg, I had to explain in my meager German, that they were not books of value to anyone but my family, and that they had not been sent to me for commercial purposes. They were part of my family's history only and would not be for sale. The customs agent finally let me have the books without paying any duty, but with a warning about the value of what I had in my hands, which he suspected was very great.

Ten years later, I have finally finished deciphering and transcribing Clarissa's account of her year in Europe traveling with a party of three other girls and two older women. Her writing became easier for me to read as I progressed through the two volumes and on completion of the transcription, I decided that the text would be so much more meaningful if the finished book, or whatever it was going to become, was annotated. The diaries could be read just as they were, word for word, and they would be interesting. But with some background information one can more fully appreciate the complexities of travel one hundred years ago, and also gain some familiarity with the historical and political events in Europe at this time, which helps to bring the story to life.

I have inserted many notations directly within the text, striving to interrupt the narrative as little as possible, when I felt that the story could be quickly enhanced by a brief reference to explain a word, historical fact or event. I also included the complete names of the many artists Clarissa notes in her writing, with the dates they lived or the date of a particular work, because I believe it to be important to clarify what works and artists were noted by Clarissa, her companions and their guide in 1900. When a longer explanation was needed, the reader is asked to refer to the Endnotes at the end of the narrative under the specific chapter headings.

My main sources for research while transcribing the Diary, were the guidebooks most often referred to in Clarissa's written record, Karl Baedeker's *Guidebooks of England and Europe*, all dating from the late 1890's up to 1901. These books proved to be invaluable in looking up the sites and museums they visited, the hotels and pensions where they stayed, the tea rooms and cafés where they ate, and the stores where they shopped. Especially when I could not read a specific word or description in her text.

Direct quotes from the Baedekers also serve to set the scene in a particular country, in that time. The Baedekers used by Clarissa and the rest of her party were written specifically for the English and American tourists who were flocking to Europe at the turn of the nineteenth century and seem quite formal, perhaps a bit prim and proper. They read somewhat like lectures, but are really great reading, the volumes brimming with useful and interesting information.

Explanations and additions from Baedeker or other sources are separated from Clarissa's own words with brackets. Where parentheses are used they were placed within the text by Clarissa herself. I have also bracketed words that proved to be totally illegible and I could not determine the word from the text.

I am extremely happy my parents, David and Marilou Stewart, asked me if I would be willing to work on Clarissa's journals. It has been an educational and rewarding pastime. They also were integral in researching her history and supplying the pictures for the Biography at the end of this volume and were so generous with their encouragement and advice. Thank you.

I would also like to thank a few of my friends: Martha Fullerton, for her careful read, edit and thoughtful comments; Alison Richards for her wonderful visual interpretation of the journey by producing, *A Map of the Tour*; and Catherine and Stephen Thurman and Alexandra Johnston-Saab, for their advice and assistance, whenever I asked for help.

Finally, to my husband, Gary, for support, encouragement and the gift of time… thank you.

Deborah Stewart Weber, 2009

An Introduction

On October 20, 1900, Clarissa Sands Arnold set sail from New York City for England and Europe on what would become the adventure of her lifetime. Over the next 332 days, traveling with five other women, she toured seven countries, slept in thirty-seven hotels and pensions, hiked in the Alps of Switzerland and the hills of England and Germany, drank the waters, bathed Turkish style, lunched among the ruins of Pompeii and thoroughly enjoyed many a German beer, Italian Asti, or glass of Swiss wine. A journey of this length and scope would be an extravagant trip today, but in the latter half of the 19th and early 20th centuries such a journey became almost a rite-of-passage for young men, and eventually young women, of an increasingly prosperous middle class from the United States.

When Clarissa and her "Party" set sail for Europe, steam-powered sailing ships were crossing the ocean in just over a week and the modernization of Europe's transportation system with an ever more integrated and sophisticated train network was making travel between the different cities of Great Britain and The Continent faster and easier all the time. The advent of companies dedicated to servicing and organizing this travel in the mid 19th century (Thomas Cook & Sons of London) and the increasing availability of published guidebooks, such as those published by John Murray and Karl Baedeker in their *Handbooks for Travelers*, allowed the novice tourist the means to guide and educate him or herself while traveling through the sites and museums of Great Britain and Europe (Stowe, *Going Abroad*).

The desire and curiosity to see and experience the Old World was fueled by popular novels and travel writings of American authors Nathanial Hawthorne, Mark Twain and others, who by writing and romanticizing their time abroad, excited and encouraged their readers in the United States to go and see Great Britain and Europe for themselves. Experiencing Europe first-hand was to become the "finishing" of American upper middle class youth before they got down to the business of real life; work and raising a family.

There was a standard tour, stopping for extended stays in the major cities of France, Italy, Germany and Great Britain, where one could visit the great museums and cathedrals and gain some appreciation for the works of the Great Masters in person while also experiencing a country's history and culture. The young people were usually accompanied by parents or guides, who insulated them from contact with the local populace, especially the young women. The city stays were relieved with sojourns in points of natural beauty for rest, relaxation and walking.

The travelers stayed in hotels and pensions that guaranteed a certain level of service and comfort, with particular hotels often frequented by clientele from one nationality, as is often noted in the Karl Baedeker *Guidebooks*. They passed their days when not being educated and informed about the local art, architecture and history, exchanging information about where to go, what to see, who was "in town", and presenting engraved visitation cards as a record of their "call".

Clarissa's trip was to follow this formula exactly and she documented her sojourn in England and Europe in diary, scrapbook, and picture album. The Diary is her account of the day-to-day joys, frustrations (at times) and wonders of what a journey of eleven months would have been like for a young woman in 1900. The Scrapbook is filled with ticket stubs, pamphlets, receipts and mementos from the journey. The Picture Album, which she titled, *Four Girls in Europe*, is filled with photos of Clarissa and the other members of her Party on their journey. I am so glad she took the time to write, almost every day, about what she saw, thought, did, ate, read and learned. She strove to become educated about what she was experiencing, and her Diary served as the means for committing to memory the art and historic sites visited.

Her account also illustrates the realities of young women traveling in 1900. Their evenings, when not attending an opera, play or musical performance, were passed working on mending or needlework while listening to one of the group read aloud either from a guidebook, usually Baedeker, or some author or traveler's account of what the group had just experienced or was to visit the next day. They also read popular novels that were set in the country where they were touring, and so served to enrich and romanticize their experiences. Other evenings they were occupied with playing games, dancing and writing letters.

The logistics of their travel were so cumbersome. Baskets, trunks, books, all to be transported with the women or, with the larger "hold-all" trunks, shipped ahead of the party to be at a location when they arrived for an extended stay.

Meals were almost exclusively eaten at the hotel or pension where they were currently lodging. Accommodation generally included three meals a day, whether they ate them or not. Restaurant meals were uncommon for the women, except for tea or coffee and cake in a café or tearoom. On day excursions the hotel or pension packed a picnic basket for the group and perhaps only coffee and dessert might be enjoyed in a restaurant or hotel along the way.

Clarissa was twenty-three at the beginning of her journey and the eldest of the "Girls". The Party was made up of three other young women of about her own age and station; Misses Marion and Leslie Buckingham, sisters from Boston, nineteen and seventeen respectively, and Miss Mary Sawyer, also of Boston and eighteen at the time of the trip. The girls were accompanied by two older women; Mrs. Charlotte Elizabeth Hurd, Clarissa's companion-housekeeper, whom Clarissa fondly refers to in her Diary as "Auntie", and who had lived with Clarissa since the death of her father in 1890. The other member of the party was Miss Charlotte S. Cadwell, or Miss C., as Clarissa refers to her most of the time. In Clarissa's obituary, it states that Miss Cadwell had been an instructor at the college Clarissa attended from 1894 to 1896, Lasell College, near Boston, but Lasell has no record to that affect, so I do not know how Clarissa became acquainted with her prior to their journey. Miss Cadwell was their guide and teacher during the year abroad, instructing them in all matters academic and cultural, while handling all of the practical particulars and logistics connected with their travels. It is apparent that Clarissa was very fond of her and valued her knowledge and advice throughout the year.

They sailed for England on October 20th, 1900, aboard the *Royal Mail Steamship Lucania* of the Cunard Steamship Company, departing from New York City. The Party traveled first class, landing in Liverpool, via Queenstown (Cobh), Ireland, seven days later.

When launched in 1893, the *Lucania* was the largest passenger liner afloat and, until 1898, the fastest. The *RMS Lucania* offered... "The most luxurious 1st Class passenger accommodation available...Victorian Opulence at its peak." (Wikipedia. "RMS Lucania". http://en.wikipedia.org/wiki/RMS_Lucania)

Stuck into Clarissa's Scrapbook, I found a note, not in Clarissa's handwriting, so perhaps written by Miss Cadwell. This note is a list of proposed sites to be visited. Some are underlined and I am not sure if by Clarissa before, during or after her travels. I include it here as a glimpse into what they had before them.

List of Proposed Places
Liverpool, Chester, Leamington, Stratford-on-Avon, Kennilworth Castle,
Warwick, Oxford, London, Ely, Petersboro, Lincoln, York,
Fountains Abbey, Durham, Melrose,
Antwerp, Ghent, <u>Brussels,</u> Bruges, <u>Cologne,</u> The Rhine to <u>Maynce,</u>
<u>Heidelberg,</u> Baden Baden, Lucerne ,
Vitznau - headquarters for excursions about (two) weeks.
<u>Grindelwald</u> - the same length of time for excursions from there also.
Across to Germany by Lake Constance "The Passion Play" by the
Oberammergau peasants to be voted on by the party,
<u>Munich, Dresden, Berlin, Nuremberg,</u> Munich,
Bremer Pass to Verona, <u>Venice,</u> Padua - a days excursion,
Bologna, <u>Florence,</u> Siena, Orvieto, <u>Rome,</u>
<u>Naples</u> - about three weeks there for excursions.
Pompeii, Capri, etc, etc. - Rome, Pisa, Genoa,
Milan, <u>Paris</u> & home.
A month in <u>London, Paris, Rome, Florence, Munich</u> each & a month between
Dresden & Berlin.

The above is the list only of what is comprised generally,
& not the order of visits, as the date of sailing &
other circumstances regulate that, as well as the wishes of The Party.

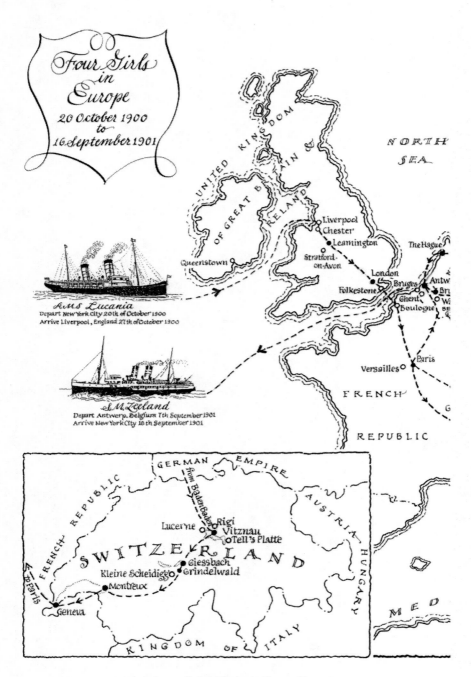

Four Girls in Europe

20 October 1900
to
16 September 1901

NORTH SEA

UNITED KINGDOM OF GREAT BRITAIN & IRELAND

Queenstown

Liverpool
Chester
Leamington
Stratford-on-Avon
London
Folkestone

The Hague
Antw
Bruges
Ghent
Boulogne
Br
W
BE

FRENCH

Versailles
Paris

REPUBLIC

G

RMS Lucania
Depart New York City 20th of October 1900
Arrive Liverpool, England 27th of October 1900

SS Zeeland
Depart Antwerp, Belgium 7th September 1901
Arrive New York City 16th September 1901

GERMAN EMPIRE

FRENCH REPUBLIC

from Baden Baden

AUSTRIA

SWITZERLAND

Lucerne
Rigi
Vitznau
Tell's Platte
Giessbach
Kleine Scheidigg
Grindelwald
Montreux
to Paris
Geneva

HUNGARY

KINGDOM OF ITALY

MED

A Map of the Tour * Great Britain

and Europe * 1900

The Itinerary

October 20, 1900   <u>New York City - Departure</u>
     Royal Mail Ship (RMS) Lucania,
     to Liverpool, England, via Queenstown, Ireland
     Days at Sea - Seven

October 27   <u>Liverpool, England</u>
     Arrival in England

October 27   <u>Chester, England</u>
     En route to Leamington

October 27 - November 2   <u>Leamington, England</u>
     The Lansdowne - Mrs. Kirk, Proprietor
     87 Clarendon Street
     Leamington Spa, Warwickshire

October 29   <u>Stratford on Avon, England</u>
     A Day Trip from Leamington
     November 2 - November 24   <u>London, England</u>
     Mrs. Phillips
     No. 10 Duchess Street, Portland Place

November 24 - December 15   <u>Paris, France</u>
     Hotel Louis Le Grand
     2 Rue Louis Le Grand

December 16 - December 22   <u>Milan, Italy</u>
     Hotel France
     Corso Victor Emmanuel

December 22	Genoa, Italy
Hotel Smith	
Vico Denegri	
December 23, 1900 - February 7, 1901	Rome, Italy
Hotel Molaro	
56, Via Gregoriano.	
February 8 - February 22	Naples, Italy
Hotel Britannique	
Corso Vittorio Emmanuele 133	
February 23 - February 25	Sorrento, Italy
Hotel d'Europe [Villa Nardi]	
East of the Small Marina	
February 25 - February 26	Naples, Italy
Hotel Britannique	
February 26 - February 28	Rome, Italy
Hotel Molaro	
February 28 - March 1	Orvieto, Italy
White Eagle Hotel	
March 1 - March 5	Perugia, Italy
Hotel Brufani Palace	
Piazza Italia, 12	
March 5 - April 3	Florence, Italy
Pension Camerini	
Via Castatone	
March 25	Pisa, Italy
A Day Trip from Florence:	
Lunch, Hotel Nettuno	
April 3 - April 14	Venice, Italy
Hotel Milan et Pension Anglaise	
Grand Canal, Opposite S. Maria Della Salute	
Calle Traghetto	
April 13	Padua, Italy
En Route to Verona: Lunch, Gold Horse	

April 14 - April 16 　　　Colombo D'oro (Golden Dove) 　　　Via Cattaneo	<u>Verona, Italy</u>
April 16 - May 6 　　　Pension Glockers 　　　5 Maximillianstrasse	<u>Munich, Germany</u>
May 6 - May 8 　　　Nurnberghof (Hotel/ Pension by the Bahnhof) 　　　Koenig Strasse	<u>Nuremberg, Germany</u>
May 8 - May 25 　　　Weber's Hotel 　　　Ostra-Allee 1	<u>Dresden, Germany</u>
May 17 　　　A Day Trip from Dresden: Dinner, 　　　Berg Kellar	<u>Meissen, Germany</u>
May 25 - June 10 　　　Mrs. Gerling's Pensionen 　　　Wilhelm Strasse 49	<u>Berlin, Germany</u>
June 10 - June 12 　　　The Grand Hotel Hartmann 　　　"Near the station"	<u>Hanover, Germany</u>
June 12 - June 14 　　　The Victoria Hotel 　　　Damrak 1-5	<u>Amsterdam, Netherlands</u>
June 14 - June 18 　　　The Toelast 　　　Groenmarkt	<u>The Hague</u>
June 18 - June 22, 1901 　　　Pension Kern-Loos 　　　Longue Rue d'Herenthal 35	<u>Antwerp, Belgium</u>
June 21 　　　A Day Trip from Antwerp	<u>Ghent, Belgium</u>
June 22 - July 1 　　　S. Bernard Private Hotel 　　　Quartier Leopold	<u>Brussels, Belgium</u>

June 26	<u>Waterloo, Belgium</u>
A Day Trip from Brussels	
June 28	<u>Bruges, Belgium</u>
A Day Trip from Brussels	
July 1 - July 2	<u>Cologne, Germany</u>
Dom Hotel	
Domkloster 2a	
July 2 - July 3	<u>Bonn, Germany</u>
Hotel Rheineck	
"At the pier"	
July 3	<u>The Rhine</u>
A Day's Cruise on the Rhine, en route to Mainz from Bonn.	
July 3 - July 4	<u>Mainz, Germany</u>
Stadt-Coblenz Hotel	
Rhein-Strasse 49	
July 4 - July 5	<u>Heidelberg, Germany</u>
Darmstaedter Hof Hotel	
"Near the station"	
July 5 - July 9	<u>Baden-Baden, Germany</u>
Hotel Müller	
Lange-Strasse 26	
July 9 - July 29	<u>Vitznau, Switzerland</u>
Hotel & Pension Rigi-First	
July 11	<u>Lucerne, Switzerland</u>
A Day Trip from Vitznau	
July 20	<u>Rigi, Switzerland and The Rigi Kulm</u>
A Day Trip from Vitznau	
July 24	<u>Tell's Platte, Switzerland</u>
A Day Hike from Vitznau	

July 29 - July 30 The Giessbach Hotel	Giessbach, Switzerland

July 30 - August 10
     Hotel Pension Burgener
     Berner Oberland
	Grindelwald, Switzerland

August 4 A Day Hike from Grindelwald	Kleine Scheidigg, Berner Oberland, Switzerland

August 10 - August 15
     Hotel Pension Breuer
     Bonport, Montreux-Vernex
	Montreux, Switzerland

August 15 - August 20
     Pension Richardt
     Rue de Montblanc 8
	Geneva, Switzerland

August 20 - September 6
     Hotel Lord Byron
     No. 6 rue Lord Byron
	Paris, France

August 31 A Day Trip from Paris	Versailles, France

September 6
     Hotel St. Antoine
     Place Verte 40
	Paris to Antwerp

September 7, 1901 The Voyage Home: Antwerp to New York.	*The Steamship Zeeland*
September 16, 1901 Days at Sea - Nine	New York City

The Tour: 332 Days

"The Party" is Complete!

Part I * England

"Expenses. The cost of a visit to Great Britain depends of course on the habits and tastes of the traveler. If he frequents first-class hotels, travels first-class on the railways, and systematically prefers driving to walking, he must be prepared to spend 30-40s (shillings) a day or upwards… Persons of moderate requirements, 20-25s…while the pedestrian of moderate requirements may reduce his expenses to 10-15s.

Money. The English gold coins are the sovereign or pound equal to 20 shillings. Foreign money does not circulate in England and it should always be exchanged on arrival. A convenient and safe mode of carrying money from America or the Continent – is in the shape of letters of credit or circular notes readily procurable at the principle banks.

Passports are not necessary in England." Baedeker, *Great Britain*. 1897, 1-2.

*

Liverpool - Chester - Leamington.   October 27, 1900.

To think we are really across the Atlantic and have but to look around to find ourselves hurrying to be off the Steamer onto the tug to be brought into Liverpool! At 9:45 in the morning we are landed, as the night was so very windy the water being left so rough it was impossible to come onto the pier and the passengers had to be transported.

We were all seated in the station until the baggage could be arranged alphabetically and in we went to the Customs Room as we thought to unpack as the officers might wish, but to our consternation not a thing was touched and we marched as pleased as punch to the carriages.

The driver put us in there, up on the top went all our baggage, the whole thing being drawn by one immense horse directly up to the London and N. Western Railroad to the hotel. Everything along the way did look so strange to us – beautiful large horses on all the carts – the signs and shops, and the most startling of all were those policemen, little less than telephone poles, with their caps held on by straps down below their mouths, and the dignity

1

of them was awe-inspiring to say the least. The tiny donkey and ponies also impressed us, and the two-story cars were odd.

We found we had some time to wait, so we were very comfortable in the hotel parlor while Miss Cadwell was busy attending to tickets, etc. By getting tickets thro' to London, the trunks were taken off at Leamington and we stopped in Chester for the day.

Such a revelation as that beautiful old city was! ["Chester … is perhaps the most quaint and medieval looking town in England." *Britain*, 274.] The glimpses of the cottages along the road out, did not even prepare us for what we were to see. After all running beyond the corner, we caught the funny little horse car and paid our fare to a conductor not more than fifteen years old I am sure.

We then went directly for lunch up in the funny row of buildings – the Rows or Arcade to [blank], where we had a most delicious luncheon of cold beef, excellent mashed potatoes, the most dainty rolls – luncheon rolls, then some of the famous Cheshire cheese and crackers with celery.

From luncheon we proceeded directly to the [Chester] Cathedral – our first glimpse of a real true English Cathedral and a feeling of reverence crept over us all, and almost of awe, where, after a glance around, Miss C. pointed out [to] us the principal divisions that we would find in nearly all the churches. After strolling about and going through the portico to the Refectory [Dining Hall for Monks from the 13th c.], we passed out through the side entrance to the back, where looking back we got an exquisite view of the building and yard with the light of the setting sun upon it.

Our walk along "the Walls" was very interesting passing the Phoenix Tower from which Charles I watched the Battle of Rowton Moor ["… circuit of the Walls is nearly 2 m and the paved footpath on the top, 4-6 ft. in width, affords a delightful walk…" *Britain*, 275].

The houses are most peculiar with their carvings, beams, etc.

After having tea at [blank] we went to a jewelers for little souvenirs of the place, then going to the station, left at 4, reaching Leamington at 8:15, where we had a very nice dinner at Mrs. Kirks, The Lansdowne, The Parade [87 Clarendon Street, Royal Leamington Spa, Warwickshire] and we nearly froze in our rooms for they have only fireplaces and but two in the drawing room and dining room. Our only light was from two candles in a huge room. The bed was like ice and we sent up a prayer of thanksgiving that we had a blanket along. I was tempted to put on my feather boa for warmth.

Leamington. Sunday, October 28, 1900.

Even when I awoke I was almost congealed, for I caught a severe cold on the Steamer. Our breakfast was at 9, and such good bacon as we had, but rank coffee, all muddy and black, but I drank it right along.

The morning was spent in reading, while the girls read, dinner at one when the English bachelor, Major Masters, carved. We did about the same in the afternoon, for we were all rather tired after our day to Chester, both mentally and physically for such a lot of brand new facts went into our noodles. It also rained, so we must prove ourselves fair weather Christians. About five, the Major appeared and he was so funny we were nearly convulsed and at table we all giggled. He returned after tea and asked Marion to play, which she consented to do, as we are the only ones in the house. When she was ready to begin he asked her if she could "turn over – alone" that nearly finished me. But in time he left and we all declared he made the evening pass quickly and he certainly was most refreshing!

A Day Trip - Stratford-on-Avon. Monday, October 29, 1900.

This is our day of days for we go to Stratford-on-Avon as a party of pilgrims to the Bard's resting-place!

After trying for money, which I finally obtained… [1]

We took the 10:40 train for Stratford, reaching there about 11:15 and starting immediately for Shottery, which is reached in fair weather by the most charming walk of a mile and a quarter through the fields. Every little way we would come to a gate opening like this [drawing] or to a real old stile where we had to step over the top of the fence; such lovely little lanes heading off and huge trees in a yellowish dress of foliage. Then all at once we came to the gate of an ideal English home belonging to the poorer class, the yard being filled with flowers, thatched roof, stonework floor, birds in the windows, the old well and the stone walk around the door in little broken fragments, and while we were drinking all the beauties of the picture, the dearest little child appeared in the doorway, all smiles but when the girls spoke, she vanished. Then the mother came with her and the girls snapped her picture with the child in her arms.

We then went to Ann Hathaway's home and such a bower of flowers as we found, roses, and all in bloom ["Anne Hathaway's Cottage is still standing here in substantially the same condition as when Shakespeare courted his future wife. It was purchased by the nation in 1892 for 3000£." *Britain*, 250]. A nice woman showed us through whose husband was a descendant. Mrs.

Baker, who was a great-great niece [and previously occupied the cottage], of whom I have the picture, having died last year from Shottery. After I begged for a rosebud, and such a beauty! we went directly to Holy Trinity Church [Stratford-on-Avon] where Shakespeare is buried. This is down by the river Avon, and is led up to by a walk, going through the "Lime Walk" which is surrounded by a churchyard. All the stones are covered with a green moss or mold.

We then saw the Harvard House [High Street, Stratford-on-Avon], which is one of the oldest. The school and church which Shakespeare attended, passing then on to the Red Horse Inn, where we saw Washington Irving's room and his belongings [American author, Irving, wrote an article about the town.]. We had luncheon at Shakespeare Hotel [Chapel St.], a main feature of which was pickled walnuts.

The Museum [Shakespeare Memorial Building] we passed on our way to Shakespeare's House, stopping at the Theater, which is to his memory, and seeing the beautiful monument [The Shakespeare Monument] by the side of it looking toward the Avon. Then we went to his house and were shown through it. The garden back was so pretty [the house "... in which the poet was born on April 23rd, 1564, is in Henley St.; it is now national property, and is kept in scrupulously good order." *Britain*, 248].

The Childe Fountain is beautiful and needs hours to fully appreciate it. The low places for the dogs to drink from I think are so humane [Shakespeare Memorial Fountain, presented to Stratford-on-Avon in 1887 by American philanthropist, George W. Childs].

The station is next, and we reach Leamington awfully tired, but did a bit of shopping, then drank tea, dressed for dinner and then went early to bed.

Here endeth a lovely day!

Leamington. Tuesday, October 30, 1900.

This is the day we have been looking forward to for a number of days and off we started in a wagonette about 9:30, and drove through the most beautiful country, and all looked like one large park all marked off by the hedges of hawthorn. As we drove through the gate the whole scene was like a dream. Before the carriage ran a deer and later we saw a herd of them run along the brow of the hill. The tree trunks were the largest things I ever saw and fully came up to the description of the English Oaks.

We drove along the road quite a distance lined on either side by the beautiful foliage and rhododendrons, till finally we came to an open space which was well filled with carriages and fine horses with their riders, and looking up on the rise of ground ahead of us we saw the end of the stone mansion, and before which scattered the red coated hunters and the hounds. At about eleven the procession started down the road toward us and across the bridge then on to the left. We followed as soon as possible, but they were soon lost in the woods, and after following some way, we turned and went up to Stoneleigh Abbey [large mansion erected in the 18th c.] and thro' the grounds consisting of between 14 and 15000 [?]. We could get a very good view of the castle and the stables were fine enough in construction to be dwellings.

By this time, it was pouring, but we had capes and umbrellas so we did not suffer at all, and reached the house by luncheon. In the afternoon Auntie and I went shopping in Leamington and had a fine time.

Leamington. Wednesday, Oct 31, 1900.

Oh, such a nice morning for all of the sights planned for today! Marion and I went out with Miss C. early and saw such cunning stuffed kittens, then we went to a florist's with Miss C. and went back to the "fernery" and such taste as someone displayed in the arrangement of the ferns in the rocks for the whole interior was lined with rocks and stones. Then from there we went down to the renowned Leamington Pump House [Royal Leamington Bath & Pump Rooms] and had a drink of the water, which is said to cure all the ails to which flesh is heir, but I thought it simply rank. It tasted like the water in which Irish moss has been soaked ["Leamington ... a well-built watering place... owes its prosperity to springs discovered here in 1797." *Britain*, 243].

Returning, we all started at eleven up on the top of the "tram", which was such fun to clamber up the little narrow winding stair, but I felt like a queen after I was once seated, for we could peek over the walls into the gardens and so see all the lovely varieties of roses, geraniums, holly hocks, holly trees and bittersweet growing up the sides of the houses, and such beautiful roses all climbing and in blossom. The Jasmine is so pretty on the walls, and the tops of many of the walls are simply covered with the English Ivy and so thick. Then in other parts we see holly hedges which are shiny and such a rich green.

The [Leycester] Hospital was very interesting being founded for old soldiers (Lord Dudley) by the Earl of Leycester in 1571 and but twelve soldiers are supported, each having two rooms for himself and all was so quaint. Of course it is the only thing of its kind in existence and being so old adds to the interest.

Soon after luncheon we started for Kenilworth Ruins, and with the beautiful day, sun out, our afternoon there is simply beyond words, so I am not going into detail but just remember our two hours - no, an hour and twenty minutes - and during that time the ruins became quite familiar and I must go there again as soon as I can come over again, for it would not be lost to spend a day there just absorbing the beauties of the country from the upper windows of the castle and then I will have read [Sir Walter] Scott's *Kenilworth*, [1821] and so make both the book and the ruins very real.

A Day Trip to Warwick Castle. Thursday, November 1st, 1900.

Today we have set apart for Warwick Castle. Auntie seemed so tired after yesterday that she had about decided not to go with us, but Miss C. said it was not a hard trip so both she and Mary, who has trouble with her tooth, put on their wraps and off we started about 10:30. We wanted to go on top of the "tram" but it was so damp we stayed inside, and after a ride of two miles perhaps, we came to the wall, which is but a short distance from the hospital we were at yesterday. The lodge at the gate is nothing remarkable but the driveway is a dream, as it is cut through the solid rock whose sides are lined with English Ivy and drooping shrubs and as it winds around it seems like a fairy story.

Finally, after the last curve, the view of the castle bursts upon us – and we see Caesar's Tower and almost opposite it we see Guy's Tower. The remains of the old moat are nearly filled with different shrubs and in the spring must be beautiful. We passed under the arched gateway leading to the court of the greenest grass, and here and there a peacock pecking away. We walked through here, around to the gardens and into the conservatory where the wonderful Warwick Vase [copy of a classical Roman vase] stands. This was brought from Tivoli and belonged in Hadrian's palace. It is said to be one of the most valuable art treasures to be found from Italy. Then going back to the part of the building, which is in use, the Guide showed us through a lot of rooms and relics, also pictures. The Earl and Countess of Warwick and Lord Brook, their son, who is 18 and just back from So. Africa, live here.

We tried to get into the Beauchamp Chapel [Church of St. Mary, Warwick], but as it is All Saints, services were being held in St. Mary's Church, so we did not wait but Marion, Leslie, Miss C. and I returned after luncheon and were so glad we did.

Auntie and Mary got their basket trunks and ours were ordered.

Leamington - London. Thursday, November 2, 1900.

"Expenses. The cost of a visit to London depends, of course, on the habits and tastes of the traveler.

Season. The "London Season" is chiefly comprised within the months of May, June and July, when Parliament is sitting, the aristocracy are at their town residences, the greatest artistes in the world are performing at the Opera…

Restaurants. English cookery, which is as inordinately praised by some epicures and *bons vivants* as it is abused by others, has at least the merit of simplicity, so that the quality of the food one is eating is not so apt to be disguised as it is on the Continent… At the first-class restaurants, the cuisine is generally French …". Baedeker. *London*. 1898, 1-13.

*

Today we leave Leamington for "Town", and although we had a fine time there and Mr. and Mrs. Kirk were as nice as could be, still I was so anxious to see what London was like that I did not mind leaving at all. Miss C. went down in the afternoon and ordered our compartment to be saved for us, which the Railway Co. does for six. So at 9:30 we left the house for the 10 o'clock train, and they couldn't get a 3rd class carriage and the guard asked Miss C. if she would be vexed should he give her a 2nd class for the same money and it's needless to say we came 2nd.

About 12:55 we reached the "Town" and we were all smiles from top to toe, so in and on we piled and drove to Mrs. Phillips, No 10 Duchess St., Portland Place, N., near the Langham Hotel and it looks like a fine place. Auntie and I have a palatial room on the second floor, which is fine, for it's very large and beautifully furnished. Then we have gas, too.

After we unpacked, we danced out to see the shopping district and look in the windows, which are one glare of beauty, and are so alluring we could hardly get by. We walked down Regent St. and went all through Liberty's, which is so tempting, but we aren't going to buy much till we return [Liberty's; fashionable English department store since 1875, 142 & 218 Regent St. *London*, 24].

When we had seen a lot, we turned down Piccadilly Circus and turned off and went in for tea and we were nearly convulsed over our cake buns etc. … Mary and Marion were rich. Then up we came thro' Bond St., and if we didn't feel grand marching up as if we "owned the Standard Oil Trust" to our house and after dressing we went down to dinner and every one stared at us and when they got thro' we stared back at them, and a lot are all right. I think there are about 25 here, a good many foreigners etc., which make it interesting to watch.

London. Saturday, November 3, 1900.

Breakfast is at nine, and it is just what I love to get all slept out, and I am ready to get up when it is time.

We went this morning to the National Gallery [established by an act of Parliament in 1824] up Trafalgar Square riding in one of the noted London busses for they have no cars here.[2]

We tried to get a general idea of the "lay of the land" and then we are to take it up room by room and study the paintings of each artist separately and get each impressed in our minds. I know I shall be glad of the little I did do in History of Art. It was just a drop in the bucket, but all these things do not seem quite so new or the names so unpronounceable as otherwise they would have. Auntie and the others got terribly tired, but for some reason I seemed to stand it the best of any, and was ready to start out after luncheon for the House of Parliament, but the weather was so dark and doubtful that Miss C. thought we had better go the National History Museum and those beautiful little humming-birds made a lasting impression for the rest was more or less familiar to me. There were about sixty-five cases of just those birds – The Gould Collection. We later had tea and came home [The Gould Collection; taxidermist John Gould, exhibited in 1851 at the time of the World Exhibition in London].

London. Sunday, November 4, 1900.

In the morning we all went down to the Foundling's Hospital, and attended service there, which was so impressive. The Hospital [founded, 1739] is such a great and good institution as it takes within its walls only such children as are known to be represented, and gives them a home until they are fifteen years old, and then sends them out into the world with a good start in life and on the road to become good men and women.

We sat in the gallery opposite the children, who filled the other corresponding side, and in all there are about five hundred.

After the service we went through some of the rooms and saw the keyboard to the organ, which was given to them by Handel and he also wrote music for the institution on several occasions.

From there we went in to see the boys at their dinner and one could not help shedding a tear or two when they all came marching in and then sang the blessing, for the little fellows were so pretty and well taken care of. After we had watched them a while we went to see the little girls and some of them are beauties.

London. Monday, Nov. 5, 1900.

The people all went to Westminster in the AM and to the British Museum in the PM, but I stayed in all day.

London. Tuesday, November 6, 1900.

Today really has not been a real brain splitting one, but we have had a good time. Miss C. went out early to see about seats for the parade on Friday and did not get back to go out with us until 11:10 but we went to the [National] Gallery and went around and so brushed up some of the dim points of last week. Of course every time we go, some of the important facts we become more sure of. It is a most overwhelming thought that we are really standing before the very works of those wonderful men who lived so many hundred years ago and whose works are among the world's most treasured art that remain.

In the afternoon Auntie and I went shopping and it seemed quite like our tours in Boston. We had pretty good success as a whole and I do hope the waist Auntie ordered will be nice!

In the morning we had a note from Miss Ivyes and she wants us to come to spend Sunday with her, but I rather think we won't go for fear we will miss something we should be sorry to, so I fancy we will wait until our return if she wants us to come then [The intention of the Party was to make the return voyage on the *RMS Lucania* at the end of their year of travel.].

London. Wednesday, Nov. 7, 1900.

McKinley is elected and that is all we know, still that is enough to satisfy us [William McKinley was elected for a second term, defeating William Jennings Bryan on November 6, 1900.].

This morning we started out and first went down to St. James Palace to the Friary Court and saw the Change of Guard at 11:00 [Friary Court. The new Sovereign of Great Britain first appears here before his/her subjects on assuming the throne]. That was most interesting and the men did look perfectly ridiculous in those fur hats that just about covered their whole heads and red coats with all the paraphernalia, and the way they strutted up and down was killing. The Cold Stream Band was there, consisting of fifty or more pieces, and called the crack band in the army. In the same locality is Marlborough House, Buckingham Palace, White Hall, York House, etc.

After the Change of Guard we went to the Flower Show at the Aquarium. It reminded me of the Chrysanthemum Show in Boston. The fruits were fine, but I did not care especially for it.

The four of us were in the Nat. Gal. for a couple of hours this PM. Mary and I went around together and during the early part the thing in general seemed like one huge joke, but finally we settled down and learned a lot before we came out and saw so much to think of and try to study out for ourselves. Miss C. came for us after hunting for a window to use on Friday for the Parade.

We had hare for dinner and Leslie and I had such a laughing time before we were through that I was really quite ashamed of ourselves but "Miss Patty" came and patted us and said that was just what they all enjoyed. Miss Phillips also did not mind but liked it, too.

Then, all came in our room & Miss C. read aloud about the pictures etc.

My green shirtwaist came home and it fits very well, much to my delight.

London. Thursday, November 8th, 1900.

Today we had our first ride on the top of a London bus and it was a great experience to us all. The only trouble with our front seat was the cigarette smoke from the driver. I don't mind the smoke from an American but I do draw the line when it comes to a driver!

We rode and rode and finally after going through Cheapsides, past "Bow-Bells" Church of which it was said, to be "swagger" [true Cockney or true Londoner. *London*, 131], one should be born within hearing of them [the bells of St. Mary le Bow Church, designed by the architect, Sir Christopher Wren], High Holborn St., etc. We got out by the Lord Mayor's House by the PO, Bank of England and in the neighborhood of a number of state buildings.

Then we walked down to "The Tower", which was truly astonishing, for I had a most indistinct idea of the whole plan [" The ancient fortress and gloomy state-prison of London, and historically the most interesting spot in England." *London*, 152]. When we reached there, it struck me so forcibly that we were really in London. At the gate the girls had to give up their cameras and chatelaine [decorative belt hook or clasp, worn at the waist] but we were allowed to carry umbrellas, which seemed incongruous. I am going to get a plan to paste in which will save space. I was so sorry not to have gotten on the [London] Bridge, for the view must be fine from the upper bridge.

This afternoon we started for our first drive and it was delightful. We went through swell shopping districts out to Hyde Park and drove round and round and saw some stylish turnouts but all the real important personages are out of town at this season, but it was quite enough for the first dose. Auntie could not go and I was so sorry, but we reached home by five and had tea and read our home letters.

London. Friday, November 9, 1900.

We had an early start for the Albert Memorial [Monument to Albert, the late Prince Consort of Queen Victoria] and in going rode on the top of a bus part of the way in a shower. But they are very nice here and only last a moment, so no one minds them. I did not care especially for it but still the frieze about the base was interesting for it consisted of the sculptors and artists, etc. arranged, which gave a good idea of the dress of their time and each had some symbol by him as a clue. Then the groups at the corners were fair, all but America, which was simply absurd as it consisted of a group of three Indians, one on a buffalo with Liberty at the front checking the progress with her wand, but the features were no more characteristic of the Indian, altho' it was done by Bell [John Bell, English Sculptor, 1812-1895].

We had an early luncheon and started for the Lord Mayor's Procession.[3] Having a fine balcony on the Strand directly opposite the Charing Cross Monument [to view the parade]. [The Monument was] erected by Edward I [1239-1307] when his wife was removed to Westminster. One of the halts was made there and at each, the King erected a cross and with the inscription meaning Charming Queen, which has been corrupted to Charring Cross.

At quarter to three the street was a perfect sea of humanity and such an interesting and pitiable crowd as a whole. One mayor wished to do away with the Parade and devote the funds toward an immense dinner for the poor, but the lower class rose up in arms at the tho't, so since, the Parade is a regular occurrence and it seemed as if everything that marched was out as the list shows [Scrapbook]. The procession took half an hour to pass and I am so glad we could see it. After it was by we had to wait some time for the crowd to dispense before starting home.

We were home so early that all felt uneasy, but tea was served soon and then a "hurdy-gurdy" came by and struck up and we all went on the balcony and motioned for him to play just under us. While Mary rushed up for some change, the maid next door came out to order him off, for they must have been having a reception there. Mary came down in the meantime and before she knew of the tragic situation, threw six pence to him, which seemed a sin to waste.

That wasn't enough: so Leslie asked Miss C. if she minded did we go around the corner on Regent St. to do a bit of shopping, so off we started to forage for fruit, candy and cake. The fruit was out of the question, but we found cake etc., and bought a round fruitcake with nuts on top, macaroons, and four kinds of chocolates besides barley candy in a cunning glass jar. Our shopping proper consisted of a cake of R & G Soap and toothpaste. Tonight we are counting on a feast in the Bucks' room after listening to some reading.

London. Saturday, November 10, 1900.

This was another lovely morning, so off we started and at first went down to Covent Garden, which was lots of fun to see the carts and donkeys starting out with their loads of provisions. Then we went upstairs and saw the birds, snakes, fish, etc. [Since 1500's site of "London's principal vegetable, fruit and flower market." *London*, 227].

Our next stop was at St. Paul's Church [St. Paul's Cathedral, London's most prominent building, completed in 1710], which was very interesting, and I think I now have the parts of the church nearly straightened out in my mind. The Nave, North and South Transepts, Ambulatory, Choir, Triforium, Clerestory, Choir and Crypt.

The Crypt was such a weird place and on one of the first slabs we came to there sat a puss as happy and contented as you please. The guard unlocked the gates and let us through where we saw an endless lot of tombs including the Duke of Wellington, the base being designed by Landseer [F. C. Penrose; Edwin Henry Landseer was the sculptor of the lions in Trafalgar Square and is also buried in St. Paul's], which had a lion's head at each corner. Further along we came to the hearse made expressly for the Duke's funeral. It was a beautiful thing and drawn by nine horses. It seemed so foolish to spend so much on a thing to be used but once!

After hurrying back to luncheon, we started out and visited the Houses of Parliament. I was a bit disappointed, but probably because we only went through such a small part of the whole building, going in at the Victoria Tower entrance, up the marble stairs to the Queen's Robing Room, which is decorated by wall paintings, which reminded me of Abby's in the Library. From there we went to the Victoria Gallery, which was decorated by two beautiful paintings on glass [Daniel MacLise, 1806-1870], which seemed to nearly cover each wall, the subjects being *The Death of Nelson*, and *The Meeting of Wellington and Blücher*. Then came the House of Lords [House of Peers], in which was the beautiful seat where the Queen sits, on her right, the Prince of Wales [the Heir Apparent], and the sovereign's consort, on her left. In front of her is the Woolsack [Seat of the Lord Chancellor of the House of Lords; a red velvet cushion]. Next in order, is the House of Commons. Then we passed around to Westminster Hall, the oldest portion of the whole.

After coming out, we went around by the Corinthian Column [Westminster Column] into the Westminster School [St. Peter's College, founded by Queen Elizabeth in 1560] and Cloister and Inner Court.

Then Buszard's, for cake [Confectioners, Oxford Street. *London*, 19], home and dancing amongst ourselves, which was fine.

Sunday, November 11, 1900.

This morning we did nothing special but wrote letters, etc. Then in the afternoon we all went to Westminster [Abbey] for service. It was so very crowded that we had to go in to the South Transept and consequently could see very little of the main part of the Abbey. The singing was very fine and we all enjoyed it very much, but it wasn't quite up to my expectations, I must say.

Monday, November 12, 1900.

This morning we went down to the Portrait Gallery, which is joined to the National, only we went in by another entrance. The collection is fine, but I feel I have a very blurred idea of it all. We went through it all and Miss C. told us which were the best in each room and it made me desperate for like as not I would pick out one in my own mind and it wouldn't be right at all. To remember the artists is more then I possibly can do and so I am not going to try.

This PM I went and had a shampoo on Regent St. and this dapper looking man in a prince albert came forward and gave me the scrub. It seemed so absurd and he didn't put on any apron but just went at it without even rolling up his sleeves. It took him about an hour and [he] crimped it for me and for that charged a shilling extra, besides loosing my hair string and trying to cheat me out of most of my hairpins. The charge was 8/6, but it looked very well and I wish I could get it up that way myself.

Tuesday, November 13, 1900.

This was a great day, my first morning at the British Museum and it was perfectly fine. We took only a few rooms of course, seeing the mummies and their cases, which was so strange to see these bodies that were human beings in 1300 BC. As Miss C. says, it hardly seems as if we were born.

We first went into the "Elgin Marble Room," for there was the model of the Parthenon on the Acropolis of Athens and we got a very good idea of the form and different parts viz: pediment, or tympanum, triglyph, metopes, cella, and frieze. The Eastern Pediment is the best preserved which shows the rising sun at one end and the sinking moon at the other corner [The Elgin Marbles; sculptures from the Parthenon in Athens from 440 BC, which were transported to London in 1801-1803 by Lord Elgin, British Ambassador to Constantinople. *London*, 301].

From there we went to the 1st and 2nd Egyptian Rooms, and lots of jewelry and stones, i.e. intaglio [incised, negative image, for wax seals; opposite of a cameo] and cameos, The Portland Vase, etc. [1st c. AD cameo Roman vase, made of blue glass, which became an inspiration to glass and porcelain makers in the 18th c.]. Then just before leaving, I went into see the Mausoleum [Mausoleum at Halicarnassus, "... was reckoned among the Seven Wonders of the World." *London*, 304] and the "Rosetta Stone", which is the keystone to all Egyptian hieroglyphics and of course is very valuable [The Rosetta Stone; 196 BC stele, with carved text in three languages. Discovered in 1799 and part of the collections at The British Museum since 1802.].

The Tanagra Figures from Tanagra [Greece] are one of the most wonderful little figures [terracotta figurines, 4th c. BC].

Powell's Greece, for reference.

Wednesday, November 14, 1900.

This morning we all went down to the Law Courts through Chancery Lane to the old Gatehouse to Lincoln's Inn, built in 1518, which led into the old court, which is all built up around the barrister's rooms. After trying to get into the Chapel, we went over to Lincoln's Inn and into the dining room, which reminded me of Memorial Hall and such a nice Englishman showed us around through the Library, Counselor's Room and Drawing Room and then through a long hall where we could peek down into the kitchen. In the Hall there is a large picture by [William] Hogarth [1697-1764] and a beautiful one taking up the end of the dining hall by [George Frederic] Watts [1817-1904].

Then we went all around the new buildings into the Temple Church, which was most interesting and around at the side of the church where [Oliver] Goldsmith was buried [1774]. We then went to the Middle Temple Hall where the carvings are beautiful and from this Hall the Lincoln's Hall was copied, this one being built in 1535.

The guide took us all thro' the building, for tonight is Grand Night, where there is a great banquet in which all the ambassadors attend and from the window of the room to which the men adjourn for dessert & smoking, we looked out into the garden in which the red and white roses of the War of the Roses are said to have grown. In this Hall, Shakespeare's *Twelfth Night* was first acted on the little stage at one end. The table is also there which was given Queen Bess from the Armada by [Sir Francis] Drake. We afterwards went to the Embankment on the Thames, passing the Somerset House [The Embankments; Victoria, Thames, Albert. Constructed in the 19th century to cover tidal flats, sewers, utility lines, providing level ground for the construction of promenades, roads, parks and gardens. *London*, 147].

This afternoon we went to the "Zoo" and it was ever so nice [The Zoological Gardens, founded in 1826]. It reminded me of Barnum's[4], and the snakes were wonderful but I didn't look at them much, the longest being 24 feet.

Thursday, November 15, 1900.

This morning we saw the [Gustave] Doré Collection of Paintings [1832-1883] on Bond Street and I am sure I can never lose the image of that most beautiful masterpiece, *Christ Coming from the Praetorium* and really it seemed as if the artist must have been inspired. The others were beautiful, but that one stands out preeminent, and Auntie enjoyed them so thoroughly. We then went to the [Royal] Arcade [28 Old Bond Street], which is down Piccadilly and it was delightful to look at the beautiful things in all the shops there and it was such a temptation to spend every cent, which I did most successfully before I [ran out] on collars. Auntie and I took a hansom [two-wheeled horse-cab] home, for it was pouring and I do think that's such fun.

This afternoon we went to the Kensington Museum but saw such a tiny bit of it before the bell rang at four for us to go out. We saw the ivories, silver, carved wood boxes and such fascinating jewelry [South Kensington Museum; renamed The Victoria & Albert Museum in 1899 by Queen Victoria.].

We then went to the A. B. place on Piccadilly for tea where we first had tea on our arrival in London [A chain of Tea Shops called the ABC; Aerated Bread Co.].

We have been here nearly two weeks and I just love the mud, rain, crowds, push and everything that goes with London. 10½ for Irvil Paper. It's terribly cute, but now I don't dare send it to any one.

Friday, November 16, 1900.

Auntie and I stayed in all day as it was a horrid, rainy, muddy day and we were not sorry to be indoors. In the PM I started my Scrapbook but I don't think it is especially pretty for there is not color enough to the material to be bright.

Mrs. Vickery took Auntie's ticket for "Herod", which was very kind of her, for it would have been a shame if Auntie had been obliged to pay for it and not use it [ticket, Her Majesties Theatre, Haymarket, 5 Schillings, Balcony; Clarissa's Scrapbook]. Miss Vickery was able to get one on the same row and next to ours so we all dressed in our pretty things. I put on my gray for the first time, Mary her black and white foulard, Marion her pink and Leslie her gray and pink. Miss C., Leslie and Mary went in a hansom and Marion, Mrs. & Miss Vickery and I followed in a four wheeler and being our first night out we were crazy over London lighted, but it was not the light we have in America, being gas and very little electricity, but the colored lights dotted here and there made it most attractive.

"Her Majesty" is one of the best theatres in London ["… in the Haymarket, English Comedy and romantic drama." *London*, 64] and the entrance there seemed like NY, but instead of boys to hand programs, women in caps and white aprons were at the door and ushered. So many ladies were in low evening dress and the men are allowed to sit with their tall hats on until the curtain rises, which looked most inappropriate. Between the acts the maids passed through the aisles with tea, sugar & cream and candies on a salver, but the tea did not seem to be in great demand.

As to the play itself, I can't say I cared for it, because it was most harrowing and kept one nerved up to the last degree, which is not my idea of the theatre. The setting was most perfect and I imagine true to the time, 36 BC. The skylights were beautiful, especially the slow change and appearing of the stars, one by one, seemed natural. But the acting I did not like, as Miss C. says, when the English voice is a bit strained it is very disagreeable and the broadest English did not seem in keeping with a scene in Jerusalem and the details in acting were not so perfect as in America.

Saturday, November 17, 1900.

This morning we all went to Westminster to go through the Chapter House [Westminster Abbey], but as I had not been thro' the main, we all followed the guide who was just to start with a party. Our group stuck close to him and he was excellent but not being prepared I feel I have no clear picture in my mind of it, simply little snatches here and there and I am so sorry for I did want a perfectly clear picture of the Abbey to carry away, but next time I can do it. We went through the South Transept into St. Faiths Chapel, which is intended for silent prayer and has been open but a short time. From there we went by a small door to the Cloister Walk [13-15th cent.] about the Green in the Chapter House where the Monks used to meet to talk over the affairs of the monastery and then it was used as the House of Commons at one time. In the floor we saw the original drawing, supposedly, for the Rose Window in the North Transept, which is very fine, but we were told is to be taken out to be replaced by a memorial to The Duke of Westminster.

Miss C. stopped on the way home to get two little bouquets of violets and lilies of the valley for Mrs. and Miss Vickery before leaving us. They were lovely people who live in Devonshire and asked us to visit them on our way back. Mrs. V. said she could take three and Miss V. three, which was lovely of them to ask. I also found that Florence and Mrs. North [from Unadilla, N.Y.] had been here most of the morning and I was so disappointed not to see them but wrote them to come to tea Sunday and I hope they can.

We went to the Kensington Museum in the afternoon, going first to see Raphael's *Cartoons* for the tapestries in the Vatican which he did for Pope Leo X in 1513, but we could not see them at all as bookcases have been moved in there and cut off every chance of a distant viewing of them. I was disappointed [Raphael Santi da Urbino, 1483-1520; *The Cartoons*; preparatory drawings for a series of tapestries for the Sistine Chapel in Rome.].

We saw the wonderful miniature collection, the most noted being by [Jean] Petitot [1607-1691] and really it did not seem as if anyone could do such exquisite work. The Limoges Pottery is very beautiful. It is painted on brass or metal of some kind, which gives it a transparent appearance. [Leonard] Limousin [1505-1577] was the artist who first made it in Limoges, France, and we saw a great deal of the Grisaille or the gray work such as we saw in the Dome of St. Paul's [painting in shades of gray, emulating the relief in sculpture].

Andrea Della Robbia – blue and white

Lucca Della Robbia – fruits, and colored

[Della Robbia - family of Renaissance artists known for their sculpture and ceramics of glazed terra-cotta bas-reliefs, mostly of religious subjects.]

Three things to surely remember are–

Savoy Mirror, Jamnitzer Vase of silver (He is to Germany, what Chellrin [?] is to France) [Wenzel Jamnitzer 1508-1585], and the Gloucester Candlestick [from Gloucester Cathedral, 1110 AD].

In robes - Chasible-plain. Dalmatique sleeves and cape hood.

Monday, November 19, 1900.

As the girls [Marion and Leslie] were going out to Hampton [The Palace of Hampton Court] in the PM, Mary and I started out with Miss C. for Smithfield [Market-place]. We first went into the Court of St. Bartholomew's Hospital, which is one of the oldest institutions in London, which was founded by Rahere in 1123, and the present built in 1730 [Rahere; Court Minstrel and favorite of Henry the Ist]. The hospital contains over 675 beds and thousands are helped who come for migraine [?]. We saw an old man brought in, held by four policemen, who must have been in some accident. A statue of Henry VIII is over the entrance and on beyond, toward the church, is a tablet erected on the site of the burning of three protestant martyrs during the reign of Queen Mary.

Across the street is the entrance to St. B. Church [St. Bartholomew the Great], which was erected about the time of the founding of the hospital. It is a beautiful example of Norman work and the restorations are very good. This is the oldest church in London with the exception of the Chapel of the Tower.

From there we went and saw Pye Corner, where the great fire was stopped in 1666 near Cock Lane. Then we went through the Market and saw St. John's Gateway and where [Dr. Samuel] Johnson is said to have written.

The Charterhouse was next visited. Originally it was for the education of forty boys and the support of sixty men. Now there are sixty-five men there and each may have sixty schillings a year of his own. We passed through the entrance to the green and there a man took us through the Cloister, containing tablets to Roger Williams, [William] Thackeray and many others and to the Chapel. Then we went up the old staircase, quite nicely carved, to the Great Hall where we pushed out a door and saw the boy's school of 500, which is owned by the Merchant Tailor Co. The Dining Hall is well carved and considered a fine specimen of 16th cent. work. Coming home we passed through the Meat Market, which is a sight.

Miss C. and I went with Marion and Leslie to the bus. Then we took the 2-d Tube down to the Consulate's office to see if Auntie and I needed Passports to find that they were not necessary [Metropolitan, or Underground Railway, commenced carrying passengers in 1863. "The Underground Railways convey over 110 million passengers annually, or upwards of 2 million per week." *London*, 58].

From there we went into Barings [Bank, founded in 1762, 7-9 Bishopsgate Street, Within] and after doing a little shopping came home to get ready for *The Message from Mars*, which was really very funny because Hawtrey was so odd in himself [Sir Charles Henry Hawtrey, British stage actor and director, 1858-1923]. The moral was a strong one, showing this most selfish of men staying home from a party, much to the sorrow of his Aunt and fiancée, to read a scientific paper on Mars. He drops off to sleep and during his nap a messenger from Mars appears who scares him so he does all he suggests going through the most awful scenes of loosing Minnie, his house, money, etc. Finally he awakes and on their return they find him out aiding the inmates of a burning tenement and so changed on his arrival they hardly know him and "all live happily ever after." [The Message from Mars; Play written by Richard Ganthony in 1899, described as "A Fantastic Comedy in Three Acts," played in theatres for over 30 years and made into a silent movie in 1913.]

Walter held the kicking horse's hind leg! [Walter; an employee of Mrs. Phillips' boarding house.]

Tuesday, November 20, 1900.

In the morning we all went to the Hertford House, which is this beautiful collection, the result of three generations' gathering, the last of which left it to London, house and all [The Wallace Collection, Hertford House, Manchester Square]. Three years the city has been at work to get it in order and it is now open to the public [1900]. The collection includes armor plate, pottery, miniatures, furniture, stationary boxes, and a beautiful art collection. The house is around a court and is very near being a castle.

In the afternoon we went to Guild Hall [Council Hall of the City]. But it was so dark we couldn't see the woodwork in the ceiling at all in the large hall. The guard allowed us to go into the Gallery and see the images Gog and Magog [mythical creatures who were the traditional guardians of the city of London], which used to be carried in the Lord Mayor's processions. They were terrible looking creatures. From there we went into the Art Gallery where we saw some excellent pictures including [John Maler] Collier [1850-1934] & [Sir John] Gilbert [1817-1897].

Wednesday, November 21, 1900.

Auntie and I went driving out to Hyde Park for an hour in a swell four-wheeler.

In the afternoon Mary and Marion went with Miss C. to hear [Eugene] Ysaÿe (the violin player) [1858-1931] so Leslie and I were in part of the afternoon and then we went out to get some cakes, etc.

First we hunted all over the neighborhood and at last found a store where we bought a cunning tin stew-cup 3½ d [denarius, a penny]. We then went to Haywoods and got some macaroons, madeira cake and a penny loaf of bread for Auntie. When we reached home Walter said, "a gentleman in your room."

Everything and body rushed thro' my brain and when I opened the door there sat Mr. Juyrs [?]. He had met the Norths in the Gallery, who told him we were here, so he came up to call and stayed until six. It was very nice to see him again and we talked over everybody in town in whom he was interested. Auntie choked at dinner and Amy swatted her on the back so hard that I thought she would go right through the door, glass and all.

Thursday, November 22, 1900.

I did not go out with the girls but instead Auntie and I went down to Peter Robinson's [216-226 Oxford Street, women's fashionable clothing store] and I got another vest. Then we walked on to the glove store where she bought some gloves and I saw some fur lined ones that I shall take home as gifts to the various men I want to remember. In the PM, Auntie asked Marion to go for a ride with her so I went with the others to the British Museum. We saw some very old manuscripts, including St. Jerome's Bible, and a great many illuminated book leaves.

Friday, November 23, 1900.

Our last day at the Nat. Gallery, so we went around and tried to get some of the principal pictures fixed in our minds. The art students nearly monopolized the place with the easels and it was very interesting to watch them at work. On our way home we stopped in the bank and then I gave Auntie her Christmas gift after luncheon. We did not do anything special in the PM, but rested for our next day's trip.

Saturday, November 24, 1900.

I am truly thankful that our stay in London is over and to see some real true sunshine again will be bliss personified it seems to me. We had breakfast at 8:30 and at 9 all started off in the bus for Charring Cross Station for Paris via Folkestone to Boulogne [Boulogne, France; "Folkestone to Boulogne, twice a day, in 1½-2 hrs. (Railway from London to Folkestone in 2-4 hrs.)" *London*, 5].

Miss C. sent us all in the 1st class waiting room while she did some last things and when we came out I couldn't pay the woman her penny, but I did not have to stay, and so left her scolding away at a great rate. Then we all rushed out to the gateway expecting to be let right through and when he asked all round for our tickets and we just looked blankly at him. Finally he said in despair, "Well, who has got your tickets?" and Mary piped up "Miss Cadwell" as if he knew her. Then fortunately she appeared and we were saved.

Our trip to Folkestone was very comfortable and at 12:30 we reached the Channel. As soon as we got on board we went down and had a nice little lunch expecting to lose it all in no time, but we were very happily disappointed and none of us were a bit sick. The sea was so calm we couldn't mind it.

At 2:30 we reached Boulogne and had to say in the Customs House that we had nothing dutiable and so got through. We had a nice compartment to ourselves and I enjoyed the scenery all the way to Paris. The mistletoe in the trees was lovely and so were the tall slender trees. We got to Paris at 6:30 and so had to go to the Custom House with our trunks. Mine was the only one, besides Miss C's, that was opened. The first thing the officer did was to unearth my package that was done up in tinfoil and asked if it was "tea". I nearly burst out laughing, but Miss C. came to my rescue and said, "Not at all, not at all, quite different."

We then came in a bus that rattled from one side of the street to the other up to the [Hotel] Louis le Grand, 2 Rue Louis Le Grand, Emile Blut Prop. It was or is such a nice place. We are at the top floor and have our own salon and that first dinner shall I ever forget! So dainty and all served in courses and I tell you our eyes just stuck out! Then we had such nice rooms and the beds are comfortable and of course the rooms are pretty cool outside the salon, so capes and the steamer rug come in handy. We were just nicely in bed when we heard an uproar in the street, so both jumped up and rushed to the windows, but we just saw a crowd of hoodlums singing and cheering for Kruger, who just arrived that day, and his hotel is near our hotel.[5]

Part II * Paris

"Expenses. The cost of a visit to Paris depends of course on the tastes and habits of the traveler.

Language. For those who wish to derive instruction as well as pleasure from a visit to Paris, the most attractive treasury of art and industry in the world, some acquaintance with French is indispensible. The metropolis of France, it is true, possesses English Hotels, Eng. Professional men, English 'valets de place', and English shops; but the visitor who is dependent on these is necessarily deprived of many opportunities of becoming acquainted with the most interesting characteristics of the place.

Money. Banknotes of 5000, 1000, 500, 200, 100 and 50 francs. Coins, 100-40-20-10-5 francs. English bank notes are generally received at full value. The currency of Belgium, Switzerland, Italy & Greece is the same as that of France.

Season. Spring and Autumn are the best seasons for a visit to Paris.

Passports, are now dispensed with in France, but are often useful in proving a traveler's identity." Baedeker. *Paris*. 1900, xii – xiii.

*

Sunday, November 25, 1900.

And now for bliss! Breakfast in bed, which is the height of my ambition. About eight the waiter came in and put the tray on the table, with a long fat roll and a crescent on each plate, then a little pot of coffee, a pitcher of hot milk, butter rolled out in little balls and a sugar bowl. I had gotten up and washed so all I did was to put on my jacket kimono and slippers, put the tray on Auntie's bed table, drew up a chair for myself and then we went at it. I was so happy I simply couldn't help smiling to myself. Then I went back to bed and stayed till eleven when we dressed for breakfast [lunch] at 12:30 or "dejeuner" as they call it. That was just like luncheon. Mary's friend, Miss Allie, invited her to a tea in the PM.

One of the Girls, Miss Cadwell & Clarissa, Paris.

We had a regular Russian tea, which is in glasses and is fine. Miss C. bought a little box of fancy cakes, which was extra for the tea. Our salon looks very pretty with the large bunch of mistletoe in the center from the lights and the chrysanthemums.

Dinner is at 6:30 and I felt lost all day because I left my ink on the drawing room table in London and so lost it, to my sorrow. I went to bed early to have something to do.

Monday, November 26, 1900.

The same joy of eating in bed again this morning and it's as nice as ever. I didn't get up until 9:30 and then I didn't go out, for the girls went to their bank and brought letters.

In the PM, Miss C. and I went to my banker and drew and bought a notebook and pencil.

Then we walked around and looked in the windows & bought .40 spoons for our tea. Mary's friend called early, so we did not get out so very early, but it was just great to look in the windows and see all the lovely things.

Pirmir = Buttons [?] Berthe = chamber maid

Paul = waiter

We got terribly near getting into a Kruger crowd in front of his hotel and Miss C. hurried us along out of it because they can't tell us from the English whom they just hate. The night before there was a crowd out whom they tho't English and they began to hiss etc. making it so disagreeable for them. Then the crowd found they were Americans and they began to cheer and we were afraid if they spotted us we might be treated in the same way.

Had Fan's letter saying she had sent the soap by express, so we went to see if the bundle had come and it hadn't and probably wouldn't be here before next week and it most broke my heart. "Finis"

Tuesday, November 27, 1900.

This morning Auntie started out with us and we first went over to see the flowers at the Madeleine [Church of St. Mary Magdalen] or by it, walking around to the front way entered and stood by the door a few moments for there was a service. It is called the most beautiful edifice in Paris with its beautiful Corinthian columns. In the colonnade are niches containing statues. The bronze doors are very fine containing subjects of the Ten Commandments.

Then Auntie came home and we walked down Avenue de l'Opera to the [Grand Magasins du] Louvre, where Miss C. bought some gloves. As we were coming out there was a rush to the door and there went Kruger by followed and proceeded by a mounted guard. He was bowing and scraping at a great rate, I really think I only saw his driver's hat, but then...

The Palais-Royal was such fun for the shops were fascinating. It was there we saw the dogs' outfits, pretty posters and such things [Fashionable in the late 18th & early 19th centuries, "The Palais-Royal, long a favorite rendezvous of visitors to Paris, is now becoming gradually more and more deserted." *Paris*, 60].

In the PM we went over to the Panthéon etc. over thro' the Place du Carrousel to the Pont Royal Bridge then walked a way till we came to the Panthéon, which is such a large memorial in the shape of a Greek cross to the Memory of Genevieve [422-512 AD], the Patron Saint of Paris. The walls are decorated with beautiful paintings giving incidents of her life, also of Jean d'Arc and Louis XIV.

We then walked around to the side and saw the belfry - the only part remaining of the convent as it was in her time - to the St. Etienne-du-Mont Church, where we saw her Reliquary [vessel containing St. Genevieve's remains] and the Rood Screen [a carved screen in stone or wood used to separate the clergy from the parishioners], which is very elaborately carved of white stone.

Wednesday, November 28, 1900.

We all started at about two for the Art Gallery of the Louvre through the Pavillon de Rohan to the [Leon] Gambetta Monument [Statesman, 1838-1882]. He was a great orator and writer and his friend, Madame Adams, has gone on with his works and is said to be the only woman whose salon teas come near to the gatherings of the famous men years ago [Parisian Salons; fashionable gatherings of men & women for intellectual discussions covering politics and art, etc.].

We also passed by the Statue of Lafayette, which was unveiled on the last 4th of July and given by the DAR [Daughters of the American Revolution]. Then we passed under the [Pavillon Sully] to the oldest part of the Louvre where we saw the white circle within which stood the little house connected with the story of the origin [of the Palace] where the traps for the wolves used to be placed and could see where Francois I, Father of [Henri II], Louis XIII, XIV, and so much by Napoleon III and Catherine de Médici built.

Going in under the clock tower, or Pavillon Sully, to the Gallery of Apollo (Henry IV), we saw such lovely paintings in the Salon Carré, which contains the gems of the collection by Rembrandt, Titian, Veronese, Correggio, Raphael. Murillo's *Immaculate Conception*. Da Vinci's *Mona Lisa*. Veronese's *Marriage at Cana* and so many others. I liked the Louvre better than the National Gallery in London.

In the afternoon all went to the Gobelin Factory of Tapestry [state manufacturers of tapestries since 1630] where it's all a man can do in one-day to make a piece six inches square. After, we came home and then walked to the burying ground of the Madeleine, where 800 Swiss soldiers are buried who defended the Tribunes and the dust of Marie Antoinette and Louis XVI is still there, the bones having been removed leaving simply the dust.[1]

Thursday, November 29, 1900.

Thanksgiving Day! In the morning we all went to the Notre Dame [Cathedral, 1163], which is so impressive inside, but I was terribly disappointed in the façade. The carving was wonderful to study and decipher the various designs, but for some reason the towers did not impress me as remarkable, tho' of course they are not finished as the law does not require unfinished churches to pay taxes. But the rear and the sides to me are by far superior to the front. They give a fine idea of the flying buttress & [blank].

In the afternoon just Miss C. and I went out and spent our time until three in the Louvre shopping, getting back just in time to rush around and dressing to go to Miss Lilly Alley's for tea and as the girls were invited to dinner with Miss Heywood in the Latin Quarter, we had to hurry off for them to get there.

Miss C. had such a lovely surprise planned for us for a Thanksgiving Dinner but the girls' friend coming just at breakfast, Miss C. had no chance to tell them of her plans, so it was terribly upset and all were disappointed, but we four enjoyed it all. The place was trimmed with holly and flags and the plum pudding was brought in burning with a pretty silk flag in the center and it was a splendid dinner, Sans Krueger!

Hotel Louis-Le-Grand
Menu
Diner du 29 Novembre, 1900
Consommé aux pates
*

Truites Sauce Crevettes
*

Dinde Farci aux Marons
*

Crème Berry
*

Filet de Boeuf Roti
*

Salade Celeri
*

Petits Pois aux Beurre
*

Plum Pudding
*

Glace aux Framboises – Gaufrettes
*

Dessert

[Hand written Menu, Clarissa's Scrapbook, Thanksgiving Dinner 1900, Hotel Louis-Le-Grand, Paris; A Clear Noodle Soup, Trout with Prawn Sauce, Turkey with Chestnut Stuffing, Cream Soup, Roasted Beef Filet, Celery Salad, Peas with Butter, Plum Pudding, Strawberry Ice Cream & Wafer Cookies]

Friday, November 30, 1900.

This morning we went to the statuary division of the Louvre, and really the only things I remember distinctly are Michael Angelo's [Michael Angelo Buonarroti, 1475-1564] *Fettered Slaves* and *The Venus de Milo* and I thoroughly enjoyed both of those and I do wish I could remember more but after getting more used to them I shall.

In the afternoon Mary, Leslie, Miss C. and I went to the Luxembourg Gallery and there we saw the modern works from the French artists ["The works exhibited at the Luxembourg are generally transferred to the Lourve about 10 years after the death of the artist." *Paris*, 256]. I enjoyed them. I remember Rosa Bonheur [1822-1899] *Cattle Ploughing* and the impressionistic pictures by [blank], and *Whistler's Mother* [James McNeill Whistler, 1834-1903], of whom it is said is the most like Velasquez of any of the modern paintings and I have a vague remembrance of loads, but can't remember them especially and it nearly drives me frantic but I have hopes that before the year is over I shall have a speaking acquaintance with them or at least know who did what.

Saturday, December 1, 1900.

In the morning we went down to the Louvre [and] as it was such a queer dark morning we couldn't pretend to see anything in particular, so we went to the second floor and just walked around the triangle of the Old Louvre so as to get a general idea of the "lay of the land" and it is a help I think, but really I can't see how there can be twelve miles of pictures there!

In the PM we all went to the Louvre Magasins and invested in gloves for the year until we come back. Then Auntie and Mary came back and browsed around looking for postals. The rest of us went over and saw President Their's Collection. He was one of the Presidents of the Fr. Republic [Louis Adolphe Thiers, 1797-1877]. It consisted of beautiful bronzes, china, antiques, but it was very dark, so we could see nothing well. Then I went and got a ruff for Auntie and had tea and coffee.

Sunday, December 2, 1900.

We went this morning to the Greek or Russian Church [?], which was a most interesting service & the music fine. In the PM, Irving Moller called on Mary at three and we all helped entertain him. I amused him while Mary went and had her tea just before we left for Mrs. Whiting's to call. Marion and Leslie went to tea at Miss [blank] who invited us all. Mrs. W. showed us all through her beautiful new home, which is a dream of an apartment. When we reached home, the water was up and it was nearly time for dinner, so I hurried and dressed. Then Mr. Walter Allen & his wife arrived for dinner, which was very enjoyable.

Monday, December 3. 1900.

We took today for a rest day and did up odd jobs. Auntie and I bo't postels in the AM and I had a good time. It rained in the afternoon and we wrote & darned. When it was time for tea, we four sat on the floor around the fire & told stories until six o'clock. I think tomorrow I shall try to take a notebook along and get some facts in my noodle to stay there.

Tuesday, December 4, 1900.

It was so dark and rainy looking this morning that we decided it best to go to the statuary department of the Louvre, for that is the easiest to see when it's not bright. We went to the rooms showing the earliest form of work, which is detected by the low relief and as they learned more of it, gradually it grew to the rounded forms. We did not see any works of special note but just before coming out passed through the corridors to see *Venus* with Leslie.

In the afternoon we all went to the Cluny Museum or the Hotel de Cluny (founded 1500) which contains a most wonderful collection of all sorts of things in marble, wood, stone, ivory, enamels, terra cotta, prints, stained glass, pottery, etc. Joining it is the old Palais des Thermes and is the old bathing house on the order of the Roman Baths and is the most picturesque place we have seen since Kenilworth. It is of stone, Norman style, and the garden is toward the street, fenced in, and is decorated with old pieces of carved statuary in stone that have been brought from other places and are arranged as if they had always been in those places. The walks wind around through the garden and under the stone archways. We then went through the front entrance where the old well remains that has a monster's head for the water to run thro'. The ceilings inside are of rafters and the fireplaces looked so pretty with the wood fires in them.

Wednesday, December 5, 1900.

Miss C. and I used the morning up in going for the mail, to the bank and for theatre tickets. In the PM we went to the Louvre and it seemed as if we accomplished more in this one afternoon than in all the other times we have been there, for we fixed so many items to remember in our minds.

I especially remember [Constant] Troyon's picture of the cattle being driven home and the dust rising in the background, opposite which is his large picture of the cow going down to the pond to drink a big dog is jumping up and on one side is a flock of sheep [Troyon, 1810 – 1865, *Watering the Stock*]. Watteau's famous picture *The Embarkment for Cythera* [Jean Antoine Watteau, 1684-1721, *The Pilgrimage to Cythera*], [Jean-Baptiste] Greuze's *Broken Pitcher* [1725-1805] is so lovely of the sweet maiden holding the jug with a piece of the side broken out and hanging by the handle on her arm. The Corot's and…

We then went to the Long Gallery in the Catherine De Medici part. I think I know Botticelli by the molasses candy curls, Giotto by the almond eyes, Ghirlandaio by the beautiful reds in his drapery. St. Margaret has the dragon, St. George on the horse & killing the dragon. St. Michael… Ingres' were fine in the room with the Luini's something like Chevaue's [?] of our day [Bernardino Luini, 1480-1532]. Only Luini's were done in the XVI Cent. There is a fine Memling in that room, too, a votive picture [Hans Memling, 1430-1495]. Solario's *Madonna* is lovely of the little child getting his coffee lying on a green cushion and holding onto his toe. The virgin's expression is divine [Andrea Solario,1460 - 1515].

In the modern Sculptors' room, we saw Canova's *Amor & Psyche*, which is very pretty. That is really the only one I seemed to care for [Antonio Canova, 1757-1822].

Thursday, December 6, 1900.

Auntie and I went out and bought Post Cards for Christmas and found some real fancy ones suitable for Paris of dancing girls, etc.

In the afternoon we all went to the Hôtel des Invalids, which was founded in 1670 by Louis XIV for soldiers who were wounded in the army. It was intended to support 5000, but at present there are only 101 inmates. It is a most wonderful place and seems rather awe inspiring for it's so unusual with its huge court guards, etc., the church which is imposing being so high and decorated with rows of battle flags like the Chapel of Henry VII in Westminster. Services are held there at 8 o'clock Sundays. It's fortunate we do not have to go for it would most awfully upset our order for coffee and rolls, which we simply live for I must admit, and the Madeleine & Notre Dame isn't to be mentioned the same day with it. Yes, it's terrible I know, but it's fine.

The Tomb of Napoleon I is really the most beautiful thing I ever saw or ever expect to see, it is so massive and simple but grand [Hôtel des Invalides]. Down in the tomb proper it was so pathetic to see the old soldiers guarding the entrance. The light in the main part comes through slightly tinted from blue stained glass windows and up in the altar the glass windows throw a warm yellow tinge. Back of the altar is the church separated by a window.

We nearly had fits in the museum part looking at the figures of natives from all parts of the world. We saw lots of models for war equipment and armor.

We drove to the Santa Chappel [Sainte-Chapelle] in the Palais de Justice, but it was so dark we could not see a thing.

For dinner Mary had Miss Alley and the girls had Miss Lucy Hayward and Miss Ariel Cotton to dinner. We had such fun playing all sorts of catching games until late in the evening; Guessing the name on ones back by asking questions, and who has the hdkf, because someone who is in the place takes the same position. Laying the 10 matches down so all will be on the table at the 10th count.

Friday, December 7, 1900.

In PM we rushed off to the St. Chapelle to see it while the light was good. The glass is the most beautiful, dating from the 13th cent. I liked the reds so much. We went through the great big hall where the lawyers consult and walk up and down with their clients [Salle des Pas-Perdus of the Palais de Justice].

The old clock on the corner of the building is the first public clock in Paris and runs at "present writing." We came home and Miss Cadwell went to call on a friend and after I had written some sweet nothings on my postals for Christmas, I came in the Salon where the girls were writing and so I made tea & had a great time; the alcohol burned out as I was heating the water for Leslie's tea as I made mine thinking it was hers, but she wouldn't let me fire up again, and so hers was made of warm water. The dear good girl said it was <u>fine</u>.

Saturday, December 8, 1900.

Auntie and I went out on our own hook this morning and bo't little things for the girls "not to exceed 5 Fr. in value." When we got in, all had flown, so we didn't see them until dejeuner. After that we all started for the "Bon Marche" and fussed around all the rest of the PM trying to shop [Bon Marche; one of the Grands Magasins of Paris, Rue de Bac 135 and 137].

Miss C. went over to dinner with Mr. & Mrs. Allen after our call from Mrs. Whiting and her daughter. Mary and I had three helpings for dinner of chicken. Marion broke Auntie's glasses when she went to kiss her, which seems a downright shame, but no one could help it. Still that doesn't help the matter any.

Sunday, December 9, 1900.

Today is a "rest day" which means getting up late in time for dejeuner. In the PM I had a fire in the grate and a fine shampoo. Poor Auntie had to wear her dark glasses all day and it is horrid. Mr. & Mrs. Leach came from Rome and it is a shock to see Mrs. L. for it is painful she is so thin. Miss C. has known them 12 years but she has not seen them for two, so that when she came up to her in the hall she did not recognize her. Miss C. felt terribly for in a recent letter from Mrs. L. she asked her not to say whatever she might think of her.

Monday, December 10, 1900.

Miss C. took Auntie's glasses out the first thing to be repaired. Then we five went to the Louvre and I got three more pairs of gloves while we also went in the Arcade, and Marion and L. bo't a poster.

In PM Miss C., Auntie and I went first for her glasses, which were 75 Fr. much to our joy. Marion insisted upon paying for them and gave Miss C. 60 Francs, so it is a fine surprise. We then went to the Bon Marche. Our horse to begin with balked when we turned around from the opticians & another cabby had to hop off his box and pull him along until he got under motion and we were in terror lest he should come to a block, but he went on finely. When we came to the store & Miss C. told him to wait, he wanted her to pay him and she wouldn't. Then he insisted upon her giving him her umbrella. We decided that during the Exposition[2] people had gone out other entrances and left the cab.

In the evening we went to the Theatre and saw Mde. RéJean in *Sylvie*. We had heard that it was immoral, but as long as we did not hear the remarks to know them, it didn't make any special difference. We had a box to ourselves and it was ever so nice. The play was terribly long, 4 acts, and my toe ached so I tho't I would go wild [actress Gabrielle Réjane, 1856-1920 - program in Scrapbook]. We got home at 12:30, then had our apples. I have enjoyed my new opera glasses very much so far and am rather glad I have them even from that source [?].

Miss L. [Linderfelt], Josh's friend, called just as we were making tea and really I was so scared when she was shown up I could hardly stand up. I do think he might have prepared me for it as I knew nothing of such a person. She came on the same steamer as J. and the Count and he must have quite liked her, as when she stood up I caught sight of his Duke [University] Pin, which he said he got for me and I am really glad he has decided I am not the only girl who is worthy of it. I sort of hate to think of it, for it's queer. Still, I am relieved way down in my heart I know [Mr. Joshua E. Sweet, friend of Clarissa since a young girl. She makes reference to him throughout her year abroad.].

Tuesday, December 11, 1900.

Ten years ago today was the ending of one period in my life and I wonder what these last two years have amounted to! I sometimes feel they have been lost, and then again, I think possibly I have learned more that will help to make my life in the end be of some benefit. But as yet, I have not been tested, but I do so trust I won't fail when that time comes. But I must come back to real cold Parisian facts! [On this date in 1890, Clarrisa's father, Frank Arnold, committed suicide in Unadilla, NY, following an unsuccessful election campaign for the US Senate. Clarissa was 13.]

This morning we all went to the Louvre and just stayed in the Apollo Gallery, looking at the pottery, "bric-a-brac," as we would say. In the PM we went down again and spent most of the time in the Dutch [Rooms]. Rubens stands out most distinctly because we saw so many of them that were done for Marie de Medici, wife of Henry IV, but I don't like them at all. They seem rather coarse and uncouth to me for some reason or other [Peter Paul Rubens, 1577-1640].

We went for tea after coming home and fixing up in our best togs to [blank] where all the swells go and it was lovely to see all the pretty clothes and people. The tea wasn't as good as we have in our rooms, but the cake was splendid but awfully rich. Mary and I went out and selected it for the party. I had two cubed shaped pieces; one was chocolate; a layer of plain white cake then a layer the same thickness that seemed like some whipped cream thickened and chocolate flavored, the whole thing being dipped in chocolate icing. My other piece was about the same only with coffee cream and flavoring and a little coffee cream rosette on the top [petits fours]. I do just love those swell places and that's all there is about it and I hope someday I can go to them all the time and be so well dressed that people will notice when I come in the door about where Miss C. wants Sara [?] to be and I am wondering which will reach that point first. The only reason I am looking forward to the end of the year is to select all the dainty and refined little things to take home.

Wednesday, December 12, 1900.

The first thing this morning was Miss C. to tell us about Marion's experience of the night before after we were all in bed. She had not more than finished when Leslie came for me to come to their room, so I hustled into my kimono and there was Marion in bed, Mary curled up at the foot and I crawled in by Marion & Leslie by Mary.

It seems about eleven, Marion started up to the closet [water closet or WC] and then got to sort of wool gathering so that she didn't remember coming down the stairs distinctly but when she got by her door she suddenly heard the water running in the room which corresponds to the WC on the other floors and she was radiantly happy thinking she had made a discovery, so back she went to tell Mary her find. When she reached the door, which was ajar, she said in a loud whisper, "Mary!" no answer. "Mary!" a little more imperatively, and all she saw was what she supposed to be M's wrapper on the bed. After a second, this head and shoulders of a man appeared, who was sitting with his back against the footboard reading under the light. At that, Marion was transfixed and seemed to lose her senses entirely and stood perfectly still and looked at him then she finally said, "I beg your pardon." and backed off. The next thing she realized was reading "Salon" over the door, she then knew she was on the 2nd floor and turned and rushed upstairs on a run all in her kimono, and by his door on the 3rd floor, where he was still sitting looking out in the same position and on up to our floor where she had to relate it all to Mary and Leslie then to Miss C., who took it seriously and told her what might have happened if she had strayed into a Frenchman's room, for they are ready for anything & anybody. It does seem as if Marion had more ill fortune than she deserved. I dreaded luncheon today for Mary was away and I had to sit facing him alone but nothing happened. He is a dear American and must be a real gentleman from his build and manners, but tonight at dinner we all were hysterical and had an awful time not to laugh out. Mary had a little moist spot on her silk lining to her grey dress when we got upstairs.

This morning at ten we all started out & went to the Exposition Grounds and it was a splendid morning. At first we took the tram-car down the Boulevard Haussmann to the one that said "Madagascar", which Auntie and I saw when we went to Mrs. Whiting's. We got a splendid view from the Trocadero Piazza above the fountain right in front of the Eiffel Tower which is enormous [Built in 1889 by Monsieur Gustav Eiffel; "… the loftiest monument in the World, attaining a height of 984 Ft." *Paris*, 282].

We rode a ways, then crossed the beautiful new bridge, Alexandria III, to the bridge by the Rue of Nations and looked a long time at that view from the bridge. We walked home down the Champs Elysee after riding part way. We also went to a cemetery [Cemetery of Passey] and saw Marie B [Bashkirtseff] Tomb, which is very fine.

In the PM we all went to the Louvre and finished the Dutch & Flemish paintings that are in the little rooms at the side of the Rubens Salon. Franz Hals [1584-1666] I love, and Breughel [Peter 1520-1569, or Jan, Peter's son, 1568-1625], the man who puts bugs and insects in everything I like to see. We sort of reviewed all of the principal ones, which is a good way to fix them in our minds from Giotto to the 17th & 18th cent. ones.

Wouwermann distinguished by a white horse usually [Philips Wouwermann, 1619-1668].

The girls had shampoos. Auntie and I had tea and looked at the stores on the way home.

Paris. Thursday, December 13, 1900.

In the morning we went to the new church that is not finished yet and does not look as if it would be for some years to come. It is Sacré Coeur [begun 1875, consecrated 1919]. We reached it by going out in the tram through Boulevard Haussman and making several changes. Then we had a climb of 262 steps from the street to the top of the hill on the brow of which stands the church. A most glorious view of the city can be had from the façade, but as it was so misty we could but get a general idea of the city. We went in while service was going on, then we went to see the bell, which is next largest to one in Moscow. It is in a temporary house, but is rung. In the afternoon it rained and we all stayed in.

Paris - Milan, Italy. Friday, December 14, 1900.

Auntie and I went to the Louvre at first then around to the stores in the neighborhood and I tried to find a Napoleon hat for Leslie and I had my heart set on a gold book with a place for a photo and a magnifying glass in it, but as they were 80 francs and more I couldn't think of getting one and was awfully disappointed. But maybe they will be cheaper next year and then I shall have one if I can get it.

At 8:30 we started for Milan and it was an awfully tiresome trip, as we did not have a sleeper for they were so expensive we all tho't we would rather use it for something else.

En Route - Milan. Saturday, December 15, 1900.

We were roused at seven o'clock at Basel [Switzerland] & as I did not get to sleep until four, I was in a killing condition to get off, but I won't go into detail as I guess I'll remember it without any trouble. We changed again at Lucerne [Switzerland] at nine, and then had coffee & rolls on the train. All I can say about the trip thro' the Alps is that it's beyond words and anything I had ever expected to see.

We reached here at 4:30. Went to the Metropole, but did not like the rooms so came to Hotel [de] France which is nice and very comfortable on the Corso Victor Emmanuel (the grandfather of the present King). We all were glad to go to bed early, as it was a hard trip and I was real carsick.

Part III * Italy

"Expenses. The cost of a tour in Italy depends, of course, on the traveler's resources and habits, but, as a rule, it need not exceed that incurred in other much-frequented parts of the continent... When ladies are of the party, the expenses are generally greater.

Money. The French monetary system is now in use throughout the whole of Italy...

Season. As a general rule, the spring and autumn months are the best season for a tour in Italy... The height of summer can hardly be recommended for traveling. The scenery, indeed, is perfection and the long days are hailed with satisfaction by the enterprising traveler, but the fierce rays of an Italian sun seldom fail to impair the physical and mental energies...

The traveler entering Italy for the first time should do so, if the season be favourable, not by rail, but by one of the Alpine passes, as only thus will he obtain an adequate idea of the full ethnographical significance of the Alps, which conceal so new and so strange a world from northern Europe.

Passports, though not required in Italy, are occasionally useful." Baedeker, *Northern Italy*, 1899, xi-xiv.

*

Milan. Sunday, Dec. 16, 1900.

"Milan, Milano, ... the capital of Lombardy, the seat of an archbishop, the headquarters of an army corps, the chief financial centre of Italy, and one of the wealthiest manufacturing and commercial towns in the country... 425,800 inhabitants. There are numerous German and Swiss residents..." *Northern Italy*, 109.

*

We decided our time here was too precious to take out a rest day and so we started out soon after our coffee and rolls and first went to the Milan Cathedral just as the procession was starting for High Mass. The people by the side of the huge columns looked like so many flies. There were lots of people there for it but they seemed like only a handful. We stayed there and heard the singing and saw the procession of priests and all sorts of robed people from green silk gowns to dress suits. They went down the center aisle into the south transept through the ambulatory to the north transept and back to the High Altar by the middle isle. The sight was a beautiful one - our first cathedral in Europe [Italy].

From there we went to the Church of S. [Santa] Maria delle Grazie. The choir, transept and nave are attributed to [Donato] Bramante [1444-1514]. Then we went into what used to be the Monastery of Santa Maria delle Grazie into the refectory where the remains of Leonardo's *Last Supper*. It is nearly beyond recognition as it has been repeatedly restored [Leonardo da Vinci, 1452-1519].

After luncheon we went to the [Palazzo di] Brera Gallery, which was formerly a Jesuit College founded, the Library, in 1170. There we saw some beautiful Luini frescoes; *Preaching of St. Mark at Alexandria* by [Gentile] Bellini [1421-1507], Raphael's *Sposalizio* painted in [1504] for the Ch. of S. Francesco in Citta di Castello, and so many beautiful ones [Raphaelo Santi da Urbino, 1483-1520].

Milan. Monday, Dec. 17, 1900.

We started out and took a succession of churches, first going into the crypt and seeing the Chappello San Carlo Borromeo with the tomb of the St. in the Cathedral. We then studied out the representations in the three stained glass windows back of the High Altar. Then we went to the <u>Church S. Eustorgio</u> [Sant' Eustorgio], where Peter Martyr is buried in the chapel back of the High Altar.

<u>St. Lorenzo</u>, the oldest church in Milan, near the Colonnades, octagonal in form, back of the High Altar is the tomb of Giov. Maria Visconti, one of the old families in Milan.

<u>St. Giorgio</u> al Palazzo to see the frescoes by Luini. We went up in threes to see his St. Geo. There were such dear little twins by the entrance.

<u>St. Celso</u> [Santa Maria presso San Celso] contains an atrium attributed to Bramante.

In the PM we went to the <u>Ch. S. Maurizio</u> [Chiesa del Monastero Maggiore], which contains a fresco from the life of St. Catherine by Luini. That is where the awful old woman let us into the Nuns' Choir where we saw the frescoes by Luini [*9 Frescoes of the Passion*] of SS. <u>Apollonia</u>- forceps, Lucia – eyes, Catherine – wheel, Agatha – breasts, Sebastian – Arrow, Rochus – stocking coming off. Shell & pouch.

S. Ambrogio is on the site of the temple of Bacchus founded by St. Ambrose in the 4th century. St. Ambrose baptized St. Augustine in 387. In 389 he closed the doors against the Emp. Theodosius after the massacre of Thessalonica (389). The Lombard Kings and German Emperors were crowned in a carved marble seat we saw with the iron crown.[1]

The pillar at which they took the oath is in the piazza, which we passed. The crypt contains the tombs of SS Ambrose, Portasius & Gervasius. The little guide blessed our handkerchiefs on the remains of the column where the SS Gervasius & Protasius were beheaded. Adjacent is a cloister designed by Bramante (1492).

We then went to the Campo Santo, which is the most peculiar place I was ever in, with the queer monuments and photographs in the headstones. It was interesting to go into the crematory[2.]

Milan - Genoa. Thursday, Dec. 18, 1900.

In the morning we went to the Bibliotheca Ambrosiana, which is a library & museum and the Hospital Osperdale Maggiore, begun in 1457, containing nine courts, half Gothic and half Renaissance. It is one of the largest in existence. One court to the right is attributed to Bramante.

We bought our pictures and at 2:45 we set sail for Genoa. The trip thru Lombardy was most ideal, with the trees trimmed to a stumpy short place, then shoots branching out from that point leaving the landscape clear with the exception of the tall Lombardy Poplars which are the road trees. The river added to the scene and the sunset was the most beautiful I ever saw.

We reached Genoa at seven. Came to Hotel Smith, which used to be a monastery, so queer with its entrance and stone stairs and everything is so clean it makes one feel contented. We are on the Piazza Caricamento, opposite the statue to Raffaele Rubattino, the Genoese ship owner, and directly in front of the long freight houses & Custom House ["English landlord, near the Exchange. Vico Denegri, well spoken of." *Northern Italy*, 65].

Genoa. Friday, Dec. 19, 1900.

We went for a walk this AM and visited several churches and went to the top of the Church of S. Maria in Carignano. Had a grand view of the harbor and the city. We also saw the house where Christopher Columbus' father lived.

In the PM we drove around in the better parts of the city & saw orange and lemon trees in bloom & fountains & all such picture things.

This morning we went to the S. Matteo Church where we saw our first orange & lemon trees in the court.

In the Church Santo Stefano we saw the *Stoning of Stephen* by Giulio Romano [1492-1546], which is one of his best works. He was a pupil of Raphael, but the picture was rather peculiar I thought.

Knock-euw Stiff Flea Soap! [margin note]

Genoa. Thursday, December 20, 1900.

We all went out the first thing and went along to the Filigree Factory, which was just splendid. The workshop was smaller than I expected it would be but we saw it all never the less, and it's splendid to think we have seen how it's done. I bought a lovely necklace with pendants all around for myself and I think it's a beauty and it will be lovely to say "yes, I bought that in Genoa" and I can scarcely wait to have someone ask me about it and then I got a rattle for Eleanor [Clarissa's Uncle J. Fred Sands' youngest child] and a necklace with daisies and a hatpin on a spring that would drive me crazy if it sat ahead of me in church.

We also went into the Cathedral of St. Lawrence [St. Lorenzo] and saw the service, but couldn't go in to see things. Just as we got to the door [there was] a funeral of the Miseracordia Monks, for they bury all the poor of the city. All had on long bluish-purple gowns with heads all covered up and just holes cut for eyes. They looked terribly dreary, but it is splendid that they do take such good care of the needy.

We went to see the elaborate decorations in the Church of the Annunciation [Santissima Annunziata del Vastato] and from there we went to the Palace [?] & through it that is said to have the most beautiful entrance of any.

We had an early dejeuner and then took the electrics [electric tramways] for the Villa Pallavacini, which is seven miles out in a most beautiful spot imaginable [Villa Durazzo-Pallavacini, 19th c. park, opened in 1846].

We left the car, left the cameras and walked through a wide path walled up on either side with overhanging rose bushes in bloom and climbing geraniums in blossom. Then we came to a square place filled with palm trees, date palms, oranges, lemons, camphor trees, eucalyptus trees (which are grown in Italy to absorb the malaria), holly, cacti, fig, olive, figurine (?) cactus, and no end of beautiful shrubs of all sorts.

We walked through beautiful walks and every little while we came onto some sort of a building erected to someone who had been there in the form of a temple, fountains here and there in the rocks and in the walks, with fish in the little ponds under the bridges. At the top we went into what was supposed to have been an old fort and stormed [?]. It was a miniature affair with a kitchen and all such things. We went up the winding stairway and looked out on the water and the mountains. Then we came down and the first thing was the sort of ferris wheel for four and we all piled in a chair and two men moved it up and around we went all yelling and laughing.

Next we struck the Grotto, which is made of the rock and as black as night for a ways. We hung on to the guide and then to each other and I nearly took Leslie's skirt off at one point. All at once we came to a sheet of water in among the rocks and there was a boatman ready to take us through the rest of the way. There was just room for the boat to get thro' among all the trees and out into the light. We followed our guide along into a round green-blinded house with a wire canopy covered with vines and all at once we were in a shower of water in a spray & all ran! Miss C. knew of it and didn't go in but enjoyed seeing us at it. There were more grottoes and sprays cutting off the paths.

We had a fine afternoon and the walk up and down the mountain about used me up after the stairs in the Carignano [Church] yesterday. The man who lived in the Palace where we went this morning is at the Pallavicini all the time and is blind. We saw his private garden but couldn't go into it.

A most interesting Franciscan monk sat opposite us in the car coming home and Mary and I couldn't help but wish we knew why he had joined the order.

An American war vessel came in the harbor today, [blank], and also the *Columbus* from N.Y.

It seems hardly possible it's the 20th of Dec. and we have our coats off while in the garden and saw butterflies.

Friday, December 21, 1900.

This morning we went to the Campo Santo [Cimitero di Staglieno], but I do not think much of it, for we simply go to see the queer statuary and monuments and do laugh like everything. It was real, real exciting going and coming, for the laborers and trainmen were on a strike early, but the cars started about ten. Still, there was an air of mystery all along.

St. Lorenzo is not especially interesting but in the St. John Chapel, his bones are supposed to be [John the Baptist's].

This afternoon we visited palaces. First we went to the Palazzo Rosso, where we saw a nice collection of paintings, especially the Van Dyck's, of members of the Sale Family who used to live there [Anton Van Dyck, 1599-1641]. Also Guido Reni's *St. Sabastian* [1574-1642]. The palace was given to the city in 1874 by Marchesa Maria Brignole-Sale, Duchess of Galliera, who died in 1889, & her son Filippo.

Next, we went to the White Palace, the Palazzo Bianco, in which there is a fine collection of antiquities, mosaics, Egyptian Ware, coins, china, lace and some nice pictures.

At dinner tonight there was such a queer combination in the twenty sitting there. The woman & her little boy appeared who were so very amusing.

Genoa - Rome. Saturday, Dec. 22, 1900.

In the morning I didn't go out but stayed in and packed, writing Josh [Josh Sweet] a note also. We had an early luncheon, then we all made a rush and got to the station where we had of lot of bundles including luncheon. The funny woman and the boy were in the bus and it was great sport to hear them fuss and worry for fear they weren't on the right road etc.

We had a great time with luggage and Miss C. called a porter & gave him her books to carry and told him we wanted "Roma seconda classe", so off we paddled and when we got to the gate, he dropped the book bag and rushed ahead. Mary snatched them and we all filed along, but could not get a compartment for six and the man told us to go to the other side & then we met Miss C. in our agony & Mary pointed to "the man with the bottle". Miss C. struck [assailed] a Cook's man [Thomas Cook & Son, Travel Company], and as she had gotten our tickets through to Rome [with them] we could call on him. So he kept track of us & as soon as another train backed up, he sent us on and there was a compartment marked "Cook Reserved" so in we all popped. No sooner than [that] a man in a light overcoat came along half frantic, declaring it was for his Cook's party, but as our man belonged at the station, he had the upper hand, so the man nearly had a fit, but we stayed there and were the only ones all the way to Rome. We wondered where the lady and the young woman were who came on because we were going to Rome from Genoa.

We had our dinner of Hotel Smith's concoction at six, & it was fine: buttered rolls, boiled eggs, broiled chicken, salt, pepper, oranges & nuts with wine and it was just as good as it sounds. We reached here at two AM after coming thro' 80 tunnels by the St. Gottard Railroad by the Italian Riveria which was fine [St. Gothard Railway Guide in Scrapbook].

We went to bed at once after reaching the Hotel Molaro[3] and such a cozy compartment with our lovely stage-setting salon and all but Miss C.'s room opening off it. We had our coffee, rolls, brown bread and toast on the round table in the salon and nothing could be [better].

Miss C. went for our mail. I heard from Eugenia, Uncle Fred, Aunt Belle, Mr. B. & Mr. F. and was as happy as could be. We rested all day and were very glad to.

Rome. Monday, December 24, 1900.

"Rome (Roma in Latin and Italian), known even in antiquity as 'the Eternal City', once the capital of the ancient world, afterwards the spiritual empire of the Popes, and since 1871 the capital of the Kingdom of Italy, with 489,965 inhabitants (31st Dec., 1897)...

The city proper lies on the Left Bank of the Tiber, partly on the plain, the ancient Campus Martius, and partly on the surrounding hills. Modern Rome is principally confined to the plain, while the heights on which the ancient city stood were almost uninhabited in the middle ages and the following centuries... these are the far-famed Seven Hills of Rome..." Baedeker, *Central Italy*, 144-145.

*

The first thing after breakfast and we were all in bed, Raphaello brought the Bishop's and Father Murphy's cards up & I told him to send them up, but next came two tickets [an Orange "Pass", is in Clarissa's Scrapbook] for the service at St. Peter's for the Closing of the Holy Door[4]. [Visitation cards; Rt. Rev. J.J. Monaghan, D.D., Bishop of Wilmington, Del. and Rev. William G. Murphy, New York, N.Y.]

Well we rushed for it was at 10:30 and [here] it was 9:30. Miss C. came in & we three took a carriage and rushed over to the Vatican to St. Peter's and such a sight! [St. Peter's (San Pietro in Vaticano); "... said to have been founded by the Emperor Constantine... in the form of a basilica ... on the site of the Circus of Nero, where St. Peter is said to have been buried." Baedeker, *Central Italy*, 306.]

Approaching St. Peter's, Rome

The whole front was guarded by soldiers all in front and along the side, and they looked fine. We saw the people with orange papers coming from the façade towards the side, so we followed them asking the sentinels along [the way]. When we got along by the last on the side, they told [us] to go to the front so we had to go by everyone of those fellows to the break about a mile & in front of the main door and going up there I was so scared for fear they would see my gilt and color, for the tickets said to wear black gowns. When we reached the door they told us those places were full, to go back, which we did & broke thro' the line of soldiers. There was a crowd there, but Miss C. left us and we went with the rest & finally got in the door.

The first thing was a six foot guard all decked out in his uniform as all were, & he was bound to take my ticket, but at that point another guard came & began to talk & presently a priest appeared who was so interested and interceded for us, so they let us by.

Then I ran into another soldier of the same sort & he wouldn't let us by, so back I rushed to the old priest & beseeched him to help us again & after a lot of talking we were sent around to the side, the priest following and I was so glad I didn't know what to do. He was tall and slim about 60, I should say, from Sidney, Australia. We talked along and followed the crowd & got near the railing opposite the Holy Door, but in front of it were heavy red curtains.

Finally we could see the candles & the procession forming and going out toward the right & then the curtains near us were drawn so we couldn't see anything. Of course we all hurried back to the right & there we could see it well. The Pope was splendid in his red velvet chair, carried by men under the gorgeous canopy. He was in white satin & gold & so pure & holy looking as he sat there raising his two fingers, as the figures of Christ do, giving his blessing. The people cheered & waved frantically as he passed to the high altar, which was one blaze of candles & glass pendants. Way up at the top in the balcony, three brought out articles, which he blessed [Pope Leo XIII, born Vincenzo Gioacchino Raffaelle Luigi Pecci of Carpineto, 1810; the 256th Pope, 1878-1903].

By that time Auntie had nearly fainted, for it was stuffy in the crowd, so she went back and sat down in front of an altar & I tho't she was going to faint dead away & I rushed to the priest and begged for his furry silk hat which he gave me to fan her with, he following. Then he disappeared and presently returned with a sister who had another woman with her & no one could make the other understand, but Auntie was better then, so she got up to see the Pope go back, and I went behind a soldier guard who was so tall I hardly showed up to the railing nearly, which they passed with the Holy Relics.

Then a lot of priests went by & one lost something which I saw was a long brass cross & I was crazy to have it, so I stood over it so no one could get it, and then I had a most horrid experience with the large stunning Italian who I was frightened to death of, & who would not let me stir until I finally squeezed in front of a peasant. The man had his hand on her shoulder to push by when a Swiss Guard came by who he knew, so I went on a little further & so escaped him. Then I felt a knock on the top of my head, which proved to be the priest & everyone made way for me to pass, and after hunting for a carriage we then got his card & came home alive after a most thrilling time!

Everyone went out to finish Christmas shopping in squads & I went for a plait & brush. We all hung up our stockings around the fireplace.

Rome. Tuesday, <u>Christmas</u>. 1900.

We were up at eight and opened our packages before coffee and every one did seem so pleased. Auntie gave me fifty francs for a buckle. Fan sent a sweet note and [blank]; Mary's was one of the sweet Roman blankets in blue, yellow & green, just what I love; Leslie, a box for pens etc. with a bunch of mistletoe on the corner in brass; Miss Cadwell gave me a veil case with veil & two pins in it and a sweet filigree dagger hatpin from Marion. By mail I had a collar from Florence and Harold, a tie from Aunt Belle & a little calendar from Mrs. Beard, so I felt that my friends at home did not forget me.

The Procession of the Bambino at the Santa Maria in Aracoeli [Church of the Altar of Heaven]. It was very strange. The bambino is a little swathed image, carved of wood, as the legend goes from a tree from the Mt. of Olives by a Franciscan pilgrim and painted by St. Luke while the pilgrim was sleeping. It is supposed to possess great power over disease and needs to be taken in state to the homes of parents to heal the children.

The procession started from the high altar where the Bambino was at the very top when we went in. The Bishop carried it and as it passed all fell down & crossed themselves. They went finally and deposited it in the crèche in the Virgin's [arms] or in front of her & left there until the 6th of Jan. when it is returned to its original chapel. The children speak pieces from a platform in the rear of the church & the tragic gestures were so funny.

In the afternoon we went to Santa Maria Maggiore, where there are the remains of what is said to be [five] slats from the Savior's manger [the Santa Culla or Cradle of the Infant Christ]. There we heard the Pope's Angel[5] sing & it's like a woman's voice. We saw Father Murphy & a friend.

We had an elegant dinner with such pretty table decorations. Antonio had on a white vest and everyone looked fine. I nearly burst by the time we were through, but it was well worth it.

Hotel Molaro
Menu du 25 Dec. 1900
Huître au gratin
*

Potage
*

Fish - Sauce *Tartare*
*

Roast Beef - Sauce Bernaise
*

Galantine de Faisan a' la Gelee
*

Ris de Veau - Sauce Truffes
*

Petits Pois au beurre
*

Dinde Rôti
*

Plum Pudding ay Sabayon
*

Glace a' la Napolit
*

Congolais aux Amandes
Dessert

[Handwritten Menu, Clarissa's Scrapbook, Christmas, 1900; Baked Oysters, Soup, Fish & Tartar Sauce, Roast Beef & Bernaise Sauce, Cold Pheasant Terrine, Sweetbreads with Truffle Sauce, Peas with Butter, Roast Turkey, Plum Pudding, Napolitan Ice Cream & Almond Petit Fours]

Wednesday, December 26, 1900.

We went to the Rag Fair in the morning and such a mess as they did have. It's held every Wednesday and the people bring everything imaginable to sell from embroidered underwear to old rusty nails. Each one had their own stand and it was terribly funny to see the odds and ends. We none of us saw a thing we wanted, much to our sorrow.

In the PM we went to San Giovanni in Laterano, where there are the heads of St. Paul & St. Peter, and also heard the Pope's Angel again. We saw the Bishop that day and were tickled to death to squeeze his hand again.

Thursday, December 27, 1900.

We all went to the Capitoline Museum up by the Santa Maria d'Aracoeli and there we saw the *Marforio,* a river-god in the form of a fountain & some sarcophagi. Then the *Dying Gladiator,* found in 16th cent & the *Marble Faun* by Praxiteles [*Resting Satyr*], which is the foundation of Hawthorne's *Marble Faun* known as *Transformation* over here, which we began reading aloud last night [Nathaniel Hawthorne; 1860, while residing in Rome].

In the next room is a Faun in red marble. The old woman's statue was very good. In the Philosopher's Room *Socrates, Homer, Young Barbarian* are good. *Endymion,* asleep in relief with his dog is good. The vase was interesting to pick out the characters around it.

Doors on a Fountain Basin, mentioned by Pliny.

Capitoline Venus, which is fine. Her back is especially beautiful, but *Venus de Milo* is to me more beautiful in her face and this one is called a perfect type of the female figure.

The Forum was our afternoon trip and so much straightened in a short time, but with the recent & present excavations the whole section is stagnant & seems so malarial. We paid a lira to go in, which is a new scheme.

The Roman Forum

"The systematic destruction of the Forum was followed by its systematic burial in rubbish-heaps, so that the ancient pavement is at places 40 ft. below the present level of the ground... In the 15th century, The Forum was largely occupied by gardens and cane-brakes... while a few isolated columns alone protruded from the rubbish. The very name of the Forum was forgotten; and down to our own day the famous site was popularly known as the Campo Vaccino. As early as 1519 Raphael had formed a plan for restoring the ancient city, and especially the Forum. The object in view being merely the discovery of works of art ... the excavations were soon filled up again.

At length the plan was revived by the modern spirit of investigation. In 1803... 1813... 1835 and 1848 [parts of the Forum were excavated] but from that year to 1871 the work was discontinued. [In 1871], the Italian government resumed the excavations with considerable energy; and the rest of the Basilica Julia, the temples of Castor, Caesar and Vesta and the Atrium Vestae have been brought to light... But for the present the costliness of the work and the requirement of the modern traffic unfortunately render the continuation of the excavations in this direction improbable." *Central Italy*, 244.

*

The Basilica Julia, Temple of Saturn, Rostra or Center of Rome, and of Septimus Servious. Columna Phocas, the last thing, erected in the Forum ["… 54 Ft. in height, which was erected in 608 in honor of the tyrant Phocus of the Eastern Empire." *Central Italy*, 247]. Temple of Caesar, Temple of Vesta, Atrium Vestae, Temple of Faustina, Basilica of Constantine, Church of San Francesca Romana, Triumphal Arch & Colosseum, which we hadn't time to see & the Arch of Constantine.

The Bishop called in the evening and took our names for a private audience to the Pope to be held next week when the pilgrims from England get here. We are all crazy to go and I guess they will bring it around so we can. We have asked them to dinner for Sunday and hope Father Murphy will have gotten over the effect of his wild boar that he ate and it made him sick, poor man!

Rome. Friday, December 28, 1900.

Miss Cadwell and I went out to do a little shopping and such horrid luck. It began to pour and kept it up. Neither of us could find a thing to count and when we got in at luncheon time we were soaking wet and tired. No one went out later, but mended & Miss C. read aloud from the *Marble Faun*. It makes it so much nicer being right on the spot where the scenes were.

Saturday, December 29, 1900.

In the morning I had a little sore throat so Auntie & I decided to stay in instead of going to the churches. But we couldn't withstand the temptation and so we went up to the Via Sistina and walked along buying some Roman blankets, pillows & a tie. Also a vellum frame & the Pope's picture, which I adore, for I bro't the man down 2 Fr. on it and the blankets are great.

In the afternoon we all went up on the Pincian Hill through the Santa Maria del Popolo, where the little chapel was designed & decorated by Raphael. The hill is a dream. The entrance walk is fine and the view over the wall on the one side overlooking the Piazza del Popolo, and the other the Villa Borghese and the Appian Way. The turn outs [carriages] were great and I hope we can go next Saturday for the band plays every Saturday at 3 PM [The Pincio, Hill of Gardens, "… fashionable resort in the evening, about 2 hrs. before sunset the military band plays; the Italians then pay and receive visits to their carriages, presenting a gay and characteristic scene." *Central Italy*, 149].

Rome. Sunday, December 30, 1900.

Auntie and I went to All Saints for church [English Church]. It is down beyond the Bank. They had no music because the organist was ill. In the PM we all started out and took two carriages and drove out by the Forum and along outside the wall to the St. Sabina Church to see [Giovanni Battisto Salvi] Sassoferrato's [1605-1685] *Madonna of the Rosary*, but there was a service. Still, three of us went up quietly & then waited outside and Auntie tried to pat the horse, a little black one & he squealed every time and that made us laugh. The man tried to tell her he was "multi forte" & such a time.

Then we all started & went about two [?] when he stopped & we all three piled out in such a rush, but Miss C. didn't move but motioned for us to get back and we obeyed but didn't just see why & sat a second when we discovered he (the horse) was obliged to attend to the wants of nature. It was most killing and especially so to hear of it after we got back.

We peeked through the keyhole of the door to the gate at the entrance to the Garden of the Knights of Malta through the lovely path covered with vines & with St. Peter's Way along at the end.

We then went to the Protestant Cemetery where we saw John Keats' grave, Shelley's grave & Goethe's son. Adjoining is the Pyramid of Cestius, erected 12 BC [The Cemetary ..."It is a retired spot, rising gently towards the city-wall, affording pleasing views, and shaded by lofty cypresses, where numerous English, American, German, Russian, and other visitors to Rome are interred." *Central Italy*, 277].

We then drove back through such lovely bits of country & beggars to the St. Sabina Church where we all went in and saw the *Madonna* close to. It's a gem [*Madonna del Rosario* by Sassoferrato]. The view through the grated window into the Garden is fine looking onto the tree that St. Dominic is said to have planted, for he founded that church.

From there we drove to the Pincian Hill to [Santissima] Trinitá de' Monte to hear the nuns sing at Vespers, and it was lovely and I hope we can go again next Sunday.

We expected the Bishop and Father Murphy to dinner and after we had had our discussion about paying, for the girls all begged to join us and I refused to allow it because they didn't speak of it sooner. We had just decided, when a note came that the Father wasn't well enough to come out, so we had our fuss all for nothing.

Rome. Monday, December 31, 1900.

Leslie, Mary, Miss C. and I went to the Nat. Museum of the Dioclezian [Museo Nazionale Romano delle Terme Diocleziane] and saw some lovely statues. The stucco relief was fine in the fragments.

The nude *Bronze Figure of a Man Leaning on the Staff* & *The Pugilist*, both being found in the Tiber in 1884, were splendid and so perfectly preserved. The *Marble Statue of a Kneeling Youth* is an exquisite thing, the head and arms being gone. Still it seems as if at any moment the body might change its position. The marble is lifelike in color and we reluctantly moved on from it.

The next object that transfixed us was the *Head of the Sleeping Nymph*. Nothing is known of its origins or what the rest was like, but just the head and throat are perfect in every detail as it rests on the rich brown velvet cushion.

In the PM we went to the Jesuit Church [Gesù, Principle Church of the Jesuits], where the lighting of the candles around the altar & the rest of the Church is marvelous, and the Pope's Angel sang again.

We go to St. Peter's to see the old year and century die. After tho't and consideration we decided it was worth the powder [?] even if it's rainy, for it will never occur again.

Later, when we were ready to start at 10:30, it wasn't raining a bit and as the cabman wanted 5 Francs, we went down to the Piazza di Spagna and there we saw the most sleepy cabby who made us feel that it was an imposition to disturb him, but he said, 2 Frs. and if he didn't whiz along. Mary and I nearly bobbed out, for we two sat on the little seat in front of Leslie & Miss C. There were colored lanterns hung before so many of the buildings that gave them a very gala appearance.

The Piazza was a sight in the moonlight. The doors were not open, so we stood outside a few moments, then we all went in and up by the steps down in the crypt around which are the 92 lamps that are always kept lighted. The ceremony was not especially exciting, but we were so glad we decided to go there, and stayed until about 12:30. Then we came out with some friends M. & Miss C. saw who had a gentleman to guide them through the crowd & we were so lucky, for we hadn't been in more than 10 minutes before it poured & we heard some had a terrible time getting out later.

Rome. New Year's, 1901.

This morning we went walking up by the Palazzo Regina Margheritta [Dowager Queen Margherita 1851-1926, Queen Mother of Italy and Consort of King Umberto I of Italy until his assassination on July 29, 1900] and saw

The Horse Tamers of the 4th cent. in the fountain in front of the Palace ["... colossal, marble Horse Tamers... Works of the Imperial Age, copied from the original. They once stood in front of the Thermae of Constanine." *Central Italy*, 169].

We went by the Hotel Swiss, and the Quirinal [Palazzo Regio del Quirinale, 1574] where the Pope used to live prior to 1870, and where the present King, Victor Emmanuel III & Helena, his wife, live and that's where *The Horse Tamers* stand.

In the PM we went to the Pincian Hill & sat down to listen to the music for two hours and watching the crowd was such fun, and Mary and I were so interested that before long I think we would have attracted some men.

We later went to Miss Babbington's[6] for tea.

I rested with Mary on her bed and we had a nice talk. She is a corking girl and I am going to love her dearly before our trip is over, just see if I don't! Big dinner, but I would rather have one of Mrs. Bell's "fish & 'tater" ones any day.

Wednesday, January 2, 1901.

This morning we all started out bright and early and went first to see some lovely old palaces. The [Palosso] Massimi alle Colonne was the one that looked the oldest and was used to stable horses in parts of it. We went to the Palazzo Farnese. [It] was very beautiful with its three stories of different designs and the fountains and flowers to the rear. The Palazzo della Cancelleria was designed by Bramante for Cardinal Riario and the court was beautiful because of its simplicity.

The Rag Fair at the Campo Fiorio (Field of Flowers) today was more interesting than it proved to be last week and we all picked up a number of things. I got a most unvaluable agate for a hatpin for two francs and then I found a cunning ring for 5 Frs. and a bronze frame for 3 Frs. that I rather like.

I was dead tired when I got back for lunch but we started out right after. Marion and I going ahead in one carriage to the Casino Rospigliosi, where we saw Guido Reni's *Aurora* on the ceiling. I don't care much for it. It's too glaring.

We then walked along by the Quirinal to the Barberini Palace where we saw Dürer's *Christ Among the Scribeo* painted in five days in 1506 at Venice [Albrecht Durer 1471-1528], Guidi Reni's *Beatrice Cenci*, which is most sad and impressive as one looks at it.

The most ghastly thing was the famous Cemetery of the Capuchin in the Church of the Capuchins [Santa Maria della Concezione], a little aside from the Piazza Barberini where we first looked at Guidi Reni's *St. Michael*. "An image of that greatest of future events, which we hope for so ardently at least why we are young, but find so long in coming, the triumph of goodness over the evil principal," Hawthorne. And after it we went downstairs into the crypt, and what a place! Each chapel is vaulted and arched with the bones from the deceased monks of the order. *The Marble Faun* made it so vivid as he describes it in the XXI Chapter, which Miss C. read after we reached the house.

We stood in front of the Palazzo Regina Margherita, hoping she [Queen Margherita] might go for a drive, but were disappointed [The Palazzo is presently, 2009, the US Embassy.]. We had "maritozzi" [alla panna; soft sweet buns with raisins and candied peel] for tea and then I went to sleep while Miss C. read aloud much to my shame. Antonio's afternoon out.

Rome. Thursday, January 3, 1900.

This morning we started for our first glimpse of the Vatican and took carriages down at the Piazza di Spagna after going to the bank. It was freezing cold and we were glad to hurry along. I had no idea where the Museum was and so it was surprising to go around the Church [St.Peter's] to quite the other side of the façade.

There we went into the Sala della Regia, called so because of the two horse chariot which was used for centuries as an Episcopal throne in St. Marks. The *Discobolus* or *Disk Thrower* of Myron [Greek, 5th c. BC]. From there we went upstairs to the Etruscan [Museum] founded by Gregory XVI in 1836, containing twelve rooms in which are vases of the black on terra cotta & red on black and were fine. Going through these we came to a room containing bronzes of every description, kitchen utensils to gold ornaments. The glasses dug up didn't compare with some of the other collections. We went into the Gabinetto delle Maschere, because of the mosaic with masks found in Hadrian's Villa in 1780.

The Sala Rotunda containing the bust of Zeus by Otricoli [*from* Otricoli], which is fine. From there we went to the Galleria delle Statue, where we saw lots of sort of general things, but nothing especially wonderful.

Cortile del Belvedere was the green. It is a court with truncated corners and belonged at one time to the Belvedere built by Innocent VIII. [The Cortile] is surrounded by an arcade and the cabinets at the corners contain some of the most valuable things of the collection. As we entered from the Galleria delle Statue, it is flanked with two *Molossian Hounds* [ancestor to the Mastiff]. In the center are a fountain, sarcophagi & statues.

The *Group of Lacoon*, with his two sons strangled by serpents by command of the offended Apollo, is the grandest piece of the Rhodian school of art.

Apollo Belvedere, found in the 5th cent., and *Perseus & Two Pugilists* is another and *Mercury,* found beneath the Belvedere.

Auntie and I rode home & Count Uysini helped me out and in a most startling manner held my hand but it was quite by accident.

This afternoon we went in the car [tram] out by the Porta del Popolo to the Ponte Molle under the Porta del Popolo or Flaminia Gate along the Flauvian Way, and it is such a picturesque ride between the high walls and queer odd shaped houses of plaster painted in pinks & reds with here and there an outline of some old archway or wall long ago lost to history. Sheep made it attractive & donkeys all along added to the picture. The women with faggots in bundles on their heads, short skirts, & wooden sandals were walking along by the road.

The little Chapel of St. Andrea, erected by Pius II on the spot where he met the head of St. Andrew being brought from the Peloponnesus in 1462. The bridge [Ponte Molle] was built in BC 109; the central arches are the originals where Maxentius was slain after being defeated by Constantine in AD 312.

Friday, January 4, 1901.

This morning we tried to go to the Doria Galleria [Palazzo Doria], but it was closed for repairs, consequently we were obliged to use up the morning by going to some palaces and going in the courts of them. I don't remember the names, but I guess they aren't special.

In the PM, we took the car and went to St. Lorenzo Outside the Walls [San Lorenzo Fuori le Mura], which is a most wonderful church in its combination of the architecture, for the greater part and the ceiling is perfectly ghastly, but the mosaics are perfectly beautiful in the detail and the cosmato work is fine. We then went back and down into Pope Pius IX berth [tomb] where the work on all sides is the most beautiful of the modern mosaic work. The views of the mountains from the Campo Verano at one side of the church are beyond description.

Saturday, January 5, 1901.

This morning we went to the Vatican, beginning in the Animal Room [Sala degli Animali], going to see *The Horse of Hercules,* found in the 16th cent. near the Theatre of Pompey.

The *Apoxyomenos* (Scraper) is a fine thing & there were heaps of others but those two are the principal things ["… an athlete cleaning his right arm from the dust of the palaestra with a scraping iron… found at Trastevere in 1849." *Central Italy*, 345].

In the PM, Auntie & I went shopping & got charms and rosaries for we had our tickets for the Vatican from the Bishop this morning and are going tomorrow at 4:30.

Sunday, January 6, 1901.

This morning was rather uneventful, but I was glad to get some letters written; Mrs. Sargent, Aunt Belle, Eugenia, and Uncle Fred. Then at 3:30 we took carriages for the Vatican for which Father Murphy and the Bishop got us tickets. It was so funny when the envelope came yesterday morning we found only five, and I said I guessed the other had been forgotten. But when we were in the Vatican at the gallery yesterday, a guard offered some for sale so we clubbed together and bought one so all could go. Then this morning we found another one with Father Murphy's card accepting for dinner tonight!

We got good places at St. Peter's going by one of the huge pillars and as Auntie had brought a campstool for the occasion, we felt very grand. When the Pope finally appeared from the curtains along by the front entrance, we all stood on the base of the pillar and the stool, so could see him very well. He wasn't under the canopy. Neither were the candles burning, so we didn't see his face as plainly as we did before. He had on simply a skullcap and his red robes, but it was fine to be able to see the line of soldiers. He passed down the whole length of the church.

The service lasted about an hour and we had to wait a long time for the crowd to lessen, then we had a great time getting a cab for a Fr. & finally got one at 1.25. When we reached here, I asked Count Uysini for .25 and it was such fun, then we knew we should have borrowed it from the Secretary, so Marion rushed around to get down to give it before the rest came home. They didn't come for a long time and we tho't they were obliged to wait for the second round of carriages, but finally they came and said their horse fell, breaking shafts and they had to sit quietly waiting for them to be repaired with ropes.

The Bishop and Father Murphy came to dinner and I think they both enjoyed it very much. Father Murphy is a great one when he once gets started and he does talk splendidly and in a most interesting manner. I had to laugh to hear the Bishop simply nod whenever his opinion was asked or his private secretary asked him anything. They went about nine so we had time to write after talking them over.

Rome. Monday, January 7, 1901.

This morning Miss Cadwell's throat and voice didn't seem to be any better, so we induced her to stay in and let us go out by ourselves sightseeing, to which she consented. Of course we went to the bank first, and then I bought a Holy Year charm and chain with the money Frances sent me for my Christmas (16 Francs) and I am glad I selected those for it. After fussing around up and down the Via Condotti, we went on down to the Corso. On the corner I saw a beautiful buckle in the window that just took my eye and I decided then and there I would use the money Auntie gave me for a buckle for Christmas in that way. So I went in and asked the price to be told 2600 Francs. To say it took my breath away is mild. I nearly fell over and so did the rest.

Then we went along to the Pantheon, which we could not get in as they are getting ready for the Anniversary of Victor Emmanuel, the grandfather of the present King. We went around to the back and saw the columns and dolphins carved in it, and the arches over the Baths of Agrippa, which is back and under the Pantheon. Then we saw the Tomb of Fra Angelico in the San Maria Sopra Minerva [Fra Giovanni Angelico da Fiesole, 1387-1455]. From there we went outside and saw slabs that mark the height of the water in former days.

We saw the [Domenico Zampiere] Domenichino [1581-1641] paintings on the walls in the Chapel of S. Luigi de Francesi or the French Church.

'Hilda's Tower' [Torre della Scimia] as described in *The Marble Faun* is beyond, which we saw. It is a white Madonna way up on the top of the Torre della Scimia, by which the lamp is always kept burning.

This afternoon Miss C. and Auntie both remained in and we four went up on the Pincian Hill. The band played but I really felt a little nervous as the men were so thick and watched us quite a bit. We did not stay a great while but walked around and looked over the wall at the Villa Borghese [17th c. Villa of Cardinal Scipio Borghese].

Rome. Tuesday, January 8, 1901.

This morning we took carriages and tried to go to the Caesars' Palaces, but as it is Queen Helena's Birthday [Princess Helena of Montenegro; 1896 married Victor Emmanuel III, King of Italy, 1900-1946.], consequently a féte day, we could not get in, so instead went first to the Tarpeian Rock where the prisoners used to be flung over to their deaths. The view of the tops of the houses and the view over to the mountains including the Janiculum Hill [Gianicolo], and by the way, when we started out from the house we met the priest of Holy Door Day and he looked awfully nice and bowed very pleasantly at us.

I would have stopped if we had been sure of its being he. Then we went to the Palace of the Conservation where we saw all sorts of things of Bronze utensils and terracottas [The Palace of the Conservatori, or town-council]. The Picture Gallery where we saw the Guido Reni's *St. Sebastian* very like the picture we saw in Genoa, and no one knows which is the original. We saw the *Thorn Extractor* in bronze [Spinario; the Thorn Puller, 1ˢᵗ c. BC bronze. Clarissa had a copy in her home in Unadilla.].

In the PM Auntie and I took a carriage and rode to Trajan's Forum where we met the rest. All went to the Baths of Paolo Emilio or Baths of Trajan, which were entered through a gate by a smith's shop where there was a funny little pug in the midst of the fray. The Forum of Augustus was not far from there and by it were the beautiful Corinthian Columns. The Forum of Nerva (or Minerva) came next, and in just the little bit that has been excavated, we saw the most beautiful work of any so far. The statue in the centre and columns only half of which are above the ground, and the fine work is beautiful.

The Mosaics in St. Cosma [Santa Maria in Cosmedin] and Domnica [Santa Maria in Domnica] are beyond description.

We had coffee at a swell restaurant, Café Nazionale, where the men all smoked & had a beautiful time ["Usually called, Caffé Aragno, (after the proprietor), Via del Corso 179." *Central Italy*, 129].

Marion read a while in *The Marble Faun* and I made a bag for my leftover money out of some Liberty satin ribbon.

In the evening, I wrote four pages to J.E.S. [Josh E. Sweet] and these two pages and I don't see how I ever took so long to do so little.

Had to pay .50 on a card from Rob, because the stamp had come off.

Rome. January 9, 1901.

This morning we took the tram for the Vatican and Auntie didn't go and Miss C. only paid for four of us instead of five. The woman got in with the funny little dog that she kept in her fascinator all the way so the conductor wouldn't see it [a fascinator; woman's hair accessory worn in place of a hat].

We went directly to the Raphael Tapestries, the Cartoons of which we saw in the South (1540) Kensington Museum. We took each one as a whole and studied it all out. They are in the following order; * *Christ's Charge to Petro;* * *The Healing of the Lame Man;* * *Paul and Barnabus at Lystra;* * *Paul Preaching at Athens;* *Elymas Struck Blind* (not the original); * *The Stoning of Stephan;* *the Conversion of St. Paul;* * *Death of Ananias;* *Paul in Prison;* * *Miraculous Draught of Fishes;* *Christ Appearing to Mary Magdalene;* *Supper at Emmaus;* *Presentation of Christ in the Temple;* *Adoration of the Shepherds;* *Adoration of the*

Magi; Ascension. (Those marked * are from the original cartoons of Raphael and the others were designed by a pupil.)

We then went through to the Court of the Belvedere and took a hurried view there, then passing through the Atria del Meleagro, to the Atria Quadrato where the *Torso of Hercules* is [1ˢᵗ c. BC]. Then through the long Museo Chiaramonti to the Braccio Nuovo to see *Augustus Demosthenes, Wounded Amazon,* the colossal *Group of the Nile, Head of Juno* and the splendid *Apoxyomenos* (Scraper).

In the PM, Leslie and I took Auntie and Marion to the Baths of Diocletian while Miss Cadwell and Mary went calling. (Had 1 doz. Maritozzi for tea)

Rome. Thursday, January 10, 1901.

We had an early start and went directly to the Raphael's *Stanza*, which are the frescoes done by Raphael in 1508-1520 in the State Apartments by order of Popes Julius II & Leo X. He did not at first expect to do them by himself, but to assist older artists [Pietro] Perugino [Raphael's teacher, 1446-1536], [Giovanni] Sodoma [1477-1549] and other Umbrians and painters from Siena, but Raphael soon became so prominent that it was all given to him, but finished after his death by his pupils.

The *Incendio del Borgo,* representing the fire as it raged in the 9ᵗʰ century & was extinguished by Pope Leo IV by the sign of the cross as he stepped on the balcony in the loggia of St. Peters, the *Disputa,* the *Parnassus,* showing Apollo surrounded by the Arts & Sciences.

The *School of Athens,* a companion to the *Disputa,* represents an assembly of scholars.

The *Miraculous Expulsion of Heliodorus from the Temple of Jerusalem* alludes to the deliverance of the States of the Church from their enemies. The *Mass of Bolsena* shows an unbelieving priest convinced of the truth of the bread being the Savior's body.

Attila Repulsed from Rome by Leo I, from the expulsion of the French from Italy after the Battle of Novara in 1513. The Pope sitting on a mule surrounded by Cardinals etc., above is seen Paul & Peter who are visible to Attila and his Huns who are struck with terror.

The *Liberation of St. Peter* over the window & on the sides in three sections; showing Peter asleep in the dungeon, on the right he is conducted away by the angel and on the left the awakening of the guards.

Battle of Constantine Against Maxentius executed by [Giulio] Romano [1492-1546] is most interesting as it shows the Ponte Molle, which we know.

Domenichino's *Last Communion of St. Jerome* (1614); Raphael's *Madonna of Foligno* (1512); Raphael's *Transfiguration* are the pictures we noted especially.

In the afternoon we went up to St. Giovanni in Laterano to the Baptistery where Constantine is said to have been baptized in 337 [Il Battistero, San Giovanni in Forte]. We saw some beautiful mosaics of the 5th century.

Then we went to the principal Basilica & took it in detail [St. Giovanni]. It has a picture said to be Giotto's [di Bondone 1276-1337]. In the burial-vault of the Corsini is a *Pieta* by Bernini.

The Monastery Court of the Benedictines, founded in the 6th cent., is beautiful. Then we went to the Scala Santa of twenty-eight marble steps from Pilate's house in Jerusalem over which the Savior is said to have gone up ["Brought to Rome in 326 by the Empress Helena [Constantine's mother], and may be ascended only on one's knees." *Central Italy*, 298.].

Rome. Friday, January 11, 1901.

In the morning we went directly to the Vatican and through Raphael's Stanza to Fra Angelico's frescoes in the Chapel of Nicholas V, showing scenes of frescoes from SS Lawrence and Stephen. From there we passed to Raphael's Logge or Raphael's Bible [thirteen sections of painted Biblical scenes]. Then we went directly to the Sistine Chapel and had all our expectations realized by the beauty and grandeur of the place. We took it in a general sort of a way.

In the afternoon we got pictures only of the Vatican, then we five went for a lovely drive through the Villa Doria-Pamphili getting a fine view of Mt. Mario & St. Peter's, also of the city from different points. That is where Marion said the little boys had thrown the burrs on the trees. Oh, Marion. That's one on you!

Rome. Saturday, January 13, 1901.

This morning we went up to the Museum at St. John the Lateran [Museum Gregorianum Lateranense], which contains the antiquities that were crowded in the other museums.

In the PM we drove out through the Villa Borghese and into the room containing the Antiques then into the Picture Gallery and saw some lovely pictures. Afterwards, Auntie and I went shopping for waists & I got five.

Rome. January 13, 1901.

Three weeks today since we came; it does not seem possible! I wrote Nellie, Edna, Uncle Fred, Harold and Aunt Belle in the morning. After luncheon, Auntie and I started about two and walked up on the Pincian Hill. There were a great many people there and at three the band came, but it was pretty cold, so we did not sit down but came down home soon. Met Mr. Molaro [of Hotel Molaro] and his daughter going up.

At 4:15 Auntie and I started up to hear the nuns singing, but we reached there at about the same place in the service as the Sunday before, so were disappointed a little.

Monday, January 14, 1901.

This morning we got a good start for the Palatine Hill to see the Palaces of the Caesars and all the early Emperors of Rome, except Nero, who went off on his own hook and built his "Golden House" only the site of which remains ["The Palatine did not afford scope enough for the senseless extravagance of Nero, who built himself the Golden House." *Central Italy,* 265]. We took carriages and it was so cold even driving, Auntie was most frozen all the morning, but some of the others think it too warm for fires etc., so we are going to say nothing for a time and see how long it will be before they are shivering around.

We went through the little house at the entrance and walked up a hill between the rows of budded rosebushes to the ruins, the foundation, as I understood it, of Caligula's Palace or the Caesars, from which point we saw where his bridge is supposed to have spanned across to the Capitoline Hill. We walked through the old paved street flanked by odd shaped rooms that may have been shops, up some stairs to the top of the garden of Tiberius from which we had a fine view of the Forum and Miss C. read to us while we sat and stood in the sun - blowing away.

Then we walked over to the other side or the northwest side & got another view. Then we went back to the other part and went to the House of Livia [Wife of Augustus Caesar, mother of the Emperor Tiberius], to the Domus Augustana [Imperial Palace], which includes the Tablinum or Throne Room and Peristylium & Triclinium, then the Stadium, and the Palace of Septimius Severus to the Belvedere, where there is a fine view, around by the Paedagogium [school for the imperial slaves] and around by the altar & the cave where the wolf lived, and home ["... behind it (part of the original wall of Roma Quadrata) is a grotto, quite erroneously supposed to be the Lupercal in which the she-wolf sought refuge when driven from the twins (Romulus & Remus) by the shepherds." *Central Italy*, 271].

Rome of Today and Yesterday, The Pagan City, by John Dennie. 27 No. 23rd St., New York [note by Clarissa]

In the afternoon, Miss C. read to us awhile about what we had in the morning seen. (Poor Leslie has just announced that she has lost her scarab pin that Mary gave her for her Christmas, and is in a perfect flood of regrets.) Auntie was awfully cold and so were we all, but two of the girls do not want fires and so we will say nothing about it for a while, then we must see about it if it keeps so cold.

Auntie was so tired she decided not to go out again and so lay down, and we all went to the Mamertine Prison, which is up by the Forum under a church. It was really more awful than I had imagined. We went in through a bed quilt and turned to the left where a man lit two candles, Miss C. taking one and the man the other. He went down a long flight of dark stone stairs all covered with candle grease and at each landing he held his light so we could see where we were going.

Finally we got to the bottom and there we were in a room cut out of solid rock where we could distinguish an altar, and a hole with a grating over it through which they used to drop prisoners into the lower vault. We went down stairs and on the way, behind a grating in the wall [there is a rock], which is said to bear the imprint of St. Paul's head and we could easily imagine it for we could make out the side of a face. He is said to have used that stone as a pillow while he was imprisoned nineteen months in the cell under.

When we got in the under cell, which was scarcely high enough for us to stand in, we saw the pillar to which he was chained and in front of it the well, which is said to have sprung for him to baptize his jailer and the door through which the bodies were thrown into the big drain and so carried to the Tiber.

We had just time to dress when we reached Molaro's to go to the Quirinale for tea [Hotel Quirinale, Via Nazionale; "... a large hotel in "the Swiss style with restaurant in the winter garden." *Central Italy*, 127]. Auntie was too tired to try it and so we five took carriages, and were helped out at the door by "buttons", passed through a little office to the reading and tea room which reminded me of the same room in the Metropole in Milan but much nicer and Mrs. Metcalf with her "gal" [?] must have created quite an excitement when they were dropped there the night they reached Rome!

Well, after a while, Mrs. Howard and her daughter finally came without Mr. H. so we all went to the further corner and had our tea; bread and butter sandwiches, cake with two pieces of something that proved to be a sort of apple-pie and it was pretty good, too. It was fine to listen to music again from the balcony.

On our way home we stopped in a branch of Baker's [Chemist, Piazza di Spagna 42] up on the hill to get Spirits of Camphor for Leslie's chilblains, and on the little table by the door was a copy of S.S. Pierce's "Epicure", which looked like Boston. Pierce sells their beef extract I believe [Boston Grocery Store opened in 1831 by S. S. Pierce, selling gourmet foods and choice liquors.].

When we got in we found two tickets for the services tomorrow for the Mass for Victor Emmanuel at the Pantheon and it was decided Auntie and I should go, and start at 9:30 in the morning [King Victor Emmanuel II; " D. Jan. 9, 1878. An annual funeral mass is celebrated in the Pantheon a few days after Jan. 9th, to which the public are admitted by tickets, to be obtained from the consuls or other influential persons." *Central Italy*, 209].

I found Auntie so cold when I went to bed, having caught cold on the Palatine in the morning, so I got in with her for a while.

Rome. Tuesday, January 15, 1901.

When we were at breakfast Raffaello brought in another envelope from the Consulate General containing two more tickets so Marion and Mary hurried and we all set off for the Pantheon. We had to go around sort of back of the Pantheon to drive in between the rows of soldiers all like this [drawing], where the dots are, and after we got out we had to pass through the line of soldiers who presented arms as we four went in. We couldn't and can't imagine the reason why it was done.

We found our seats in B & Mary said we would scarcely recognize it with the top covered, floor carpeted and divided by railings for the different lots of people. In the center was an immense catafalque [raised, decorated platform] built for the occasion with a coffin on the top and surrounded by candles and hanging Roman lamps, which would spit every once in a while. From the entrance up to it and around to the side were the Roman Guards with their brass armor and breastplates with white pants, their helmets with the lamp chimney brush in front and long white hair hanging off the end of their helmets. They were the King's Guard in the above dress. The music was on a big balcony at the left consisting of voices and instruments, which was fine. They had [Luigi] Cherubini Requiem, and then some priests talked awhile, then followed a good deal more of the same sort.

When it was over we waited a while and then walked around by Humbert's Tomb [Umberto I, King of Italy 1878-1900] and to see the flowers around Victor Emmanuel's catafalque and to my surprise the flowers were all artificial, which made the whole thing seem like a farce as the body was not in the center at all but in the niche at the corner.

We finally got in at 11:30 and Miss C. & Leslie started out to see the place we had just left. I trotted down to Baker's and bought a water bottle all alone, and to my sorrow I fell short a franc and Mr. Baker said to drop in and pay it some other time. It was awfully nice of him I thought. Then I had to come back for more money to get the chocolate.

This afternoon we had the most splendid time down at the Colosseum[7] all the afternoon. We rummaged around and saw all the things on the ground and under it, getting an idea of the form and construction of it. The circumference on the outer side being 1/3 of a mile around, 205 yards through the long way & 170 the shorter and seated 40-50,000 spectators. The first row of the seats, called the Podium, was for the emperor, senators, & Vestal Virgins. The Emperor occupied the top raised seat called the Pulvinar. Two other divisions rose above this where there were wooden seats & still above sat the common people & on the edge of the wall on top sat the sailors.

We went up 176 stairs to the top and sat down on parts of the bases of columns in the sun overlooking the whole place. We sat there an hour while Miss C. read aloud out of Mr. Dennie.

It was so funny when we came down ready to get in our carriages, Auntie popped up as if she had come out of the ground and we were all so shocked to see her, for we thought she had gone home long before.

Miss C. stopped & got some sugar and Maritozzi and in the evening Miss C. & Leslie went and called on the Chamberlains.

(Head Waiter = Michaele dei Fiori da Capri. Such a fall from Antonio.)

Rome. Wednesday, January 16, 1901.

This morning we all took carriages and drove to the Villa Farnesina where Auntie and I left our man while we went in and then were going on.

The ceiling and lunettes are very pretty indeed and although they have been freely restored, they show Raphael's touch very decidedly. The figures around the border are better than the two large ones covering the ceiling proper.

Directly to the left is a room, which contains Raphael's *Galatea* and *Cupids*, a copy of which we have at home in the large engraving on the parlor wall. It is very sweet in colors and I think I shall like it better when I get home then I ever did before.

Auntie and I then went out for our carriage and for the life of me I didn't know which was our driver as I had not thought there would be more than one there, and I guess there were half a dozen standing around. We piled into one and then I saw another that looked familiar so we went over to him and there was a little man bobbing around us trying to talk French but we finally got in and I was so afraid he would take us to the wrong place, and then to my horror the little French man bounced up on the box, too. Then I was floored, but we did not have far to go and I saw St. Peter's to my joy looming up. Then the little man jumped off & lifted his hat in the most friendly manner. I had 10 centimes to give him but he was so grand I felt it would insult him. I made the driver understand where we were to get out and expected as much as could be to have to pay 2.50 for the minute or two overtime but gave him the 2 Francs for which he was duly grateful and we then went in and I bought the two tickets, and in we went, for I had my Baedeker, which we had all gotten down at Piale's [Bookseller] before starting to ride this morning.

I took Auntie all around through the Tapestry Rooms and then we looked at some of the statuary and walked around St. Peter's to the street where the bus was just ready to start for the Piazza del Spagna and I got out and paid Mr. Baker the Franc I owed him, then met Auntie on the corner and came up, and soon the rest came in from getting little bronze figures that are BC.

To my delight my coat from Marie came today, forwarded from Paris that I sent for on November 5th, which letter Marie didn't get until she got home on the 29th of November. It came in fine order.

In the afternoon we went to the Baths of Caracalla, which were splendid for the afternoon was ideal and the sun as it shown through the windows and over the jagged walls. We could easily see the divisions of the baths and found daisies in blossom.

We had our tea in the girls' room and then sat on the bed and talked and laughed. Marion insulted Mary all as a result of "How d'do Old Chappie", which was the song that was sung up on the Colosseum, and seemed so absurd.

Rome. Thursday, January 17, 1901.

We took this morning to visit St. Peter's and see it thoroughly ["St. Peter's is the largest and most imposing, if not the most beautiful church in the world." *Central Italy*, 308].

We took the tram, getting out a block this side and walked in. We did it pretty thoroughly and I liked Melozzo da Forli's [1438-1494] angels the best of all. There were the four large pictures, which are frescoes, which were originally done and framed in a big gilt frame and it shows them off well. The ones above these four are not especially striking with the exception of the one in the further corner, which is sweet with the little head peeking over the instrument. Then there were a few others about the room, and some of Giotto's, but not noteworthy.

When we were coming out, we were by the chapel containing the queer looking place which was a fort [?] and there were five - no four - children standing around & one woman had a little tiny baby hanging over her arm and Miss C. said there was to be a baptism so we waited and soon a man came & got out the priest's robes & the ointment & powder, etc. They had a great time for the priest put something in its mouth and all over its face in spots. Then they turned it over & looked as if to put its whole head in the tank but I think the priest only wet the back of its head. The child has to be baptized before it is 48 hrs. old and this little one had earrings on and was "real cunning."

Mary and I stopped for the mail and the others went on and we couldn't find them, but all the time they were just on the other side of the street watching us.

This afternoon Marion and I rode in the carriage over to Santa Stefano Rotondo, which is most peculiar in every way being round, and the walls covered with the most blood curdling frescoes of the martyrdom of the various saints. There must have been twenty-five. In the entrance was a chair in which Gregory the Great sat [Saint Gregory I, Pope, 590-604 AD]. It is a very old church as it was started in the 5th century.

The day before, we went to San Gregorio Magno built by Pope Gregory the Great in AD 575. We saw a chair and the niche where he slept and a marble table in the Chapel of St. Barbara where Gregory entertained twelve poor men daily, which is very beautiful, each place being marked by a cross & with beautifully carved supports.

From the round church we drove to the Villa Mattei, which is out in the direction of the Caracalla Baths and the view from some parts of the grounds was grand and there were so many bits of classic art scattered all about that it made it have an air of being so very substantial.

We walked home. Then Marion and I went down and got the Maritozzi for tea and all the afternoon we were bubbling over & at dinner when Marion took the poor leg, we simply exploded.

Rome. Friday, January 18, 1901.

This morning, all but Auntie went to the Villa di Papa Giulio, and we walked all the way for it was such a perfect morning, and we thoroughly enjoyed the walk. It's beyond the Porta del Popolo on the Flavian Way and then turning to the right we soon got there.

It's very beautiful in the court and all around the fountains. Then we went through the museum part and it was most instructive for among the collection we saw a coffin which was made of a tree hollowed out and must have been one of the earliest forms, but no date can be gotten at of course, and all the bronze ornaments etc. are arranged as nearly as possible in the order the things were in the coffin.

When we were through there we came out and took the road in front heading to the left and walked along through the country and everything we met seemed picturesque. The oxcart, soldier riding along, and that awful old beggar that discovered us as we were nearly by him, and whose curses we could hear until we were out of sight. Then we came on the road that leads to the Ponte Molle and caught a car that brought us to the Piazza del Popolo, and there the artists' models were so funny, urging us to give them money for the girls to take their pictures.

Soon after luncheon we walked to the Piazza Venezia and took an electric car after standing on the curbing about 15 minutes. The car was filled with people hand in hand with Baedeker and those who didn't own them borrowed them, so one woman proved. When we were nicely started the power gave out and then we waited for half an hour and the people were so funny to watch.

Finally we reached St. Paul's Outside the Wall [San Paolo Fuori le Mura] and went through the Church which is a Basilica and very beautiful in the sacristy. It was founded in AD 388 by some men on the site of a church of Constantine, and is still being built, having been started after the fire of 1823. The facade is going to be very imposing when it is finished. We saw the workmen cutting a block of marble and an American would drop dead in his tracks to see the slowness with which they worked. The Cloisters are very beautiful, like those of the Lateran with the cosmato work in the twisted columns.

We then just missed the car coming in so waited some time for another; in the meantime the girls bought fifty postcards for "half a franc", then we went up to the Café Nationale for coffee and cake and then hurried home.

This morning was rather cold and around the fountains at the Villa the maidenhair fern was all covered with ice. We are having awfully cold weather; there is no getting around that!

Mary and Leslie got mixed up with the scarlet robed German Priests, and did look so absurd, for they had six ahead and six behind them and there they marched in step and everything for about half a block. When they finally discovered where they were, their expression was something great. Then they crossed their path at the Piazza Cologna and again on the return trip at just the same place.

Rome. Saturday, January 19, 1901.

Nothing special for me today. Stayed in bed till noon and read all that's been going on for the year in Marion's transcript.

Rome. Sunday, January 20, 1901.

Rest day, taken up in writing. Just as we were ready to dress, Marion came rushing for me to come and see the Count dressing and there he was primping away!

Read more in *The Gladiators*. Asti for dinner! [*The Gladiators; A Tale of Rome and Judea*, by George John Whyte-Melville, 1863.]

Rome. Monday, January 21, 1901.

Being the twenty-first of January, it was the Blessing of the Lambs at Sant'Agnese Fuori le Mura, founded by Constantine over the tomb of St. Agnes. We took the "tram" out and as usual Miss Cadwell knew the best spot and we pushed through the crowd up near the altar on the left and after waiting a little while, about eleven o'clock, a little boy preceded two priests, each with the dearest, whitest little lamb lying in a flat round basket & edged with paper flowers. Then each little lamb had a crown of flowers tied on under its chin and they looked too cunning for anything. They kept so still that there is no doubt the little things were drugged.

After the service, Auntie and I took the tram and came home by ourselves. I think we could get along pretty well alone if we had to. I was ever so glad we went up, for it was such a queer idea. The singing was very good. The man, who comes near to being the Pope's Angel, sang.

Queen Dowager Margherita [note by Clarissa]

In the afternoon we went down to the Santa Maria della Pace, where we went through so much dirt and horrid ways, into the queer little court or cloister constructed by Bramante. From there we passed into the queer dirty church and saw the lovely Raphael *Sibyls* over a chapel. It has a bad light and the surroundings detract from the fresco, but I think they are very beautiful and I shall get a picture of them. There are some other rather peculiar things in the way of frescoes & carvings.

Santa Maria in Via Lata, which does not amount to much except that Sts. Paul and Luke are said to have preached from the oratory, which is upstairs.

We tried to get into a number of other churches but without success. Finally we left the rest and went shopping, buying Roman pearls and in one store we ran into Sonny & Auntie [guests at Molaro's Hotel]. Sonny bowed, but A. glared simply.

Miss C. was to meet her friend at Miss Babington's for tea at four and she never came until 4:45.

Tuesday, January 22, 1901.

In the morning we simply took on the whole city-microbes in the lead, too [?]. First we tried to see the Doria Gallery [Palazzo Doria], but it is closed as the pictures are being arranged in schools.

Then Auntie and I drove to Santa Maria in Cosmedin, which is over by the Tiber. It is an interesting old church and in the entrance there is a big round marble slab with a face carved in it showing hair, etc. with a big mouth into which the Romans, it is said, used to thrust their right hand when taking an oath [Bocca della Verità; the Mouth of Truth]. The pillars are very old and up back by the altar is an old chair very beautifully carved with lion arms and beautiful cosmoto work in the back

We then looked at the campanile, crossing to the Round Temple, to the remains of the old bridge or arch remaining of the Pons Aemilius, built in 181 BC, and below is the mouth of the Cloaca Maxima ["... ancient channel for drainage of the Forum." *Central Italy*, 272]. Casa di Rienzi is across the way from all this and the bits remaining are very picturesque as they are hid among all the other old buildings.

The Theatre of Marcellus is such a great surprise to come on to and we got tickets and went all through it, coming out in the yard of the Orsini Palace. We passed through what was originally the Ghetto or Jew Quarter and it was horrible to me, but still interesting ["Jewish Quarter, which was pulled down in 1887... in 1556 Paul IV, assigned this quarter to them, and until the end of the papal rule (1870) they were forbidden to settle elsewhere." *Central Italy*, 223]. Still I have decided I do not like dirt long at a time unless I am driving.

When we tried to go to the Palazzo Colonna for the pictures, etc., Auntie was getting pretty tired, so she and I took a carriage & drove up home. Bishop had called.

We went up to [the Palace of] Dowager Queen Margherita and waited an hour and a half for her to start for her drive without success. Then all went down to Miss Babington's for tea and teacakes, which were nice. Girls had shampoos and we got more pearls.

Rome. Wednesday, January 23, 1901.

Miss Cadwell read to us about the Catacombs, then we went toward the bank first and at the Piazza de Spagna saw a big funeral coming up the Via Condotti, which we waited to see. First came the band playing a dirge followed by a line of monks entirely in white with little peek holes cut to see out of, all carrying lighted torches. The hearse was drawn by four big black horses. Around and extending back were the mourners, mostly men in tall silk hats who looked like gentlemen. Then a school & nuns, followed by a great many fine carriages, the first few filled with beautiful flower pieces. The deceased was a member of the Municipal Council.

We then took a ten-seated Victoria and all six got in and drove out the Appian Way to the Catacombs of St. Calixtus and such a drive as we did have for we drove by the Circus of Maxentius [constructed for chariot racing], the Tomb of Caecilia Metella, and going as far as the Casale Rotondo [a tomb], and when we were up the steps by the stable we were shocked by the announcement that it was one o'clock, just luncheon time. We started home in a few moments, and enjoyed imagining what the old ruins of the tombs must have been that were all along the road and picturing the [carriages] that used to drive over the very same pavement of which we saw now and then. It was perfectly fine and we were so sorry when we had to get out of our carriage at two o'clock.

We found Capt. [Horatio] and Mrs. McKay had been here to call and had waited until late before giving us up, as Michaele assured them we would be in as we were <u>never late</u>, and he was so funny when he told us about them at the table.

We were all ready to go to see the Queen [Margherita] go out to dinner and got downstairs just as the Capt. and Mrs. McKay came again, so we all went in the Salon and we three girls, Marion, Mary and I, talked to Kenneth while Miss C. talked to the others.

We finally went over and only waited a few moments before out she drove [Queen Margherita] with a lady & man-in-waiting with her, the harness in dull black and all the equipment, also the four bicycle riders in the same. Then we went to the Santa Maria degli Angeli and San Bernardo, after which we had some lovely Maritozzi & tea.

The Catacombs[8] were fine, going through with the oldish monk who carried a taper wound around a stick while we all had little bits of ones, and I did expect any minute to set fire to the whole party. It seemed awfully good to get up to open air again and in the sunlight again. We went in the little house at the entrance and the girls bought postcards and the monks wanted us to buy some of the chocolate that they made, but Marion's was more inviting by far.

Rome. Thursday, January 24th, 1901.

In the morning Miss C., Marion, Leslie, and I went to the Capitoline Museum for Leslie missed it before. So after going to the bank, we started down, Miss C. and I walking. When we got there, Miss C. expected Marion and I to tell about things, but there was a silence, for I did not pay any special attention to the old reliefs, etc., so Miss Cadwell had to go through it again, but when we got up to the statuary, then I felt at home with the *Marble Faun* and all his companions.

In the afternoon Auntie, Marion, and I went for a drive up around the Monte Mario seeing Mr. Sebasti's Villa on the way up and lots of other funny things, including the woman with her donkey, which Marion tried to get a picture of but she persisted in staying in the shadow of the bridge. But she did take the little children who were standing at the gate of a house. Then at another gateway there was a group of peasants and children standing. Just as the oxen came out, one little child plunged forward and nearly went under the oxen's feet, which was a narrow escape as it could easily have hooked the little one.

We were out until after five and the man instead of coming right up through the Piazza del Popola went way around by the Corso making time. Marion paid him and we tho't it was all over when off he bounced and we had a great time in the entry with the old porter and the "boy who fights" as witnesses, ending by giving the man 5 Frs. instead of the 3.50 we started with. We nearly went in fits after it was over, and Marion and I went for Maritozzi, and when we got in the people announced that they were all looking out the window and saw the proceedings and it was because the money wasn't ready that we had such a time. But I think a dollar was none too much for the lovely drive. We went out through the Porta del Popolo and back by St. Peter's.

Rome. Friday, January 25, 1901.

The girls didn't go out and so Miss Cadwell took Auntie to the places she had missed; first we went to the Mamertine Prison, then dismissed our horse, which was the funniest thing, all the way there he would not go or stay in the middle of the street or do anything we wanted him to. Then we saw Baby Stuart [?] in the S. Luca Gallery [Accademia di San Luca], going from there over to the Capuchin Church to see the Campo Santo again. When we came out the queerest little donkey was braying for his dinner in the most human tones.

In the PM we all parted company and went in different directions, meeting at the photograph store in the Piazza di Spagna [Piales]. Then Miss C. and I had tea at Miss Babington's and from there went to have a shampoo. I tho't Miss C. would too, but she was a bit hoarse, so waited for me.

In the evening Marion read aloud to us in *The Gladiators*, which was fine.

The girls' pictures are fine and I guess I must buy some too.

Rome. Saturday, January 26, 1901.

I made up my mind that instead of going to Mr. Vedder's in the afternoon as I had expected to I would rather spend the 15 Frs. for photographs of Rome instead of just one of his pictures. The girls felt badly because I had to give it up but I didn't mind so very much [Elihu Vedder; 1836-1923; American painter who had a studio in Rome in the late 19th century. Via San Basilio 20].

We went to the Museum Kircheriano, where we saw costumes and instruments from different countries. The Ficoronian Cista [cylindrical toilet-casket 4th c. BC] and the bronze objects are interesting.

In the PM we did not do much because it sort of rained, so after doing some mending Mary and I ran up to the Via Sistina and got a lot of the tiny pictures of places and statuary. When we came in and had tea, Marion read and at dinner we all had our worst laughing spell of the trip and were nearly convulsed all during the meal.

In the evening I stuck in some of the little pictures. Mary got the idea from Miss Howard. [Clarissa has "stuck" many of these small pictures into, and sometimes on, the text in her Diary.]

Rome. Sunday, January 27, 1901.

We heard from Uncle Fred of little Eleanor's death at 5:45 AM, January 14th and it is needless to say that our hearts went out to poor Aunt Lou and Uncle Fred in their sorrow, which is ever more than we can possibly realize and I wonder if I could lessen it were I at home! [Uncle Fred, J. Fred Sands, Clarissa's guardian. The baby, Ruth Eleanor Sands, was the daughter of J. Fred and his wife, Clarissa's Aunt Lou.]

Monday, January 28, 1901.

My cold didn't seem to be much better, so my day was spent in bed for I had a splitting headache aside from being "[illegible]" as Leslie said.

The people went to a lot of churches in the morning and saw Michelangelo's *Moses* [San Pietro in Vincoli] in which they were disappointed. Baby Stuart again and the chains by which St. Peter was bound. In the afternoon they went to the [Villa] Doria Pamphili grounds and walked around, fed the ducks, sat on the grass and brought me home some pretty crocuses that they picked.

Rafaello brought me my dinner with such a prettily arranged dish of fruit on it that I put 1 Franc on the tray for him and he saw it as quick as a flash.

Leslie and Mary bought photographs, so Leslie let me take a list from her of the ones I want, which makes it so much easier and then I have the advantage of seeing how they look at home.

Read in *The Gladiators*, by Whyte-Melville in our room.

Rome. Tuesday, January 29, 1901.

We first went to the dressmaker, taking my shirtwaist, which she is to have done Friday. Returning we found the maid with Mr. Vedder's pictures, which were not as Marion ordered. Mary and I sent in orders and I think I shall give the one I ordered to Julie Sherman for her wedding present as it has Mr. Vedder's autograph on it.

We then tried to see the sarcophagi at the Laterni [Museum Gregorianum Lateranense, within the Palazzo del Laterano] but it was the wrong day so we had our tickets and went in and saw Sophocles, which I love ["... one of the most beautiful ancient portrait-statues in existence, found at Terracina in 1838." *Central Italy*, 294].

Auntie and I then bo't my photographs and got home in time for luncheon.

In PM we went to Doria Galleria, but it's not open yet, so took car and rode over to the Queen's, but she didn't go out. Then Leslie and Mary bo't a little basket of oranges and went to [Hotel] Eden to see the McKays and such a funny time as they reported. The bird fell out the window & was "quite dead!"

It was a lovely moonlight night so we decided to go to the Coliseum. We five went out and got a white horse that didn't look as if he could draw a thing, but we all got in and off we went and the little thing didn't stop from the time we left the corner until we reached our destination.

There was no one else there until a guard finally came, which really made it all seem more novel. The stars, moon, and fleecy clouds hurrying over the skies were perfect and it seemed a real live fairy tale to feel ourselves on that spot of so many scenes of bloodshed and horrors. The arches partly broken in regularly made a picture against the sky and one who is in Rome during the moon and [does not] avail themselves of the opportunity, miss a sight unequaled in the whole world. It was completed by Titus, 80 AD.

We gave our man 3 Francs for driving so well.

Rome. Thursday, January 30, 1901.

This morning didn't count for much as Auntie was sick and we called Dr. Baldwin who is the physician to the Duchess of York and whom we found came from NY and last summer drove through Unadilla while he was in Oneonta. His father was a minister there. Auntie felt as if a cyclone had visited her when he left.

In the afternoon we drove out to the Monte [del] Grano through the Porta San Giovanni. From the Monte we got a superb view of the surrounding country.

We then read in *The Gladiators* after dinner and finished it.

Received letter form Uncle Fred giving details of little Eleanor's funeral. Dear little girl, she shall be missed in that family!

Bags came, 11 Francs and oh how they do smell!

Mr. Beatty & Mr. Ferrie hoped to land [Mr. Harrison Beatty, a friend of Clarissa's from Bainbridge, NY, was to become Clarissa's second husband in 1915.].

Rome. Friday, January 31, 1901.

We went to the Sistine Chapel for our final view of it and saw the McKays following a guide around and the Captain [McKay] said, "His gabble grew very tiresome". We had a fine time looking at them all again and had a few minutes left, which we spent in the Raphael *Stanza*.

We went this PM to the San Pietro in Vincoli where we saw Michelangelo's *Moses* and I must say, as a whole I rather like it, but still I do think the pictures flatter him.

We went to the San Clemente [Basilica, predating 392 AD], which is the queerest of all queer places, and it's simply beyond description with the three churches, one on the top of the other. There was a special illumination today so the second church was lighted.

Mr. Vedder's pictures came!

Pincian to hear the music and saw some fine turnouts & people.

Rome.　Friday, February 1, 1901.

This morning the Doctor came and talked pretty plainly to Auntie and later to Miss C. and me and it seemed pretty serious, for the rest are to go on to Naples and to all those places I have simply lived for ever since we thought of coming abroad, but I think I could not have been in a better place if we had to give up [something] and it is lots better to be in this place than any other. The girls would not listen to going on tomorrow but are going to stay here a few days longer or until we know just how Auntie is going to be. It's awfully good of them and I shan't forget it.

In the meantime, the girl came with my waist, and it's sweet, so I gave her the two others to be made without linings.

We finally got in the Doria Gallery to see the pictures, which is a beautifully fitted up collection with white silk curtains at the windows and it has the appearance of a real palace. We saw the McKays on the rampage and poor Captain had Baedeker upside down.

This afternoon we went first to Santa Maria in Trastevere and it is most interesting, but somehow didn't pay much attention to anything we saw for everything has come so suddenly this week. Just before we left the Bank this afternoon I had a letter from Fan telling about little Eleanor's funeral, which nearly finished me. It's really awfully hard to take all these things and think they are for the best, but I do know it must be all for the good of us, and sometime, no doubt, it will be perfectly clear.

We next went to San Cosimato [Monastery] but was not much to remember.

Then we walked around to Santa Cecilia in Trastevere where we saw the figure of the recumbent St. very like the one in the Catacombs [Martyred St. Cecilia, by Stefano Maderna, 1571-1629]. In the adjoining chapel they show the remains of the bathtub in which she was boiled, for the church is on the site of her home.

Rome.　Saturday, February 2, 1901.

This morning the Doctor came and found Auntie so much better that he said he thought maybe we could go to Naples after all and I am simply overjoyed and the girls are all perfectly dear and seem to be so glad that we can go that it's a perfect delight.

It was then 10:35, so Leslie, Marion, Miss C. and I started out, while Mary went to Dr. Chamberlain for dentistry and we went for our permit to visit Castello Sant' Angelo by eleven o'clock [Erected AD 136 by Emperor Hadrian for himself and successors. Today (1900) Fort held by the Popes. *Central Italy*, 300].

We took a carriage after coming from the 10th Reg. station over toward the Font du Trevi ["The most magnificent of the public fountains of Rome… erected 1752." *Central Italy*, 153] and hurried along, reaching the gate in plenty of time. A funny man showed us through Hadrian's Tomb, who was a mixture of Lou Sherwood and Fred Hubbell, so he was a choice bit. The firing of the noonday gun was fine as we saw it from one of the balconies.

In the afternoon we went down to the Forum and investigated the new church, which was simply wonderful, and the skeletons in the niches like those at the catacombs were most interesting.

Rome. Sunday, February 3, 1901.

Quiloquy: Hives or Fleas! [drawing in the Diary]
The above is Marion's view of the three of us, for we are nearly dead with what Dr. Baldwin said this morning were fleas, but Miss Cadwell thinks is hives.

Dr. told us that Auntie was in no condition to keep up with us for the remaining of the year and must plan to go home when the opportunity offers and so I suppose we must make the best of it and I do hope it can be arranged so she can go back with the friends who have just come over for the Orient Trip [Mr. Harrison Beatty & Mr. Ferrie].

Rome. Monday, February 4, 1901.

This morning the Doctor was coming early to say whether we could go to Naples as we had planned, but we had most fortunately decided that Auntie couldn't possibly get ready on such short notice, and he didn't come finally until eleven o'clock. He said he wanted her to go to the oculist and so Miss Cadwell went up to see if she could go this afternoon, but he can't have her until tomorrow at ten. In the meantime, I went down to the bank and drew some more money and it does seem as if the money is simply flying and I don't know but I shall be obliged to go home C.O.D. Before we got home it began to rain and my skirt got all drabbled much to my disgust.

Right after dinner we went to the Lateran Museum to see the sarcophagi, which gave us such a good idea as to the way they progressed from the first form on wavy decorations to the more elaborate kind.

We then took a Fr. and Marion and I did a little shopping. Finally Miss C. and I got together and the tailor came and took my blue skirt to fix and the jacket to reline and he said it would be about 10 Francs, which nearly took my breath away it was so cheap.

Auntie went down to dinner.

Rome. February 5, 1901.

This is a horrid, rainy morning and the doctor didn't come until rather late and the girls stayed in bed while Auntie went up to the oculist and had her eyes tested and I went down to the P.O. Then I met Miss Cadwell and we went up to see the McKays for a little while and had a nice call up there.

It was [also] a horrid rainy afternoon, the sort of day that is pleasant one second and pouring the next. Miss Cadwell and the girls went for a walk and I went out alone to see about some velvet and had a good time all by myself. When we got in, we found the McKays had been here and the porter told them no one was in, which was simply maddening, for we had everything ready to give them tea and bought an extra cup and saucer, milk and Maritozzi, so Marion and I took theirs and left them up at the Eden. We were so relieved that the maid came down instead of Mrs. East, who "was resting". Coming home we went in the postal store and I selected three perfectly stunning ones and such a time as I had paying for them, for I couldn't understand what she said and I still think I was fooled because they came to over one franc.

We had tea already waiting for us and then began *Last Days of Pompeii* by Lytton, and it seems as if it was an awfully long book [Sir Edward G.D. Bulwer-Lytton, 1803-1873; *Last Days of Pompeii*, 1834].

Rome. Wednesday, February 6, 1901.   Mary's Birthday !!!

And such fun as we had, for Miss Cadwell had given it a lot of thought and asked Raffaello yesterday to please have one hard boiled egg for morning and bring up the largest soup tureen and ladle from the dining room and to get a lot of flowers, so he was quite interested and we howled when Miss Cadwell said she thought down in his heart he thought us mildly insane to make such requests.

Well, this morning he came and we all but Mary and Auntie went out in the salon and helped where we could to arrange the things. We moved the wiggly table up and put the big tray with a napkin on it, then streamed the narcissus and iris all over it and put the presents in among them. Miss C. wrote a poem at 4:30 AM, which was read aloud before our repast was begun. Then her chair was covered with one of the Roman rugs and on the other side was another small table with a napkin and ferns spread over it and in the middle set the tureen, covered. Leslie called Mary as usual & it was such fun to watch her surprise as she opened one thing after another. Auntie came out and we had a nice time and felt as if we all had a fiesta day.

The girls went over to the Vatican for the last time & Auntie and I drove up to the oculist, No. 5, XX September [Dr. Krahnstöver, Via Ventí Settembre 5] and he is nice, sort of like Mr. Bennett. When we got home we found the glasses weren't just as we thought, and so I went up again, but couldn't get in, so it was all useless.

The Dr. came while we were gone and said that he tho't we could go tomorrow, which meant we must do some packing. So Auntie & Miss C. went to order the [oculist].

Then later we went to a new Roman Tea Room over on the Corso and we were so disgusted to think we hadn't been there before for everything was so dainty & artistic.

Coming home I saw a buckle in Tombini [Via Condotti 2] I liked so Leslie and I stopped and the nice dark Italian let me bring it up to show Auntie and Leslie and I rushed back by the Di Spagna Steps and I bo't a little Roman lamp for 2 Frs. We met the girls on the way, saying Miss Cadwell was worried that we were out so late. So, we hurried home, and she wasn't angry, only tho't it too late for us to be out.

To think we leave "Too Bad!" and "John", Rafaello, Michaele, Count, the Boy that Fights, Bert Hilt, the Man that has Money, Porter Rosinia or Rosina and all the rest. Christmas Tree, Bambino, Dolly, Auntie, and Sonny, and Leo and I am sorry we are going and only wish my skirt would come before I go.

Rome - Naples. February 7, 1901.

The Captain and Mrs. McKay and Mrs. East came to call and we were all busy packing our new "carry-alls" ready for our trip south and it was such fun because none of us had any idea how much we could get in each, as it was our first experience in that line and so it required "careful thought". When I was in the midst of mine the Doctor came and he was so pleased to see how much better Auntie was and how well her glasses seemed to work.

After everyone went, Miss Cadwell and I went down to Cook's, the bank and did up some little errands. Then we had an early luncheon sitting at the little table in the corner with Michaele and "the man that has things" to wait on us and we had a fine luncheon; omelet, breaded chops, and potatoes fried, chicken and lettuce salad, cheese, oranges, apples, English walnuts, figs, and hot roasted chestnuts. We had to hurry and so took our fruit & nuts with us.

Then started right off and the whole corps of attendants were in the hall waiting for tips and as John didn't wait on us, Miss C. tho't he wasn't there, and did not give him anything and Marion and I were most heartbroken to think he was not remembered. As we each went out of the door, Mr. Molaro stepped up and presented each of us a bunch of flowers, so when we got in the bus we looked like six brides and felt it too.

Reaching the station we followed the man from Cook's again and he conducted us to a compartment by ourselves and then we tried to look full, and succeeded very well until a red haired chap came along and we six females couldn't faze him, so he made himself at home. All the spare room he filled with his dress suitcase, coat, hat and umbrella, which dripped a drop on me. Then he went out and found another empty place, so moved all his chattels, and so he seemed but an apparition.

We had a comfortable ride and reached Naples at seven, but it took us some time to drive up to the Britainnique from which we are going to get a lovely view of Vesuvius, but if this rain keeps up I fear we will be disappointed. We could only have rooms on the ground floor until someone [leaves]. It seems very nice here and the people look quite wide-awake. We were all tired and so went to bed early, soon after we finished our dinner. [Hotel Britannique, Corso Vittorio Emmanuele 133, Napoli. "... patronized by the English and Americans." Baedeker, *Southern Italy*. 1900, 19].

Naples. Friday, February 8, 1901.

"The life of the people in Naples is carried on with greater freedom and more careless indifference to publicity than in any other town in Europe. From morning till night the streets resound with the cries of vendors... Strangers especially are usually besieged by swarms of hawkers, pushing their wares, and all eager and able to take full advantage of the inexperienced of their victims.

Naples, the capital of the former Kingdom of Naples, now of a province with 535,100 inhabitants, is the most populous town in Italy, and occupies one of the most beautiful situations of the world." Baedeker, *Southern Italy*, 27-30.

*

Our first morning greeted us by a rainstorm and Miss Cadwell said it was nothing unusual to have it pour while she is here. We had downstairs rooms given us and Miss McPherson said she would change us as soon as some people would go who they could not get rid of.

I had a most unhappy and unpleasant morning as nothing was too unkind to say to me, and it is not surprising that in such an atmosphere I don't sleep well and have not a ravenous appetite. The more I do and look out for her [Auntie's] comfort the more hard things are said and sometimes it's pretty hard to appear happy, but when she feels better, then things run more smoothly.

Soon after luncheon we moved up to the top floor where we have such a view of the whole surrounding country. Auntie and I have a corner room with a window on each side. When it cleared and the mist lifted, the view of Capri, Sorrento, Castellammare and the surrounding country was a beautiful sight. It is hard to realize that Vesuvius is really within sight. Now it is covered with snow about a third of the way down, which does not often happen. I can hardly wait to see it really spout. We see the smoke coming out of it all the time, but no flame seems to flash and we have looked faithfully for it. The balcony is very nice to get views from and we have more than our share for there is one off both sides of the room. Auntie and I had our tea sent up.

Naples. Saturday, February 9, 1901.

This morning we took the tram and went down to the [Archaeological] Museum, which is great for they have all the choicest bits of frescoes from the remains of Pompeii and some beautiful works beside the frescoes, in the famous *Bull, Psyche of Capua, Homer* and *Flora*. Then the bronzes are the most beautiful by far that we have seen anyplace. *The Drunken Faun, Wrestlers, Apollo Shooting, Mercury Reposing, Head of Dionysus*, and in the next room the *Narcissus, Dancing Faun, Satyr with a Wine-skin* & *Silenus* make a grand row of bronzes.

When we came home we had our first experience with the Napolitan Cab Drivers and Marion and I started off alone and we tho't we were lost to this world, but we came home in good shape.

In the afternoon we couldn't go up to the Monastery [Certosa di San Martino], so browsed around and got our bearings, going to the bank and walking home. It poured and we were caught under the balcony or awning of a lemon stand and there we saw our first herd of goats that go along the streets and into the houses to be milked. The cows are also driven through the streets and up to the doors. The people bring out their little pitchers and glasses to get their pure milk, but the drivers have little bags of water up their sleeves and through a little tube the water mixes with the milk.

Naples. Sunday, February 10, 1901.

We go down to breakfast here and in addition to our coffee and rolls we have strained honey. Miss Cadwell prepared us for sour bread here but it's not a bit bad and I like the brown bread better than I did in Rome.

Soon after breakfast we started and walked up the steps to San Martino. It was an experience getting up those steps. There was no limit to the filth on them of every description and at times it did seem as if the odor would knock us over, for it was terrible. Every stage and scene of the life of the natives is exposed to view and I think the American who comes first to Italy has a good deal to overcome. I am so glad we had it shown to us by degrees, for it's bad enough now.

The view from The Belvedere is well worth the climb, the whole panorama is before us ["… commanding exquisite views of the city, the bay, Mt. Vesuvius and the fertile country." *Southern Italy*, 85]. The Museum [Museo Nazionale di San Martino] is rather interesting and especially the scene showing the natives all busy at different work [frescoes].

In the afternoon we had a two-seated carriage and Mary sat on the box with the driver going out to Pozzuoli[9] through the Grotto, which is 800 yards long, and such a queer place! We saw all sorts of sights in going there for everything is so thrown open to the public view. We were flooded with a supply of guides and finally got out at some steps, which we ascended and went over to the Amphitheatre, which are remains from Nero's time.

Coming back I sat with the driver and missed such a funny encounter. We saw a group watching some dancers and the second they spied us, out ran one while the other jumped up in the air 20 ft. and seemed to stare at us above the crowd. By that time the first man, masked and dressed in black and yellow, had reached us and had his face next to Miss Cadwell leaning over, in. The whole crowd hooted and thoroughly enjoyed the sport with the forestier. Finally, he left us and we had our laugh. We were gone all the PM.

Pompeii – A day trip from Naples. Monday, February 11, 1901.

"Pompeii was once a prosperous provincial town, with a population of 20-30,000 souls. After an earthquake in AD 63, the town was re-erected in the new Roman style and had not been long completed when it was overtaken by the final catastrophe on 24th Aug. 79 AD…

Before visiting Pompeii, the traveler is strongly advised to acquire some previous acquaintance with the place from books and plans… the more familiar the objects are to him, the greater will be his enjoyment.

The enthusiasm called forth by the [re]discovery of Pompeii [1748]... raise the expectations of the non-archaeologist to too high a pitch... in order to summon up from these mutilated walls an accurate picture of ancient life, frequent and prolonged visits and patient observation are indispensible." *Southern Italy*, 120-121.

*

We started a little before ten for Pompeii and Marion and I went in one carriage to the station where we ran into a Cook's party. Our train was late in starting but we finally got there. Marion and I were very much amused listening to the styles as told back of us.

We were one hour going the fifteen miles.

All sorts of things were out to welcome us & we went directly up to the ruins, and did it in great shape. We took our luncheon with us and ate it in the triangular Forum using an old altar in the Temple of Hercules for our table. Our feast consisted of hard-boiled eggs, brown bread sandwiches, white bread and lamb sandwiches, and oranges and it did taste so good. The pretty little daisies were all blooming around in the grass. We could see Vesuvius beautifully and by turning around had a fine view of the Campania and The Bay of Naples.

We started for home after getting some cold coffee at four, reaching the hotel at 5:30. I spoke to the Roberts who are with the Allens.

Luncheon Among the Ruins

Naples. Tuesday, February 12, 1901.

We went to the Museum in the morning and encountered Mr. & "Mrs. Philadelphia" on their way there and she asked about Auntie, which I thought very nice of her.

We saw the vases, bronze utensils, ornaments in gold & silver cups, cameos, and the Tazza Farnese, the largest onyx in existence, a sort of plate. Then we went all through the statuary department and reviewed them. That Narcissus is a gem! [bronze statue from Pompeii].

In the afternoon we fussed around and did up a lot of errands for them to leave us in good shape, for yesterday, Miss Cadwell decided to go to Capri [with Marion, Leslie & Mary] and Auntie and I will stay here while they are away. Our friends coming will break up the time and so it will go quickly. I can hardly wait for them to get here and to see what plans we can make for Auntie's return, for if it can't be arranged in that way I am sure I don't know what we will do about it for she must be sure of her companions for the trip [Clarissa is anxiously waiting the arrival by ship of Mr. Harrison Beatty & his traveling companion, Mr. Ferrie.].

Naples. Wednesday, February 13, 1901.

It was rainy this morning and Miss C. had the office telephone to see if there was an opera tonight, but there is none. We stayed in and read *Last Days of Pompeii* and it's getting so interesting I am anxious to go on with it.

This afternoon we went to the Aquarium and although it's not large it's perfectly fine and we enjoyed it very much. We should read [blank].

We then bought pictures and spent all our afternoon down there.

I spoke to Mrs. Coltrell & her daughters from Albany.

Naples. Thursday, February 14, 1901.

We nearly forgot St. Valentine's Day, but last night Marion made us all cunning little sketches from life, and Mary wrote us bits of sentiment in her own patent handwriting, so we did celebrate after all [valentines are in the Scrapbook]. I sent the Party a postcard valentine over to Capri to be there when they reached Pagano's [Hotel Pagano, "... frequented by Germans, plain, but fairly comfortable." *Southern Italy*, 153].

At last it is a nice day so we had an early breakfast and the rest took the boat at nine for Capri [Saloon Steamer *Nixe*, Daily Feb. to May at 9am; Sorrento at 10 am, Capri at 10:45 am. *Southern Italy*, 153].

I went to the stores in the morning. Then after luncheon, Auntie & I took the car and changed at "Toretta" coming out just as I had wanted to a little ways from Gutteridge & Co., where we went to look for waist-material as the cashier in the grocery store told me to do [Milliners, Toledo 192, Napoli]. We found something in another store that is pretty, but we didn't get it though.

After we came in, I made tea and began to read aloud *Agnes of Sorrento* by Mrs. Harriet Beecher Stowe [1862]. I fancy until the rest get back, news will be at a premium.

Naples. Friday, February 15, 1901.

Yesterday I ate a little pork, just why I don't know, but today I am a little under the weather and have vowed that pork shall be crossed off my list.

It is awfully cold and we had a fire in our little stone fireplace and it felt pretty good and was so cozy.

Had a card and I wrote one to Miss C. & Party.

Naples. Saturday, February 16, 1901.

A regular blizzard all night and snowing and blowing hard when we got up, so we read and looked for the [Steamship] *Adler*, which was due but on account of the storm did not come. Auntie turned the hems and I made two tea towels for Miss Cadwell and Auntie made a holder, which makes the danger of fire less when taking off the kettle.

Our larder is dry, so before we have any more tea, a new supply must be gotten.

Florence's cunning hand-painted valentine came and from the note on the envelope I think my skirt has arrived at last in Rome.

Not feeling very good in the afternoon so I am not so disappointed at having to stay in because of the storm. No boats went to Capri and so telegraphed in the afternoon.

For the first time we saw a little flame from Vesuvius and it must be lovely when there is a large eruption. I do hope so. It would be nice before we leave. [!]

Had a hot fire all day and were very glad of it.

Naples. Sunday, February 17, 1901.

It was a lovely bright morning and we kept our eye out for the *Adler*, but it did not come in the harbor until we came up from luncheon and then we watched it drawing near so very slowly and it did not get in until about 3:30.

Auntie went downstairs pretty soon and about half past four the man came up and said they were downstairs. I was all in a fluster at the thought of seeing them but got fairly composed by the time I was down the four flights of stairs. They were sitting by the fire. Mr. F. [Ferrie] & Auntie on one lounge and Mr. B. [Harrison Beatty] on the other, so I sat by him and was so sorry that they had to sail by five o'clock, for I thought surely they would be there a day or so.

Mr. B. and I joked most of the time while Auntie was talking to Mr. F. about going home when he goes. Really, he is one if not the most thoughtful, unselfish man I ever saw and he even says he will go home whenever she says if she is in a hurry to be off and I call that more than any other man I know would think of doing. He does all these nice little things in such a way that one likes to have him about.

Mr. B. was great fun, but I think he tried to be very dignified and so remind me of the drift of his conversation when I drove with him a few weeks before we came away. I think he will come around alright and be only too glad to call when we are in Germany, if he takes the proposed trip up there with the doctor before going home. He thinks he may stay until May. It hardly seems as if they have really been here, for I have been looking forward to seeing them for so many weeks. On the return I guess we will get in a longer time and then Mr. B. won't be along, so I won't need to be so careful of every look and gesture. I much prefer to have them separately.

Naples. Monday, February 18, 1901.

Auntie and I took the car a little after ten to go down and get the velvet for her waist. When we got on [the tram], there was an elderly Englishman and his daughter just on and I could see he was not sure from his movements of just what & why he was paying just that fare, and the young lady couldn't help him out. He stayed out on the platform and she sat in the cheap 10-centime side. When we changed at Toretto, he came in and sat by me and she stayed outside. He first asked me if I knew where some library was and finally I saw in his address book that he was on the right car. Then he asked me how long we had been here, all about the Museum, and if it was worth going to, all about Pompeii and even how to get there and what time the train left. Auntie was trying to talk to me on one side and for awhile I was kept pretty busy.

We got her goods and then some large bandana squares to put washing in, which are very nice. Then we walked along to Strada San Lucia and going into all the coral and shell stores looking for hairpins, lorgnettes [hand-held eye glasses], and a toilet comb, which I found and beat the man down two francs on it. I got it for Miss Cadwell's birthday on the 28th of February. I paid eight francs, a little more than we are allowed but she has been so sweet since I have had so much worry that I wanted to give her something she would surely like and use ["Coral, tortoise-shell, and lava ornaments may be mentioned as specialities of Naples. Copies of ancient bronzes, Etruscan vases, etc. ... and as a general rule bargaining is absolutely necessary to prevent extortion... The buyer should be careful to maintain a polite and unexcited demeanour." *Southern Italy*, 25].

I was also looking for nice black hair combs and one old man fussed and hunted till I left and in a minute up rushed this stranger with a comb in each hand, which the man had just found. He was breathless and hatless, and as he was the clerk he couldn't say a word of English, so I had to say no, for Auntie by that time was way on around the corner and I had visions of never seeing her again.

I then went to the bank and got the mail. Then we both took a car and Auntie came on home, while I went for crackers for tea. Coming home I bought two lemons off an old woman and I was so delighted when she was satisfied with the money I gave her for I was sure she would strike and I couldn't tell what she wanted. When I got to the hotel it was quarter of two and I was simply dumbfounded for even yet I have no idea where the money could have gone. Finished "Agnes" wrote Uncle F., Fan, Mr. F., postals to Blanche, Florence and Leslie.

Naples. Thursday, February 19, 1901.

Auntie began her waist and I helped her rip up her blue floral one. It was a great day raining one minute and sunny the next. Nothing of any importance happened. I read in Baedeker about the things I was weak on and did little odd jobs.

Had a letter from Miss Cadwell and if it was pleasant they were going to start off for Sorrento but I rather think the sea was too rough.

I read in *The Last Days of Pompeii* and it is so exciting that I can't bear to lay it down, but Auntie gets tired of listening and goes to sleep, so I have to stop.

Naples. Wednesday, February 20, 1901.

In the morning the girl came and got the waist to stitch. I went down and got medicine for Auntie, which the woman whom Auntie asked about it, said was not right. So the next morning I took it back and the druggist said he knew Dr. Baldwin well.

Naples. Thursday, February 21, 1901.

Auntie finished her waist and it is so pretty and it fits very nicely indeed.

Finished *Last Days in Pompeii* and it is so exciting towards the end.

It rained all the morning but in the afternoon I went down to the grocery store and got some tea crackers. Took the medicine.

Coming back I saw the performance of the gallant kiss the lady's hand as she put it out of the carriage door.

I tho't I would get some lemons for our tea, and so got three and dropped them in my umbrella and got the tea all ready and made ready to squeeze the juice in, when I found it was a joke on me for they were not lemons at all but sort of sweet and horrid things and I don't know what they are exactly.

In the evening I met the Cottrell's friend, Mr. [?] and I don't know which he is in love with. They leave for Spain tomorrow and he to visit some of his relatives.

Naples. Friday, February 22, 1901.

Mrs. Stoddard was very kind and asked me to go for a walk with them in the morning but we had planned to take Auntie's hairpins back and stop at the bank, so I did not accept.

We could not drive much of a bargain with the shopkeeper but Auntie got a long hairpin for a gift when she goes home.

I drew some money and got a handful of mail for the girls. It was a cold horrid day and people do complain and grumble [Auntie] so that I get awfully disgusted hearing them.

I tho't I would go and see what Mrs. S. had decided to do about the walk and found them trying to make their fire burn. Mr. S. had his overcoat on and Mrs. S. her fur cape around her trying to keep warm, but they soon had a nice brisk fire. I stayed there until about four and then came up.

Auntie said she didn't care for tea and so we were not going to have any. I had gotten nicely up when Mrs. S. came and said they thought they would go, if I would like to, down to the shops around Cook's and to the [?], but we walked down to the Villa Nazionale and Mrs. S. said she tho't it would be nice to go to the Tea Room that she had heard of [Villa Nazionale "... generally called La Villa, is a beautiful pleasure-ground, laid out in 1780... The Villa is rarely deserted by promenaders at any hour; but the busiest and gayest scenes occur when the daily concerts take place." *Southern Italy*, 33]. So we inquired and had a great time and at last we struck it opposite Sommer's [Photograhy Shop, Largo Vittoria] and had such a nice cup of tea and cake.

When I got back I found a letter from Miss C. and they are in Sorrento and she wants me to come over on Sunday to meet them and come back on Monday with them. But I decided if I went, to go in the morning and be there for Amalfi in case it was pleasant and got up the courage to decide.

Received telegraph, "A Happy Wash day to you". The [?] came by freight for I had not thought of its being a holiday until a girl rushed up and got her American flag for her table [George Washington's Birthday].

Talked to Mrs. Church and her daughter from Oakland, Cal., and to Miss [?] who met Mr. F. and Mr. B. on the steamer coming from Gibraltar. They decided Mr. B. was married and had his wife, though they didn't see her, and that Mr. F. was the only one of quite a party of men who was single, and they said Mr. F. was so kind & thoughtful and always helping everyone who needed help, which I can easily believe to be so.

Sorrento. Saturday, February 23, 1901.

"In winter, spring, and autumn Sorrento is visited almost exclusively by foreigners, chiefly Americans and English... Visitors generally bathe in the morning (swim), devote the hot part of the day to the 'dolce-far-niente' (a pleasant idleness), make short excursions in the beautiful environs in the late afternoon, and after sunset lounge in the Piazza listening to the band." *Southern Italy*, 149. [Clarissa never recorded any "bathing" by The Party.]

*

Well if this isn't a day to do! I was up at seven and ready for breakfast at 7:45 but it wasn't ready, so I waited until 8. At 8:30 the handsome door boy was ready and they called a cab and he sat with the driver and off we started and I felt to my death. We went to Castel dell' Ovo [landing location of the steamer to Capri and Sorrento] and he got my ticket and went, and I got in the small boat to go to the *Nixe* with three French people, two Germans and two Italians and myself. The porter had encouraged me by saying there were only Americans on. We rowed out to sea and the oarsman nearly frightened me to death by insisting for 30 centimes instead of 20 [as stated in Baedeker]. We climbed up the stairs and went directly up on the deck where my guard left me to my own destruction.

I finally, after the orchestra struck up in front of me, talked to an English girl and tho't she was going to get off at Sorrento, but she found she wasn't, so I went down on the next deck and finding no one else I came back. But that I knew was the place, so went down & spoke to an Officer. Just then I caught sight of Miss C. coming up to the side in a boat and if I wasn't delighted. I had to fuss and find my ticket and then made a lunge and it seemed as if it were a happen. So I landed in the boat, much to my joy, and such a sea as there was on!

When we got to shore we walked up some long steps and at the top were the three girls in blankets with their Capri hats on and waving towels as hard as ever they could from the terrace of the d'Europe ["Hotel d'Europe (Villa Nardi), 400 yds from the Marketplace." *Southern Italy,* 147].

Then they rushed along and met me with "Salve! Salve!" at the top of the steps. Then we all hugged and kissed and went into the house, which has such a terrace! Mary presented me with castanets, Leslie had a piece of the Capri sour bread for me, and two views of Capri which she bought me, a label, etc. were added to fill up the place vacated by the mail [carried by Clarissa from Naples].

We had a nice luncheon with "Carlo" and Fred to wait on the table. In the Salon, Marion played Funiculi-Funicula, Santa Lucia, Napoli, and [?], which the girls accompanied on their castanets and it sounded fine. Then I had a lesson and got the hang of it.

We went for a walk to Villa Crawford, the home of Mr. Marion Crawford, who is just landed in America, and saw their lovely terrace where they breakfast in the season [Frances Marion Crawford, American author, 1854-1909].

We got coffee - no tea - and macaroons at [?] and Marion drew our pictures in his guest book, which was fine, in the middle of the big page, and put "Washington's Birthday, 1901" under it. The Signor put a circle about it so it is there for ages. After buying some pictures Marion, Miss C. and I walked up to "The Gorge" where Agnes of Sorrento [heroine of Harriet Beecher Stowe's novel of the same name] is said to have lived and such a lovely spot as it is all the way up as far as we went with the lovely orange groves on each side.

We were crazy for a Tarantella [Southern Italian Folk Dance] in the evening, but had about given it up when Fred said it was to be at Tramontano's [Hotel], so we hurried and got ready. A boy escorted us there from the house and we all sat around the room and looked at the dancers who were great in their velvet breeches and waistcoats, sashes and long red silk capes and yellow slippers. The girls wore fancy short skirts, little satin Eton jackets, bright silk sashes, low full vests & a wide collar of silvery beads, white stockings and fancy high-heeled slippers. The dancing was lovely. The dancers played tambourines and castanets and were accompanied by the rest on mandolins, violins, guitars, etc. It lasted about an hour and a half & we wished it were longer.

I was perfectly delighted that we did have the opportunity to see a real nice one [folkdance] for I was fearful lest I was going to miss that for the girls saw one in Capri. I am glad I came early for just this day is well worth the trip and I am sure Auntie will be alright. I sent her a wire so she would surely know I got here safely.

Amalfi - A Day Trip from Sorrento. Sunday, February 24, 1901.

I slept in the room with Miss Cadwell and she was up early to see what the weather was and if we were going to have a good day for Amalfi. We all got up about half past seven and had our breakfast and were ready to leave at nine but the carriage did not come and Signor Carlo paid us a very nice compliment as a nation, saying that all nations, besides the English and Americans, were chronically behind time but we were always on time.

Finally the carriage came, a nice double-seated one with three horses and each with bells around their heads and with Antonio de Fabiolo to drive. The natives were all out in the piazzas as we passed and we all looked at one another.

The drive [4½ hours by carriage] is simply beyond description for it was cut out of solid rock and right by the sea for fifteen miles. We reached Amalfi a little after twelve and had a fine luncheon at the Capuchin Convent, which is now converted into a hotel and is exactly where the landslide two years ago was which killed the two women [Gregorio Albergo Cappuccini-Convento, "… above the town, with a fine view, frequented by English and Americans." *Southern Italy*, 170].

We had our coffee on the terrace and under the rose bushes in bloom and daffodils, narcissus, heliotrope and along the drive we saw such beautiful wild flowers, anemones & double ones, little yellow flowers something like buttercups, dandelions, bluits and wild violets that are very sweet. The little beggars would throw little bunches into the wagon for us to pay a penny for. Also the almond trees were in bloom and so loaded with blossoms. They resemble apple blossoms somewhat and have no fragrance.

We reached home [Hotel d'Europe, Sorrento] about 6:15 and after dinner Marion and I went out on the terrace for it was so mild and beautiful we hardly needed wraps. We ate my package of raisins done in bay leaves and watched the water with the moonlight on it. Beyond we could see the lights from Pompeii and Vesuvius smoking away and every now and then a small flash of fire from it. To the left Naples was easily discernable by the lights and every few minutes a flash from what we decided was a lighthouse on Ischia [Isola D'Ischia]. Then a steamer hove in sight and soon passed around the point and then a falling star completed the scene. We stayed there a couple of hours simply entranced. The girls came out after a while and enjoyed it with us.

I think taking the whole day into consideration, it was the loveliest one I can remember and the beds in Sorrento are the best we have had anywhere.

Sorrento - Naples. Monday, February 25, 1901.

We got up early and for the first time had coffee and rolls out of doors on the terrace right by the Mediterranean with an awning over us and such a lovely time with the sun just coming through the trees. The girls took a lot of pictures of us at breakfast. Antonio came for us and we left in our same turn out for Castellammare, which is a ten-mile drive through a lovely section of lemon and orange groves. We reached Castellammare in time for the 11:15 train and so got to Naples just in time for luncheon.

In the afternoon we went down & met the girls at Sommer's and went over and got tea and cake in the nice tearoom that I went to with the Stoddards.

We then walked home and listened to the most awful hurdy-gurdy from our balcony and watched a gorgeous sunset at the same time. I left my packing until morning to do.

Naples - Rome. Tuesday, February 26, 1901.

I woke up at 5:30 and got up at six, then did my packing and ended by packing Auntie's carryall for her. Breakfast at 7:30 and left the house at 7:50, leaving Naples an hour later.

The trip up was charming for it was a bright sunny day and it was so interesting to see the peasants all at work in the fields, a regular Millet *Gleaners* picture the entire journey [Jean-Francois Millet, 1814 - 1875]. We reached here at a little after two, all at Molaro's seemed glad to welcome us and I should like to embrace the whole lot.

My shirt waists came, white striped with blue and the red. Also my shirt and waist was here from home. I was glad to put that on again. (21 Frs.)

Bought Maritozzi, two apiece, to eat tonight and oh, weren't they good!

Tivoli - A day trip from Rome. Wednesday, February 27, 1901.

It was just four weeks ago today we had planned to go to Tivoli to celebrate Mary's birthday and now we are going on Miss Cadwell's [Tivoli; "Many of the Roman nobles of the Augustan age... founded beautiful villas here; under

Hadrian [Roman Emperor, 117-138 AD] the splendor of the place attained its climax." *Central Italy*, 405].

We decided to go down to breakfast for we are on the upper floor and have "John" instead of Rafaello. We went down at quarter of eight and stopped at Miss Cadwell's room to wish her "A Happy Birthday", and expected to find the violets we told Rafaello to get and take to her room early, but they were not there. When we came out from breakfast we found that John had gotten hold of them and taken them up to Auntie with her breakfast, so finally they landed in Miss C.'s room.

We took carriages for the station, Marion and I in one with the lunch basket in front of us and reached Tivoli about 10:30. Then we took such a funny old "carry-all" and drove out to Hadrian's Villa, which is quite a drive of half an hour ["Carriages to the Villa Adriana with one horse 4, two horses 6 fr., there and back, including 1½ hrs. halt, 6 & 10 fr. Donkey and Guides (superfluous) to the waterfalls, 1 fr. (3-4 fr. are usually demanded at first). Beggars are numerous and importunate." *Central Italy*, 405].

The situation is not at all as I had pictured it and while the ruins are intact, still the use of various houses is quite uncertain and the excavations are not so thorough as on the Palatine. We had a fine luncheon that Michaele put up for us and found we ate it at eleven in the Triclinium, from whose window seats we had a fine view. The big brown dog and Miss Hadrian joined us for our meal and the little dog followed us all the rest of the afternoon, but a good share of the time Mary carried him, for which he seemed duly grateful.

We found such lovely sweet violets growing all about the grounds and it was so nice to pick them.

We were through at about half past one and rode to the Temple of Sibyl in the town of Tivoli. There we left our wraps we did not need and the lunch basket and started for the Belvedere across the bridge. On the way we met two herds of the long horned cattle raised in Italy and Miss C. was afraid as well as myself, so we all took refuge by some native men lounging by the fence. The second encounter we ran up the side of the mountain. The falls were beautiful from that spot. On our return we had coffee at the hotel terrace where we sat and rested until train time.

We reached Molaro's at quarter of six and I found eight letters awaiting me having been forwarded back from Naples. One from Uncle Fred, Fan, Willie, Harold, Mrs. Louis, Eugenia, Blanche, Harriet & Josh and such fun skimming through them.

We had Asti for dinner, coffee and Miss Cadwell's presents in our room after dinner and she seemed to like all we had selected for her.

Our last night in Rome, so we all went to the Font dei Trevi and thru in our penny, taking a drink at the same time to insure our return to Rome someday, and if I tho't I should never return I should be heartbroken. It's my Mecca! [Fontana Trevi, was supplied with water by… "The Ancient Aqua Virgo… conducted to Rome by M. Agrippa (Marcus Agrippa, 63-12 BC) from the campagna (countryside) chiefly by a subterranean channel 14 miles in length… Perhaps the best (water) in Rome." *Central Italy*, 153.]

Rome - Orvieto. Thursday, February 28, 1901.

We had to get off by 8:30 AM and Mr. Molaro presented us with bouquets again. Our trip was very pretty as the day was perfect coming by such pretty scenes.

We reached Orvieto at 11:30 and rode up the hill in the cable tram where we found a bus from the White Eagle Hotel and it was such a queer godforsaken place. Cold as a barn inside but lovely on the balcony where the poor old parrot was sunning himself. They had a nice piano and the most killing hurdy-gurdy that stood on the floor and was exactly like a small sized piano. We had great fun grinding out the music ["Orvieto, a small town, on an isolated tufa rock, occupies the site of Volsinii, one of the twelve capitals of the Etruscan League." *Central Italy*, 83].

The façade is beautiful to the Duomo begun in 1290 in commemorating the Miracle of Bolsena. It is Gothic and contains Fra Angelico's *Christ & Anti-Christ* [frescoes, finished by Luca Signorelli, 1445-1523].

Went to the Fortress & saw the well [St. Patrick's Well, Il Pozzo di San Patrizio]. Japanese at dinner and it was awfully cold in our rooms.

Orvieto - Perugia. Friday, March 1, 1901.

We had our rolls, toast and coffee in bed, then went to the Chapel in the Cathedral to see the lovely frescoes, which we could not see yesterday. Left at 11:28.

Reached Perugia at 2:30 and such a swell hotel and as nice as can be [Grand Hotel Brufani, Piazza Italia, 12, Perugia]. Heard band play and saw loads of stunning officers ["Perugia, the capital of the province of Umbria, with 17,000 inhabitants… The paintings of the Umbrian School, and the fine views, make Perugia one of the most interesting places in Italy." *Central Italy*, 56].

Went for a walk and saw the poli-chrome façade to the Oratorio then walked around to get an idea of the town [Oratorio di San Bernardino]. I think it's fine here, and only wish all the places were as nice and comfortable.

Miss C. read "Orvieto" from the collection of John Addington Symond's, *Sketches in Italy* [*Sketches and Studies in Italy and Greece*, 1874].

Perugia. Saturday, March 2, 1901.

It poured all day and so we took it for a rest day and stayed in the house writing. I wrote Uncle Fred about my new Letter of Credit being from Baring Brothers, for they have been so kind to forward my mail with the others, to have my Letter from them is the least I can do. Then Miss Cadwell will write them saying I am one of her girls and that will make it very easy. I do hope Uncle Fred will understand just what I mean for I tried to make it clear to him [Baring Brothers; English Merchant Bank since 1762].

In the evening I wrote Fan a long letter and told her that Auntie has got to come home and I wonder if I ought to come home with her, but after considering all sides, I really think if it is satisfactorily arranged for her to go with Mr. F., that to have six months of complete rest will do her more good than for me to go and open the house.

Perugia. Sunday, March 3, 1901.

It wasn't especially pleasant but we had to go out and see something, so we went to the Cathedral [San Lorenzo] and couldn't get into the Chapel containing the Signorelli [*Madonna*].

We went over into Palazzo del Municipio up into the Gallery, the Pinacoteca [Vanucci, Municipal Picture Gallery], where we saw some lovely masterpieces of [Pietro Vanucci] Perugino, [Giovanni di Pietro] Spagna [1507], [Bernadino Betti] Pinturicchio [1454-1513], [Giorgio Barbarelli] Giorgione [1477-1510], etc. and they were most interesting and also Fra Angelico and others of the Umbrian School.

In the afternoon Leslie and I wanted pictures and so Miss Cadwell went out with us and we had poor success, for we couldn't find the store anywhere, so had to give it up.

Miss Cadwell read to us in the afternoon about Assisi where we hope to go tomorrow and I made tea in our room and finished our [?], which are honey letters, which are made only during Lent in Italy. Great fun watching Mr. Cannon & the Joneses from Cincinnata!

Perugia. Monday, March 4, 1901.

We had it all planned to go to Assisi if the weather seemed favorable, but it looked doubtful at seven, so we decided not to go and about two minutes after we decided, it poured much to our satisfaction.

After coffee we went out and down to San Domenico first and saw the huge window so strangely arranged and the monument [to Pope Benedict XI] with the light coming from the colored glass.

San Pietro [de' Cassinensi] contains lots of interesting things in the way of pictures, illuminated books, which are as fine as anything we have seen, and the choir stalls are beautifully carved, each different. The doors leading to the Belvedere are lovely "tarsia" [an inlay technique] while the view is glorious over the rolling plains & hills of Umbria.

In the PM the girls got their charms, which the man made of the griffin [symbol of Perugia]. We went into the Chamber of Commerce [Collegio del Cambio] and saw the wonderful inlay and carving, also the Perugino frescoes of the seven principal virtues; *Prudence, Justice, Fortitude, Temperance* in symbolical figures [utilizing portraits] of the prominent men of that day. Then *Faith, Hope, and Charity* in the *Assumption.* The prophets, sibyls, saints as the heralds of <u>hope</u> and the *Adoration of the Magi* as <u>love</u>.

We walked and saw the house in which Perugino lived. Further on the Arch of Augustus, part of the original wall of the city, and Raphael's first fresco in the Chapel of San Severo done in 1505 [Church, formerly a convent].

Perugia - Florence. Tuesday, March 5, 1901.

We left the hotel at lunch and changed at Terontola and reached Florence at three and drove directly to Pension Camarono, Via Curtatone 3 [Pensione 6-8 Fr.]. We got our hold-alls unpacked and I read letters from Aunt Belle and Uncle Fred. Then went out to the French, Lemon & Co Bank and drew, then had tea, muffins and chocolate cake.

Got the lay of the land, saw the Baptistery, Cathedral, Campanile, Misericordia House Hospital [Oratory of the Misericordia] and walked home.

Florence. Wednesday, March 6, 1901.

"Florence, Italian Firenze... formerly the capital of the Grand Duchy of Tuscany... while in ancient times, Rome was the grand centre of Italian development, Florence has since the middle ages superseded it as the focus of intellectual life... An amazing profusion of treasures of art, such as no other locality possesses within so narrow limits ... and lastly the delightful environs of the city combine to render Florence one of the most interesting and attractive places in the world." Baedeker, *Northern Italy*, 416.

*

We started early and walked by the [Galleria degli] Uffizi and it is about as large as the Louvre it seemed, before we were ready to come home. There are so many works there that are perfect gems that it really is impossible to go into detail. Raphael's *Madonna and Child* with the goldfinch and [Mariotto] Albertinelli's [1474-1515] *Meeting of Elizabeth and Mary* are the ones that seem to stand out in my mind very plainly. Of course Fra Angelico's angels around the Tabernacle with gold ground and the other Coronation are beautiful. [Raphael's Madonna is 'noted' by Clarissa in her personal copy of Baedeker's, *Northern Italy*, purchased in Florence, March 5, 1901, complete with a tooled leather bookcover. This is the only Baedeker that survived with her Diary and Scrapbook.]

In the afternoon the girls went out but I stayed in with Auntie and did nothing special. We looked at jewelry in the hall after dinner.

Florence. Thursday, March 7, 1901.

It was pouring hard when we got up, so after coffee, Miss Cadwell and the girls came in our room and read <u>Romola</u> (George Eliot, 1863).

It finally stopped raining so we all walked over to the Monastery of San Marco and saw the beautiful frescoes by Fra Angelico; his *Two Monks Receiving Christ, Peter Martyr, Christ on the Cross with St. Dominic* and in the Chaplin House is the *Crucifixion of Christ*, between the thieves and surrounded by twenty saints and the busts of monks all around it. [Domenico] Ghirlandajo's [1449-1494] *Last Supper* is fair. Upstairs at the top of the flight is the *Annunciation*, like my little picture at home by Fra Angelico, *Madonna della Stella. Coronation of the Virgin* and *Adoration of the Magi* with *Annunciation* are lovely framed pieces. Then the *Coronation* is a beautiful fresco.

The cell of [Girolamo] Savonarola contains a crucifixion by Fra Angelico, Savonarola's chair, desk, rosary, a piece of his hair shirt and a picture of him. Also, we saw the room [Savonarola; Italian Dominican priest, executed in 1498 for opposition to the Papacy].

In the afternoon went to Michael Angelo's House [Casa Buonarroti, Via Buonarroti] and saw a great many sketches that he did and a number of things that were interesting but still, the whole thing seemed rather overdrawn and uncertain and there is a good deal of discussion over its identity.

From there we went to St. Croce and saw no end of monuments and such like and the tassels at the corner of a cushion on a slab of which Ruskin has written so much [John Ruskin, 18th C. art & social critic and author].

The Giotto frescoes were nice and we had a fairly good light on them. *The Nativity of John the Baptist, Dancing of the Daughter of Herodias, Resuscitation of Drusiana, Ascension of the Evangelist.* The scenes from the life of St. Francis [of Assisi], especially his death, are very good. In the chapel of the Medici is one of Giotto's on the wall, *The Coronation.*

We hurried home and found Miss Cadwell's friend, Miss Whittier, waiting. Leslie and I took tea up to them [Miss Harriet E. Whittier, Milton Hall, Milton MA; address on her calling card].

Auntie had a nervous time and couldn't get to sleep for a long time. Too bad!

Florence. Friday, March 8, 1901.

It poured all day and we had reading, etc. Miss Cadwell went out and got lady cake, marguetras and macaroons and we simply had a feast on so many good things.

Florence. Saturday, March 9, 1901.

Rainy again, but we went to the Pitti Palace, and if there aren't jewels in the picture line here in Florence [Florentine residence of the Kings of Italy; in 1901, King Victor Emmanuel III]. Just Raphael's pictures there are enough to feast on. Titian portraits are lovely there [Tiziano Veculi da Cadere, 1477-1575].

On our way home Miss Cadwell went to ask Dr. Coldstream [noted in Baedeker] to come and to see Auntie and he made a nice long call and told her the same as all the others have and gave her another prescription to have filled out.

We then went to St. Maria Maddalena [de Pazzi] and saw Perugino's *Christ on the Cross.* <u>Beautiful</u>. Then to the Baptistery and saw two children baptized after which we had tea [Battistero or Church of S. Giovanni Battista. "All children born in Florence are baptized here." *Northern Italy*, 442]. I dropped water on "Marion" from our floor.

Florence. Sunday, March 10, 1901.

Nothing special. Miss Whittier to dine and we all fell in love with her, for she is so sweet and interesting that we could not help liking her. She has traveled a great deal and tells her experiences in a most charming manner. She described their dangerous situation when they were in India.

Florence. Monday, March 11, 1901.

Miss Cadwell wisely stayed in bed part of the morning so we four girls started over to the Uffizi Gallery by ourselves. On the way I stopped and tried to get a little handmade collar to send home to Fan for her birthday, but there were none less than six Francs and those were too wide to be real becoming to her, so I did not get any.

We had a nice time in the Gallery, but there are so many things one wants to remember that it is very bewildering. Leslie and Mary were together and Marion and I started out together, but she wanted to look at each picture so long that I soon got off by myself and we did not try to stay together.

It began to pour as soon as we got in the Gallery and did not slacken before we came out, so we took a cab, which was a good thing. We paid him 1.50, where it really should have been only 1 franc.

In the afternoon we stayed in and had reading until dark in Horner's, *Walks in Rome* [Florence], which is later then Hare and got along in <u>Romola</u> nicely [Susan & Joanna Horner, *Walks in Florence*, 1873; Augustus J.C. Hare, 1834-1903, *Walks in Rome*, Vol. I, 1871].

Mary and Marion went out for teacakes and I made tea.

Florence. Tuesday, March 12, 1901.

Auntie is losing strength rapidly and I do really think it's lack of nourishment, though Miss Cadwell is on the look out all the time for things that will help her and nothing is being left undone that will add to her comfort. But in a boarding house it is simply impossible to get things that are dainty and nice as I would like. Unless she is very much better, I have decided that by early in April, I shall break away from the party, for even though she does not realize it, I shall not leave a thing that will make her more happy undone. No one shall ever know what these days are and what the cruel words mean when I think of nothing else and do not remember anything we do in my anxiety for her.

This morning Mary and I went to the Doctor's to ask him to call today and without Mary I should have been floored, for the man did not understand English. The Dr. came while we were at the Bargello [Il Bargello, Palazzo del Podestà, residence of the Chief Magistrate of Florence] and wrote an order when she was to take food, med., etc, and this afternoon she really seems to feel quite a little better and I am so glad.

The Bargello was a lovely collection of all sorts of things and there we saw the *John of Bologna, Mercury* and lots of reliefs by the Della Robias [Luca Della Robbia, 1399-1482, & Brothers; Artists of glazed terracotta].

We went into Dante's house and saw a number of interesting things that belonged to him; fork, hourglass, chair & books [Dante Alighieri, il Sommo Poeta; Supreme Poet of the Italian language, born 1265 in Florence].

Florence. Wednesday, March 13, 1901.

The Doctor said yesterday that the very best thing for Auntie would be to go to the Villa Natalia where she could have just the very best of care [Villa Natalia, Via Bolognese]. Miss Cadwell and I decided we would take this morning to go to two convalescing homes and look over the situations.

So the girls said they would go to the Pitti and do that by themselves, so Miss Cadwell and I took the cross-eyed man with his sorrel horse and drove first up to the Villa through the Porto Gallo to Via Bolognese 48. The housekeeper, Miss Walsh, and the directress, Miss Turton, were both out but we persuaded the two nurses to let us see the rooms and they are really awfully nice and I think that Auntie would be very happy and contented up there.

We then drove out to the other home, which is out through the Porto Romano, but we didn't care for the looks of it at all and the matron was sort of talkative and I didn't like the looks of things at all.

We then went to French, Lemon & Co. and I got a letter from Josh in which he signed himself "Dr. Josh" and I am so glad his time over in Europe is so nearly over for it will do him good to get back to America again. We also met "Sonny" and I had quite a chew with him while Miss C. was busy.

At two o'clock I skipped out with Miss C. under the pretense of doing errands and went over to Dr. Coldstream's as he asked her the day before to bring me. He gave us the addresses of two English trained nurses that we were to go to see.

Auntie and I went out for an hour's ride, going around by the Duomo and giving her a general idea of the lay of the land. Then we went to the Casino, which is lovely [Casino Mediceo; site of Medici Garden and School for Artists during the Renaissance]. Auntie was awfully exhausted when we returned but after lying down for a while and having her hot milk, she felt better.

Miss [?] invited me to go and call on her friend, Mrs. [?], who lives in Del Santo's house but we only went to see Miss Ellis, Via Magio 2, and it was such an adventure getting in, for the street door was locked and the coachman had to ring and then stood with his hand against the door ready to push it in. So finally it gave way and in we poked, he yelling something upstairs and we found Miss Ellis was in [Miss Ellis was one of the woman recommended by the Doctor as a nurse for Auntie.].

She seemed very nice and right to the point. We said we couldn't tell for sure but would let her know by six the next day.

Florence. Thursday, March 14, 1901.

The Doctor came and proposed the place to Auntie and of course she said she would have to think about it. We went some place and I think to the Medici Library.

Florence. Friday, March 15, 1901.

Auntie decided to go up to the Villa Natalia so Miss Cadwell and I went up and engaged the nicest room for her, which is so light and pretty all done in pink and white with pretty tinted walls.

In the afternoon Mary and I went over to engage the Nurse while Auntie and Marion went for a little drive. The Nurse did not seem to understand that she was to go to the Villa and did not favor the idea at all but said she would come to the house and see Miss Cadwell at half past six, which she did. After talking with Miss C., she came in and saw Auntie for a few minutes and I think she will get on famously with her.

Florence. Saturday, March 16, 1901.

Miss Cadwell and I spent our morning in doing errands and getting whisky and things from the druggists and doing little odd jobs for Auntie.

Auntie tried to go into dinner but collapsed and so she had a light luncheon of eggs and things in Madame's private room. At three, Nurse came and they started off in good spirits with all her baggage.

We had the cross-eyed driver and went up to San Miniato [al Monte Church] where we got a beautiful view of the town. We had tea at the Albion Tea Rooms and came in [The Albion, Via dei Vecchietti, Florence].

That evening we had the dance, but as I was not dancing I had no special adventures, but it was killingly funny with three or four men to each girl. Leslie came down and kept me company and we did the most contemptible thing, listening to the folks next-door talk, Miss Rodgers and her mother. It was disgusting to hear such conceit!

Florence. Sunday, March 17, 1901.

The Doctor called and offered to take up any word, for Nurse sent for him as Auntie had such a poor night. He said for me to stay in bed and rest, which I did, not knowing that Auntie was poorly. I was ready to go down but the maid tho't I said I wanted luncheon upstairs, so she brought it and I ate it upstairs.

After luncheon Leslie and I let down my bag for oranges, which was such fun to do and nice oranges too! But we found it was very improper, for it was bad for the reputation of the house. Miss Cadwell went to dinner with Miss Whittier.

From now till the end of our stay in Florence I shall not go into detail for each day, as with my anxiety and planning, I must say, I became most careless.

We went to the [Giuseppe] Cantagalli Factory of Pottery out the Porto Romana and went simply crazy over the pretty things [Cantagalli, Via Senese 21; reproductions of antique Italian pottery. *Northern Italy*, 413].

One day we took the train and went up to Fiesole [Etruscan town N. of Florence] to which Miss Whittier went, going to tea at Miss McCauley's afterwards.

Another lovely afternoon we went to Certosa [di Val d'Ema], which is the most fascinating old monastery and the brothers wear the white robes and the little jugs and things filled with liquor are so stunning. We saw all of Bishop Lawrence's family there.

Villa Petraia was another lovely villa where Victor Emanuel used to visit. [Victor Emmanuel II, first King of a United Italy, 1820-1878]. In the yard was a tree 400 years old with a platform built in the branches where he used to sit. We went through the house, which is very beautifully furnished but does not compare with the Palazzo Pitti, which we went through one of the days where the beautiful [Benvento] Cellini plate and private apartments are on show. There we saw the [Sandro] Botticelli [1446-1510] painting.

Palazzo Vecchio is another wonderful building and we enjoyed it so much.

Another day we took the tram and some cake and went up to St. Miniato [al Monte], which dates from the 12th cent.. We went on up to Galileo's House [No. 13 Via Costa S. Giorgio], who discovered the motion of the sun, and from the tower we had a most lovely view of the city and surrounding country.

The Foundling's Hospital is adorned by the little Della Robbia babies over and between the arches. In the chapel is an *Adoration* by Ghirlandajo which is as beautiful a thing as we have seen. We also saw Andrea Del Sarto's [1487-1531] *Holy Family of the Sack* [*Madonna del Sacco*], which is full of grace [in the Church of the Santissima Annunziata].

In the Cathedral Museum we saw the *Groups of Singing Boys* by Della Robbia and also Donatello's [plaster reliefs; Donato di Nicolo di Betti Bardi Donatello, 1386-1466].

In the National Museum we saw John of Bologna's [Giovanni da Bologna, 1524-1608] *Morning*, also a nice bust of Michel Angelo, which is said to have belonged to one of his servants. Also Andrea Verrocchio's [1435-1488] *David* and Donatello's *David*.

In the [Accademia della] Belle Arti we saw lovely things, including Michel Angelo's *David*, which is reproduced in bronze in the Piazza Michelangelo where we had our cake and coffee the day we went to the Torre del Gallo [Tower of Galileo] and such lovely things we saw, one being Fra Angelico's *Last Judgment,* the *Paradise* being superb.

The Biblioteca Laurenziana [Library founded by Cosimo di Medici in 1444], which contains so many and such beautiful old manuscripts and the picture of Petrarch & Laura in color in a book.

The Chapel of the Princes, or New Sacristy, is for the de Medici's, in which are Michael Angelo's *Evening* & *Dawn*, & *Day* & *Night* [Michael Angelo for Pope Clement VII, Guilio de Medici, in 1523-29]. Miss Cadwell and I went there after we had been to see Auntie off.

Pisa - A day trip from Florence. Monday, March 25, 1901.

"Travellers are strongly recommended to stay at least one night in Pisa, enjoying the view from the Campanile at sunset and seeing the frescoes at the Campo Santo by morning light. Those, however, who are unavoidably compelled to hasten their visit may leave their luggage at the station and proceed on foot (20 min.) ... to the Piazza del Duomo...

The chief boast of Pisa is the Piazza del Duomo, to which every visitor first directs his steps. The Cathedral, the Leaning Tower, the Baptistery, and the Campo Santo form a group of buildings without parallel, especially as it lies beyond the precincts of the town and therefore removed from its disturbing influences." *Northern Italy*, 383, 385.

*

We had been waiting a long, long time for a nice day to go to Pisa, so finally started, getting up at seven o'clock and leaving the station at 8:45, reaching Pisa at 11:05.

We went directly to the Hotel Nettuno ["... with good Trattoria." *Northern Italy*, 382], which is sort of a restaurant & where the men sit with their hats on. We enjoyed watching the men eat macaroni.

As soon as we were thro' we walked along to the Duomo and the Piazza [del Duomo] and there we got our very first glimpse of the wonderful Leaning Tower. The grass was so green [there could not be] a better setting for all the beautiful structures ["The Campanile, or clock tower... completed by Tommaso Pisano in 1350 ... Owing to its remarkable oblique position, 13 ft.

out of the perpendicular, it is usually known as the Leaning Tower." *Northern Italy*, 386].

We got our tickets first to enter the Campo Santo [Burial Ground] where we spent a long time hunting the figures on the [Andrea di Lione] Orcagna [1308-1368?] frescoes, which are beyond imagination in their horror. His Hell is the worst thing I ever saw.

From there we went out and sat on the ledge around the Baptistery and studied the Cathedral, which was begun in the 11th century in the Tuscan Romanesque style, and by contact with the weather has become a most beautiful yellow. The doors are bronze with Bible scenes depicted upon them and the marble carving is beautiful.

The Baptistery is rather plain from the outer view but contains Niccolo Pisano's Pulpit [deceased, 1278], which is most noted for its construction. The Font is another beautiful piece and the carving has been copied perfectly in the altar. The echo is splendid there.

We all went in the cathedral. We saw a good Sodoma's *Sacrifice of Jacob* [*Abraham*] in the choir. In the nave hangs the beautiful bronze lamp, which is said to have suggested the swinging of the pendulum to Galileo.

Leslie, Mary and I went up the 294 stairs [of the Leaning Tower] where we had a most beautiful view of the city and surrounding country.

We then went back to the hotel and had coffee and some of the nicest long flakey iced pastries that are specialties of that one hotel [Hotel Nettuno].

We sat in the station a long, long time and finally got to Florence about 7:45. I found my friend [Mr. Ferrie] had called twice and would come again after dinner, so I hurried and put on my yellow waist and he finally came about nine. Miss C. went down too, and as the parlor was full and the Madame had gone to hear Mrs. Williams sing at the recital, we went in her private room. Miss C. did not stay long and left us there. It goes without saying we talked the trip over thoroughly and numerous other things as well [Mr. Ferrie will accompany Auntie on her return to America. We met him earlier, with Mr. Beatty in Naples, when the possibility of his traveling with Auntie on the return voyage was first discussed.].

He went about eleven after Marco had been and tried to put out the lights. His going now means more to me than I shall ever forget and I hope I may return it in some way one of these days and I feel that under the circumstances I am doing quite right. I am glad it was so, that he had to see me in the evening.

Villa Natalia. #48 Via Bolognese. Florence.

Oh, Auntie has gotten along so well since she went up there that it has been a delight to see the improvement each day. Nurse Ellis is very good, but slow. Miss Turton and Miss Gregory [Directresses of the Villa Natalia] have made her stay so nice that I really think she dreads leaving for everything is cooked expressly for her and the chef is so particular to get dishes she likes and it is all as nice as she would have at home. Nurse said the first two or three days she was as sick as anyone she wanted to see, simply from the lack of the good nourishing food, which we could not get, although Madame Cammarano was kindness itself.

Pensione Cammarano - 1 Via Curtatone

Emily Ellis - 5 Via Maggio

Dr. Alex Coldstream - 5 Via Femmiccio [notes by Clarissa]

One of the girls and I went up everyday to see her and stayed about half an hour making 4 Frs. for the hour and a half [?].

French, Lemon & Co. ordered her stateroom; No. 250 on the [Steamship] *Maria Theresia*, North German Lloyd, 527 Francs, the 27 francs being for the exchange in gold.

Auntie and nurse started Saturday the 30 of March for Genoa at 11:12, reaching G. at 6:10 and going to Smith's Hotel. Our friend [Mr. Ferrie] went to G. from Monte Carlo Sunday but the Steamer [*Maria Theresia*] did not sail till the 2nd. We heard by postal she stood the trip well and nurse would stay over with her. Auntie's fare there, about 23 Frs. & nurse's round trip about 30 Frs.

The girls all gave her presents and I a little steamer pillow. She took my rug, hold-all, wicker basket, Boston bag and basket trunk. She thinks her steamer trunk would have held all she had, but I fear she would have been surprised.

They had a splendid trip down to Naples, needing no wraps, and that far Auntie said all was lovely.

I gave 15£ to Auntie from my Letter and borrowed ten from Miss Cadwell to hold out.

Florence - Venice. Wednesday, April 3, 1901.

We were up bright and early and had all our little odd jobs done up so that we said "Good bye" to the people we liked; Mrs. Waitt and her daughter and Aunt; Miss Richards, from 4 Aldridge Rd. Villas, Westburn Park Rd., London; and Mrs. Williams, who sings so beautifully [Mrs. Gibson Tenney Williams, Buffalo, NY; calling card in Diary].

Mary and I went downtown and got a cake for luncheon. Madame put us up a very nice one and Mrs. Waitt gave us some chocolate crackers. Then Miss Whittier came to the train and left a little box containing the remains of the Page & Shaw [?] from yesterday at her rooms.

Our train left at 11:30 and the trip was superb, for though there were lots of tunnels, the glimpses of country between were lovely. We passed the Apennines [Mts.] and then the country was perfectly level till we reached Venice and crossed the two-mile bridge from the mainland just at six as the sun was setting.

It was so queer to see boats instead of busses. We all got in and the gondolier stood up behind and piloted us safely through the small canals to the Hotel Milan and just as we were at the door the full moon came up and we all did not want to go in for a minute [Hotel Milan et Pension Anglaise; Calle Traghetto, 8-12 fr.].

But soon after dinner, we got in a gondola and went all around to see the first of Venice in a flood of moonlight and no descriptions have been exaggerated, for it's glorious with the light pouring down on the old Venetian palaces with their stories of open arched loggias.

We finally drew up by a singing boat, in the midst of hundreds it seemed, and listened to the music; Santa Lucia, Adio Bella Naopli, Mari, Carmen, Marguerita, Funiculi Funicula, and others that we know, but not the names. The singing boats are barges with a framework from which are suspended the Jap. lanterns. There are eight or ten musicians and the music does sound lovely. There were two out, one in front of the Grand [Hotel] and the other not far the other side of us. We stayed out till nearly eleven and it was lovely for our first impression of Venice.

Venice. Thursday, April 4, 1901.

"Venice, Venezia, the capital of the province of its own name, a commercial and naval port... lies 2½ miles from the mainland, in the Lugane, a shallow bay of the Adriatic... its 15,000 houses and palaces, chiefly built on piles, and about 6½ miles in circumference, stand on 117 small islands, formed by more than 150 canals and connected by 378 bridges, most of which are stone... In winter spring-tides raise the level of the water about 8 ft., so that even the Piazza di San Marco is flooded and has to be traversed by gondola." *Northern Italy*, 252-253.

*

Marion did not go out with us, but we walked over to St. Mark's [Basilica di San Marco] and went in getting a general ideal of the style. We were in just in time to see a nice procession for it was Maundy Thursday in our church ["The Piazza of St. Mark is the grand focus of attraction of Venice. On summer evenings all who desire to enjoy fresh air congregate here… Indeed, there is, perhaps no more fascinating spot in Europe than this huge open-air drawing room." *Northern Italy*, 254].

St. Mark's Plaza

In the afternoon we walked over to the [Ponte di] Rialto and it is the queerest place. It seems out of keeping for a bridge of such historical note to be given up for such truck shops.

In the evening we all went out in our gondola for the week. Miss Cadwell had a fine looking fellow engaged, but we think he bragged about this job to the Poppies at the stand in front so they would not let him come. But I think we shall like our new one very much. When we get in he stands at the prow with his hat in his hand and his arm out for our support. ["The gondolas take the place of cabs at Venice. Their 'stands' are at the different hotels… The rower himself is hailed as Poppe… For a whole day (10 hrs.) the charge is 6 fr." *Northern Italy*, 244.]

Venice. Friday, April 5, 1901.

We get out here about half past nine, so this morning we went across the Canal to the Salute [Santa Maria della Salute], which is directly opposite us [The Hotel Milan was situated on the Grand Canal]. Next we went to St. Giovanni e Paolo, which is an immense place and full of monuments to different Doges. In the choir are four very elaborate monuments to Doges Morosini, Vendramin, Loredan [and Marco Corner. The Doge of Venice; since 700, the title of the Chief Magistrate of Venice, who was elected for life.].

The Chapel of the Rosary [St. Giovanni e Paola], which was burned in 1869, must have been beautiful judging from the remains of marble carvings.

In the Gesuiti or Jesuit [Church] we saw Titians *Martyrdom of St. Lawrence*, which is so full of life and action, but the light is so poor that one can scarcely make out anything.

We then went to the Madonna dell' Orto where there is a very good Cima da Conegliano [1489-1508] of *St. John the Baptist* with four other saints.

In the afternoon we went in the Court of the Doge Palace, which is perfectly wonderful and the two bronze well-heads, so many of which we see in Venice, are beauties.

I heard the day before from Naples [Auntie]; the trip was glorious. So I cabled Fan [in Unadilla] that Auntie had started.

We studied the relief of the structures around and on the Loggetta at the base of the Campanile, which was used as a waiting room for the guards when the great councils were in session, built 1540.

Had tea in piazza or coffee, came home and read. Going out in the evening and listened to band play Don [Lorenzo] Perosi music [Italian sacred music composer, 1872-1956].

Venice. Saturday, April 6, 1901.

In the morning we went to the Belli Arti or Academy [Academia di Belle Arti] where we saw perfect gems. Titians *Assumption* and such beautiful Bellini's.

On our way back we stopped at Mr. Browning's Palace and enjoyed that so much [Robert Browning died here in 1889; Palazzo Rezzonico]. Robert Browning's son lives in it now [Painter, Robert Barrett Browning, 1846-1912].

In the afternoon we had the gondola again and went to the island of Murano going into two interesting churches; Duomo of S. Donato, which has a wonderful mosaic floor, dated 1111 and the S. Pietro Martire [Basilica] is interesting ["Murano, a small island with 3600 inhabitants, since the 14th cent., the seat of the Venetian Glass Industry." *Northern Italy*, 301].

Venice. Easter Sunday, April 7, 1901.

We went to St. Mark's, up in the gallery, but the singing was poor and no flowers, so it was very disappointing. Went on the Balcony and saw the Bronze Horses ["... 4 horses in gilded bronze... once adorned the triumphal arch of Nero, and afterwards that of Trajan. Constantine sent them to Constantinople ... brought to Venice in 1204. In 1797 they were carried by Napoleon to Paris... and in 1815 they were restored to their former position by Emperor Francis." *Northern Italy*, 255].

Miss Cadwell not feeling well; cake and candy in the PM. No one was very hungry when our Easter dinner came. The gondolas were decorated with Jap. lanterns and red lights burned, which made a charming scene. We were in our rooms hanging out the windows, so saw and heard just fine.

Venice. Monday, April 8, 1901.

We had our gondola and went over to [Church of] S. Giorgio Maggiore, which is not used now as it belonged to a monastery. The choir stalls are beautifully carved giving scenes from the life of St. Benedict and the old sexton, who has been there thirty years, was so funny we enjoyed watching him as well as anything. The marble in the altar showed a number of little birds in the grain of the stone.

From there we went to the Redentore [Franciscan Church on the Island of Giudecca] where we saw a lovely Bellini [School of Giovanni Bellini]. The little Christ child reminded me so much of our little Eleanor.

We went next to the [Santa Maria del] Carmini Church, then to S. Sebastiano.

In the afternoon we went through the Palace of the Doges and while it's awfully nice, I thought it so dry, for the pictures on the ceilings were of battles and things I never had heard of, but we enjoyed picking some of the characters in [Domenico] Tintoretto's [1562-1637] *Last Judgment*. As Mary said, "What a mess!"

We had a nice view out to the lagoons from the balcony. In the evening we went out to hear the music and Mary and I sat in the bow and nearly convulsed watching the old Poppies with their derby hats with streamers behind.

We went on the Bridge of Sighs, but we were hustled along so we hardly knew we were there. It was a case of "on again, off again", but the dungeons were awful and also the place where they beheaded [the prisoners]. One day we saw a convict peeking through the bars at us from the prison opposite [The Bridge of Sighs connects the Palace of the Doges with the prison, or Carceri.].

Venice. Tuesday, April 9, 1901.

Out we started in our gondola and had better success than we have had any day in getting into churches. First we went to Santa Maria Formosa, where we just drank in the lovely Palma Vecchio's [1480-1528] *St. Barbara*. I do think I love it better than almost any picture I have seen. It's an altarpiece with other pictures set in the marble about it all in beautiful shades of dark rich reds.

Then we got into S. Zaccaria and S. Giorgio degli Schiavoni, which is so queer and the frescoes of [Vittore] Carpaccio [1470-1590] illustrating the lives of St. George, Jerome and somebody else [Tryphonius].

In the afternoon we went to the Lido "to the beach" and such fun picking up shells and I got some Adriatic water in a bottle that was washed up on the shore[10].

On The Lido

Don Carlo [?] went by twice with his wife and dog while we were there and it was quite a sight to see him for he is handsome as can be.

Poppe had too much fête.

Venice. Wednesday, April 10, 1901.

The morning we went to the [Santa Maria Gloriosa dei] Frari, where there is Titian's *Madonna of the Pesaro Family*, one of his most beautiful. The

Madonna is seated on the column and is lovely. Also Bellini's sweet altarpiece and this has the two dear angels playing at each side of the step.

We went to the Cini Museum (Gallery of Palazzo Cini) and saw some rather interesting things. On our way we stopped at the bank and I drew nine pounds leaving five on my letter. I do hope I will find my new one in Munich.

In the afternoon we bought pictures. Among mine was the large St. Barbara, twelve francs, music twelve francs, hatpins & postals. Coffee at the piazza then we went to the Lace Factory. We did not buy much. I got a little torchon [tea towel], but I didn't care for it. The nice [?] was beautiful.

In the evening we all went in the gondola and heard the [?] music yet.

Venice. Thursday, April 11, 1901.

I stayed in all day and it did seem such a waste of good time, for the day was simply perfect. The girls went over to the Lido again in the afternoon and there were all those funny men in the white felt hats we saw in the morning going by on the steamer.

Poppe asked if I was sick and I was hanging out the window looking at them start and he looked up and raised his hat. I was as pleased as if the King had done it, for he is fine. He presented his card to the girls before arriving home.

No. 158; Giuseppe Dalla Pietá, Gondoliere
Traghetto: Hotel Europa, Venezia

The Grand Canal

Venice. Friday, April 12, 1901.

I stayed in during the morning while the girls went over to the Venetian Glass Factory [Murano Island]. Leslie bought a number of pieces and had them sent to London. Miss Cadwell brought me a dear little violet holder from there and I shall think so much of it.

In the afternoon we went to the piazza and first met Mrs. Metcalf's friend and that voice is awful. People turned around and stared it was so nasal. When we were sitting drinking coffee and listening to the music, along came Auntie & Sonny (Mrs. Williams & her nephew, Mr. Eddy). They stopped and shook and talked. Then we saw the Rogers talking to a dreadful looking man.

After the music was done we went into the Baptistery of St. Mark. Then the girls went up the Campanile and I went to Cook's and found my letters from Auntie & Mr. – [Ferrie], which was a relief, for Miss C. had said I would not get any from Gibraltar. The passage is fine so far. Mr. [Ferrie] did not get my letter at Cook's, for which I am awfully sorry.

Tonight we go out in our gondola for the last time and I am so sorry to leave Venice for it's been one long beautiful day from the moment we arrived.

Venice - Padua - Verona. Saturday, April 13, 1901.

It blew and stormed in the night, but when we got up in the morning it was pleasant and we started from the hotel in our gondola at eight with our dear Poppe. Oh, he is so nice, even if now and then he does get a little drowsy, for his hair is so nice and sprinkled with grey enough to suit me and remind me of another.

We got to Padua about 9:30 and by that time it was pouring great big wet drops. We first went to the [Church of i] Carmini and saw - or tried to see - Titian's *Madonna and Child* [actually a Palma Vecchio] in the Baptistery outside of which is Petrarch [Monument Statue of Francesco Petrarch, Father of Humanism, 1304-1374].

Then we went to the Ermitani [Augustinian Church], where we saw good [Andrea] Mantegna [1431-1506] frescoes of the lives of St. James and St. Christopher, which are badly damaged, but still I liked them.

From there we went to the Madonna dell' Arena, because it's on the site of an old arena and there we saw the beautiful Giotto frescoes and they go beyond anything we have seen. They were done in 1306 and are superb.

We then went to the S. Antonio [il Santo], which is to the memory of St. Antony of Padua, an associate of St. Francis of Assisi, and it is very elaborate in places and the Cappella del Santo, which has lovely reliefs.

We had luncheon at the Gold Horse. There we had spaghetti and cold meat and salad and cheese. Then we went across the street and had coffee and cake.

Then walked around to the piazza and saw the style of architecture and "Il Salone" [Palazzo della Ragione], which is called the largest hall in the world and it is a big barn of a place with a wooden model of a statue [a horse] for the monument of *Gattamelata*, which is the first bronze statue made by Donatello.

We left for Verona at 3:40 & Mary and I room together at the Golden Dove [Colombo D'Oro, Via Cattaneo, "… generally well-spoken of. Second-class (with trattorie)." *Northern Italy*, 207], which we think is going to be nice and clean. We got here at 4:45 and had a funny time getting in the bus when it tried to go off without Miss Cadwell. Leslie hit the top of the bus. Mary nearly broke the glass in the window, Marion hit something else and I put my head out of the window and it was so funny.

Verona. Sunday, April 14, 1901.

Had breakfast in bed. Mary and I room together and we stayed until 11:30. Then wrote and at five slept till nearly seven, wrote more and got in bed by ten.

Verona. Monday, April 15, 1901.

We started out early and walked along where we got a view of the Ponte Vecchio [Ponte di Castel Vecchio] over to the [Church of] S. Zeno Maggiore, which is very old and in the Romanesque style. The interior reminded me of the Duomo in Fiesoli. The best picture is [Andrea] Mantegna's [1431-1506] *Madonna and Saints* in three sections.

From there we went to the [Church of] S. Bernardino in which is a nice court and the Cappella Pellegrini is very beautifully carved marble.

We crossed the bridge over the Adige [River] coming close to the large old water wheels to the [Church of] San Giorgio in Braida. The [Domenico] Tintoretto [1518-1594] *Baptism of Christ* was so dark we couldn't see it. The Girolamo [dai Libri] *Madonna*, Romanino [of Brescia] and some of the others were good.

St. Anastasia [Gothic Dominican Church] was interesting, especially the holders of the Holy Water Basins, which are deformed men. The frescoes did not look Giottoesque ["… ancient Veronese Frescoes of the 15th cent.; erroneously ascribed to Giotto." *Northern Italy*, 211].

The Cathedral has a complicated façade of the 12th Cent. In it is Titian's *Assumption,* which is perfectly beautiful, while it is much more simple, I like it better for the beauty and grace of the Virgin seems more in keeping with her position.

Then we went to the Cloisters [of the Cathedral], which were pretty, each arch resting on two columns.

The Palazzo del Consiglio or Town Hall is (& surroundings) so quaint and picturesque and the well [fountain] back of the Piazza [dei Signori] is lovely.

Then we went around and saw the Tombs of the Scaligers, which are great large elaborate Gothic things [Family Della Scala, Lords of Verona, who ruled the city from 1260 - 1387].

The Piazza della Erbe, the old Forum, is fine, with the Lion of St. Marks, the Tribuna [Seat of Judgement], etc. are fine ["The Piazza Della Erbe, the ancient Forum, now the fruit and vegetable market, is one of the most picturesque squares in Italy." *Northern Italy,* 209].

After luncheon Mary and I took another nap, then went to the Giardino Giusti [Roman garden at the Palazzo Giusti], which is lovely and where we got a splendid view of the city.

I bo't a Roman Lamp - 3.75.

Part IV * Germany, The Netherlands & Belgium

"The expense of a tour in Southern Germany depends, of course, on a great variety of circumstances. It may, however, be stated generally that traveling in this region is less expensive than in most other European countries.

Language. A slight acquaintance with German is very desirable... Those who are entirely ignorant of the language must be prepared frequently to submit to the extortion practices by commissionaires, waiters, cab-drivers, etc. ... English travelers often give trouble by ordering things almost unknown in German usage; and they are apt to become involved in disputes owing to their use of the language. They should therefore endeavor to acquire enough of the language to render them intelligible to the servants, and should try to conform as far as possible to the habits of the country.

Money. The German Mark (M), which is nearly equivalent to the English schilling... English sovereigns and banknotes may be exchanged at all principal towns in Germany, and Napoleons are also favorably received. Those who travel with large sums should carry them in the form of circular notes.

Hotel-Keepers. Those who wish to commend their houses to British and American travelers are reminded of the desirability of providing the bedrooms with large basins, foot-baths, plenty of water and an adequate supply of towels. Great care should be taken that the sanitary arrangements are in good order, including a strong flush of water and proper toilette-paper; and no house that is deficient in this respect can rank as first-class or receive a star of commendation." Baedeker, *Southern Germany*. 1895, x-xiv.

*

Verona - Munich. Tuesday, April 16, 1901.

At two o'clock a hard thunderstorm came up, but as nothing ever seems to get struck we did not mind it so very much, but soon after it seemed a hard knock came at the door, and it was just 3:30 AM. Mary and I got up and dressed as soon as we could and were down for coffee and rolls at 4:30 and it was so strange to be up so early, still not so bad after we were once going.

At five we piled in the bus and just as were ready to drive off, my soapbox was meekly handed in and I had to claim it. We were so thankful we had our hold-alls strapped the night before.

The sky was beautiful for it was beginning to get daylight and we soon got among the mountains and enjoyed the lights as the sun rose.

About seven we reached Ala [Austrian-Italian frontier], where we had to get out, for we had crossed the line into Austria and as usual, where our luggage was to be looked over and all our hold-alls nicely arranged on the counter. Miss Cadwell's and mine were the ones pounced upon, but Miss Cadwell said for me to "hold back". So he looked through hers and then said nothing more about mine, but just stuck on the label and we went along back in the car, which was a corridor the rest of the way.

We took turns at lying down for naps during the day and were ready for lunch, which was not as bountiful as we sometimes had, but plenty though.

The Brenner Pass is beautiful through the Tyrol Mountains and the country is more like ours than any we have seen so far. The houses with the top stories all open for hay are so odd and the Crucifixes along the road are a most peculiar sight.

We found after arriving in Munich that we had Prince Ferdinand of Austria with us in the same car, but 1st class [In 1901, heir to the Austro-Hungarian throne. Assassinated 1914 at Sarajevo, Yugoslavia, leading to declarations of war and WWI.].

We arrived at five o'clock after not as long a day as we all had expected and not nearly as tiresome as we tho't it might be. We took carriages at the station. Marion and I in one and drove up to Pension Glöckers, 5 Maximilian Strasse, where we found everything so nice and cozy that we were in love with it all the first thing.

We had fires in our rooms, for it was snowing and real cold when we reached here. I have a lovely room, just by the dining room, off the girls'. Mary is quite a way off with Miss Cadwell in the new part of the house. We had tea and such nice chocolate cake to eat with it. We also had [blank] to put in the tea instead of lemon or milk.

Munich. Wednesday, April 17, 1901.

"Munich, the capital of Bavaria, with 350,600 inhabitants... The lofty situation of the city and its proximity to the Alps render it to sudden changes of temperature, against which visitors should guard, especially towards evening." *Southern Germany*, 144.

*

Miss Cadwell got up and went out early for mail, etc. and brought back news that the Maria Theresia [Mr. Ferrie and Auntie] was sighted off Fire Island at 12, Sunday the 14th, and I am so anxious to hear how the passage proved. We think we will hear by a week from Saturday the 27th.

Miss Cadwell also brought me my new Letter of Credit for £305, Number 8904, from Baring Bros. Such a nice letter came with it and I was of course perfectly delighted. In the afternoon I drew my last £5 on my old Letter and gave that up.

Wednesday we went to the Bavarian National Museum where we saw a fine collection of treasures of every sort. The building is simply fine and the exhibits are so artistically arranged.

It rained and snowed all the morning and was cold and horrid.

In the afternoon, we went to the bank. Then Marion and Miss Cadwell went to Tristan and Isolde [Opera, Richard Wagner; German composer of Operatic Dramas, 1813-1883], having a lunch of tea at five and going to the Opera at six. I sat up and they came in at 10:45, so I joined them in the dining room and had my first taste of real German Beer and how I love it! And really it makes things whirl, but as I go right to bed, I don't mind.

German Beer!

Munich. Thursday, April 18, 1901.

In the morning we went to the Old Pinakothek where we saw some beautiful pictures principally of the Dutch and German painters. *The Apostles* by Dürer is especially beautiful and the others do not stand out in my mind as strongly.

We went to see the Royal Stables [Royal Coach House and Harness Rooms]. The carriages are perfectly beautiful, but I do not think any more elaborate than those we saw at the Vatican. From seeing the carriages we went to the horse stables, in which there were about 105, I believe. The stables really were nothing astonishing, but I was very glad to see them.

Then we had coffee in a café that was crowded, full of men smoking and women. The coffee was splendid and the cake very nice, a sort of chestnut layer cake.

Our Letters of Credit could easily be used in the store we went to next for the most fascinating bronzes and household furnishings that I have ever seen were there and were so artistic I could hardly help buying everything I saw. The clocks are too pretty for anything and I think I shall get two. And a lovely picture frame I saw just took my eye. We will get the things and then have them packed and sent up to London to meet us next fall.

Munich. Friday, April 19, 1901.

We walked over to the Glyptothek or Repository of Sculptures and the best in that collection are the sculptures in marble from The Temple of Minerva on the Island of Aegina found in 1811. They remind me a little of the Elgin Marbles in the British Museum, as they are the figures from the tympanum of the Temple. The *Sleeping Satyr* [*Drunken Satyr*] or *Barberini Faun* is good, also the Niobe Child [*Death of Niobe's Children*]. The *Cornelius Frescoes* done in 1820 are good, but look so new and fresh that I do not care for them [Peter von Cornelius, 1784-1867].

In the afternoon we went without Marion, who had to have a tooth filled, out to the *Bavaria* and Hall of Fame, which is a statue of Bavaria in bronze measuring sixty-two feet high with a beauty lion nestled up to her [Patron Saint of the State of Bavaria]. We went up to the top where we could see through little bits of windows that are in the hair. It's a tight squeeze and might be unpleasant meeting people on the narrow stairs.

Munich. Saturday, April 20, 1901.

We went over to the New Pinothek and there saw some most interesting modern paintings.

In the afternoon Miss Cadwell said she would go out with me so I got some new underclothes and some fit very well, but the corset covers are simply hopeless. They are so small.

We, all but Mary, went to our first Opera, having our tea and rolls at 5:30. Then, after talking at the table some time, we dressed and at 6:40 started for the Hoftheatre to *Fidelio* [Ludwig van Beethoven, 1806]. We have perfectly fine seats up in the fifth Gallery, but they are the first row and directly in front of the stage and only 2.80 or 70 a piece. (The Opera was *Fidelio* and very good.) Some woman goes and stands in line the morning of the Opera. The orchestra was superb and I liked Ficks [unreadable] and Klöpfer very much. The setting was lovely and the prison scene, or the last one, most effective [Hof und National Theatre. Max-Joseph Platz. Burned in October, 1943.].

It was out at 10:15 and we came home and found a nice supper ready for us of cold meat, salad, preserves or oranges rather, cheese, bread and butter and beer. Then I fussed around and finally went to bed.

Munich. Sunday, April 21, 1901.

This is rest day, but I finally had enough ambition to get up and give my head a good shampoo, which it needed badly and I worked fast and hard to get it done, but I felt repaid for it.

In the afternoon I wanted to write but simply fussed around, did not get much done, but went and lay on Mary's lounge and looked at her photographs with her. Then we had tea and I did manage to start Uncle Fred's letter, but I dreaded it, for it was to answer his that I received which reproved me for not going home with Auntie. I am wondering if this week will mean anything new in our friendship, which will no doubt be reviewed!

Munich. Monday, April 22, 1901.

We went to such a queer place this morning after going first to the Vegetable Market and to see the Isarthor Gate [14th c. city gate on the Isar River], which is remarkable, painted in scenes from a battle. It is a most picturesque gate.

From there we went out to the Cemetery [Southern Cemetary... "contains the finest and most artistic tombstones in Germany." *Southern Germany*, 192]. They have such a queer, but possibly a good, custom at a death, which requires that the body shall not be allowed to remain at the home for more than sixteen hours after death, but is taken to this cemetery and put on a bronze slab behind a glass front and covered with flowers and a white veil sometimes. Then a bell is placed within reach and should the person rouse, the guard, who is always present, will hear the bell. Because in the twenty years no one has rung the bell, it's said to be proof that there have been none buried alive.

All the afternoon Marion and I slept and woke up just in time for our tea at 5:30. Then we dressed and went to the Opera, which I enjoyed very much [*Herzog Wildfang*, by Siegfried Wagner, 1869-1930, son of Richard Wagner]. Feinhals was fine in his song, which he sang to Osterlind, who was Burkhart's daughter and I also liked Fraulein Koboth, for she was pretty and had a sweet voice. The plot was as usual where all the suitors are for the girl and they race and one says he came out ahead, but is proven wrong and they all have their excuses. But she finally chooses and takes Reinhart who used to love her. The music is light and parts are very sweet and pretty.

Munich. Tuesday, April 23, 1901.

We went to the bank, but I got no mail and I thought I might hear from J.S. [Joshua Sweet]. Then we were walking along [and] a man with a cape overcoat came along and took my hand in his for a second as he passed me. Letting mine lose, he took Leslie's and when we compared notes it was real exciting. Miss Cadwell says it often happens here where there are so many artists.

We then went to the Embroidery Rooms Leichnungs, Attlier Rud, Kohler, Kaufingerstrasse 12/11, and we nearly went crazy over it, for it is so artistic. I got such a lot for $4.25.

In the afternoon we all took the tram and went out to Nymphenburg [Schloss], which is a lovely chateau founded in 1663 by Max. Joseph I [Maximillian Joseph, King of Bavaria, 1756-1825]. It is so wild and beautiful. Prince Alfonzo and his family live there [Prince Alfonzo von Bayern]. All the different buildings and grounds were simply lovely. The house for the banquets after the hunt is great with room for the guns to fit in the closets and kennels under them all along the sides for the dogs to lie in.

We went for coffee over to the garden where the music was playing. The cake was so awful that we saved it & took it back with us to feed to the swans in the gardens. They were such perfect beauties. The wild flowers were so thick all over the place and the little anemones such as we have at home were in full bloom. Also little purple ones.

I thought I should be ravishingly hungry, but since we have been here, I have not wanted to eat anything.

Munich. Wednesday, April 24, 1901.

We first went to the bank, then over to the embroidery store and brought up at The Residence [Alte Residenz or The Old Palace], for it was the Festival of the Order of St. George.[1]

We all stood on the curbing under the gate for a long time and now and then a man all rigged up would appear. Then finally the soldiers marched in and took their places to keep the crowd on the walk and such splendid big men they all are. After awhile the Body Guards arrived and took places in front of the soldiers. These are all elderly men and so handsome in their chamois skin short coats with a frill on the bottom of silver embroidery, white kid trousers and long grey kid boots that came half way up to their hips, patent leather helmets with brass lions on the tops, white gloves and lace jabots and some of them were just stunning.

Finally, the band played and marched by, the drums draped in embroidered cloth and carried by lackeys. Following came the Knight in satin slippers, wearing a long sweeping robe of blue and white velvet, the train being carried by two pages.

We saw Prince Alfonzo, the favorite and nephew of the Prince Regent and then the dear Prince Luitpold, [who is] the Prince Regent [The heir to the throne, Luitpold von Bayern was Regent and de facto ruler of Bavaria from 1886 to 1912, due to the incapacity of his nephews, Ludwig and Otto.]. They all marched out on the carpet spread for them under the gateway and up to the Banqueting Hall. We followed the crowd and after they were all seated, we marched through the room and looked at them. It was a great sight, but we felt cheap looking at them all as we did. We got home at 1:30.

In the PM we did errands and then Miss Cadwell, Leslie and I went to the English Garden [600 acre park] while the others had a shampoo.

Munich. Thursday, April 25, 1901.

We started out to see some churches, but saw a crowd at the Residence, so went in and found it was sort of a continuation of the day before. A nice policeman came and told Miss Cadwell we might go upstairs, so we had to pass pair after pair of bodyguards and finally got into the large hall where the Knights finally passed thro' on their way to the Chapel [Hof or Reiche Kapelle]. In the long narrow hall beyond were the rest of the bodyguard lined up who saluted all the Knights as they went by.

Began gnome prince [needlework].

In the evening we went to the Opera, *Cupid and Psyche* [Max Zenger, composer, 1901], which was a pretty setting and the tableau good at the end.

Munich. Friday, April 26, 1901.

We went to the Old Pinakothek and pointed out the pictures to Leslie. On reaching the house I found that Josh [Sweet] had called and would come at three. I was so frustrated, I ate hardly any dinner, but I was glad to see him and we had the salon to our selves, which was nice. Miss Cadwell came in and stayed a little while and asked him to go with us to the English Garden, which he did and I was frantic, for they really got on horribly together, neither agreed with the other. He soon left us at the Pagoda and it did seem as if I never would see him again, but he came in the evening and we all entertained him in the salon and had a nice evening. Miss Cadwell stayed until he left and was as sweet and dear as could be. He had his mustache cut before coming to see us.

Munich. Saturday, April 27, 1901.

Last night after Josh left, Leslie and I wanted some beer, so we rang and had a bottle brought to us. Leslie had it in her little mug and I in my large new one, which is just fine to drink out of.

In the morning we walked quite a good deal and saw a number of churches and such things, bought some russet apples and ate along the street.

In the afternoon Josh called and all came in awhile. He stayed until I said he must go for we were to have reading. So he went and we had our tea early and Josh came back in time to go to the Opera, "*The Jewess*" [*La Juive*; Jacques Halevy, 1835]. It was the best we have seen so far and the girl who took the Jewess was fine and so young.

Munich. Sunday. April 28, 1901.

We as usual had a rest day and I stayed in bed till late. Then got around just in time for dinner.

About two Josh came. All went in the salon for some time. Miss Cadwell did not leave us until after three. Then Josh began to be serious and I did yield, so that he was very happy when he left, but he had no more than gone when I knew I had made a great mistake. Miss Cadwell and Frau Glöcker were worked up because he stayed so long and I was as sorry as could be, but it really did little good. Miss C. said he should be corrected in his manners, but after his two years all alone, I really did not take it as seriously as she, though I knew he was rude and should have known better.

I spent my evening until 1:30 AM writing a page and a half and taking back my decision. [Calling Card; *Mr. Joshua Edwin Sweet*, in pencil: 15 rue Boissonade, Paris, France. Clarissa had known Josh since they were young. He had been in Germany studying medicine for two years when Clarissa sees him in Munich. In 1901 he left Germany for Paris to study Bacteriology at the Louis Pasteur Institute.]

Munich. Monday, April 29, 1901.

Josh came and went with us through the Brauhaus and saw the people all busy drinking at ten in the morning. I nearly went crazy because he was not on the alert every minute to open doors, etc. We then went through the Royal Palace and while it was nice, I did not pay much attention. Coming out I gave him my note and told him he had better read it before giving me the one he wrote me the night before when he was so happy.

He did not come to go with us in the PM, so we went alone out to Nymphenburg to the Deer Park and it was such fun watching the fold at their pleasures. M. had her cake and coffee spilled by the deer.

Found an awful note when I reached home in answer to mine. If I thought the wound would not heal I should feel I might ruin his life. But I think if he goes back to Paris, Miss L. will get him on the rebound, for he is fond of her and she is of him I feel sure [Miss Linderfelt had arrived in Paris on the same Steamship as Josh in December. She arrived wearing his Duke University pin. Diary entry, Dec. 10, 1900.].

I was ready for dinner a few minutes ahead of time and the maid came saying, "Der Herr ist im denn salon", and I did not care to see him but pulled myself together. When the gong rang, Miss Cadwell came as she said she would, so I was excused. He tho't we had tea earlier and I was so glad to go, hardly knew what to do, for I did not feel in the least like getting into a discussion with him.

In the evening I wrote Uncle Fred and Auntie, no Fan, for no mail came as I expected it would.

Munich. Tuesday, April 30, 1901.

It poured and as there is really very little to do now, we all decided to stay in and possibly go out if it cleared in the afternoon. But it did not prove to be best, for Miss C. was "took" and Marion had said she would stay in with me to see Josh. But he came at three and Miss Cadwell came in for a while and as soon as she left he began to talk on that subject, and I thought if I could only hurry up and get it done, I should be happy. I felt so sorry for him, for he is really in earnest and I felt so cruel to be so severe, but he would not be satisfied unless I did go into the awful details. Frau Glöcker came in and it's a wonder she did not see him sitting on the piano. I was so thankful when he left and while it was an awfully hard thing for me to do, I felt there was no other way, for it did seem that it was more of a risk than I did dare take. Maybe I have ruined his life, but otherwise two would be lost.

In the evening we went to the Opera, which was light but very pretty, and I enjoyed it! [*Der Waffenschmied von Worms* (*The Armorer of Worms*); Albert Lortzing, 1846].

Munich. Wednesday, May 1, 1901.

We insisted on Miss Cadwell's staying in during the morning and Marion did, too. So Mary, Leslie and I went to the Bank and I told Herr Abber I couldn't give him the stamps from the letter of the day before, which I was so glad to get.

We then went for our clocks and I wanted a frame, but it was gone and the clocks, too, but I got one green one that was 16.15 M and now that I have it at home, I really like it very much indeed and am so glad I got it.

Josh came at three to say goodbye and he seemed to be feeling pretty good again and I was glad I did not have to see him alone.

My appetite and spirits have come back and so I really feel better that it all came out as it did and by tomorrow night the poor boy will have consolation, I hope, in Paris [Miss Linderfelt].

Munich. Thursday, May 2, 1901.

Marion did not go out, but we went over to the New Pinakothek as Mary had not been there before. I simply cannot remember the names of these modern works, but there are a number I like very much.

In the afternoon, as we could not go to the Opera as we had hoped, we just read and then went out for coffee to the Residence. Miss Cadwell found a parasol she liked, and the Bucks and I came up home.

[Newspaper article in the Diary: "Mrs. C.E. Hurd, who in company with Miss Claire S. Arnold has been traveling abroad since October, has returned to this country. She arrived in Oneonta on Wednesday night and is visiting her daughter, a member of the Normal Faculty (SUNY College at Oneonta, NY). Miss Arnold remained and is now in Munich, Germany, with the other members of the party with whom they went."]

As soon as we had tea we started about 8:15 for the Keller, which is the drinking room for the Löwenbräu Beer ["Löwenbräukeller, Stiglmayer-Platz, with a terraced garden and a large concert-room, often crowded." *Southern Germany*, 138]. The building is on the way to the Nymphenburg, but when we went in there was not a place downstairs, which seemed like a large theatre with the orchestra on the stage. Every man within miles turned to look at us, for of course they recognized us as Americans. We finally went up in the Gallery and got a table but had no view whatever.

The walls are beautifully frescoed and the whole thing was great with authors all around the sides. The mugs were plain stone ones with "Löwenbräukeller" on the side and the Bavarian coat of arms on the top. I can now drink a ½ liter or a pint.

Miss Cadwell surprised us all with big chocolate bugs on our beds and such a joke as it was we nearly burst laughing.

Munich. Friday, May 3, 1901.

We went downtown and did some errands going over to the embroidery store and I took my gnome piece and left it to have the middle stamped in. Then we went to the Museum and went upstairs where we saw lots of iron things and different costumes of Queens, etc.

In the afternoon Miss Cadwell, Mary, and I went out and selected my sailor [hat] and then got the hat Mary and I saw for her.

In the evening we went to *The Huguenots* [Opera, Giacomo Meyerbeer, 1836], which was the best thing by far that we have seen and we enjoyed it so much. The music was fine and we recognized parts we heard the night before out at Löwenbräu. The setting was very nice and comes nearer to the music I had expected to hear in Munich than anything we have so far seen or heard and I do hope this is the beginning of good Opera for us.

Munich. Saturday, May 4, 1901.

We did not, for some reason, accomplish much in the morning but did more errands and in the eve we went to a German play. It was funny, but to really enjoy it one should understand what is said [*Im Weissen Rössl* (*The White Horse Inn*), Oscar Blumenthal and Gustav Kadelburg, 1897].

Munich. May 5, 1901.

Have not heard from Uncle Fred for two weeks, but yesterday had a letter from Auntie. She is down home and I guess settling. I wrote Uncle F. if he tho't it best I would come home now, but I think rather than do that, Auntie will go up to Oneonta again.

We all had been in Marion's room and ½ liter is a little more that I can comfortably stand, I must admit.

We had telegram from Dresden and will go on to Nuremberg tomorrow and then will get to Dresden for the Opera on Thursday if all goes well. It has been so nice here that I hate to leave my room, though some of the anxieties have been unpleasant.

Munich - Nuremberg. Monday, May 6, 1901.

"Nuremberg; Germ. Nürnberg, population 142,500, a free city of the Empire down to 1806, has since belonged to Bavaria. There is probably no city in Germany still so medieval in appearance, or so suggestive of the wealth, importance, and artistic taste of a 'City of the Empire'." *Southern Germany*, 97.

*

We were up early with our trunks packed and hold-alls ready to start for Nuremberg and at 8:30 we left the house and got into the two carriages that were waiting for us around the corner and once again Marion and I brought up behind the other carriage at the station.

When we got out the man told us there was no such train, and sure enough, the timetable that Frau Glöcker [had] was not right in giving the 9:30 train, so we left our bags and sort of loitered toward Frau Glöcker's for it really did seem too bad for Frau G. looked it up and told us about it.

We were so hot it seemed like August, but after stopping at the house and waiting while Miss Cadwell went upstairs, and having everyone nod from the window and supposing we had left, we walked up the Maximilianstrasse and went in the English Garden for the fresh foliage was just lovely.

We sat there a long time, then went around by the Hofgarden and had orange ice out under the trees that we had said a fond farewell to about four hours before and it seemed as if we were in the midst of our second trip to München. [Hand drawn picture by Marion; "The Peterkins[2] in their homeless wanderings seat themselves at the foot of the Monument to Victory, in order to rest before they continue."]

We went to the Bank and then to Frau Glöcker's for luncheon and she was in a rush getting ready for people who came in the morning instead of the evening, but Frauline Etrucchen [unreadable] was dear. A maid was sent after us to tell us we had not paid for our luncheon, for Miss C. did not notice it was deducted from our bill, but off we went, saying we would write.

We left at 1 PM and reached Nuremberg and went to the [Hotel] Nürnbergerhof [Königstrasse], which is fine and just by the station and over by the side of the city wall.

We soon went out to do the town so it wouldn't seem so strange when we went out the next morning. We went into St. Lorenzo where we saw Krafft's beautiful *Ciborium*, which was fine [Adam Krafft, Sculptor, 1455-1509… "the Ciborium, or receptacle for the Host … beautifully & elaborately executed in stone, in the form of a tower." *Southern Germany*, 99]. The fountain in front, with the water coming out of the breasts of the figures like those in the Residence in Munich, which was extinct.

We saw *Hans Sachs Monument* [Hans Sachs, Poet and Mastersinger, 1494-1576] the Nassauer Haus [city's oldest private house, with one of Germany's oldest inn restaurants, Nassauer Keller.] opposite St. Lorenzo and we brought up at the Bratwurst Glöcklein (Roast Sausages at the Little Bell) and I never thought I would eat eight sausages and two helpings of sauerkraut, a mug of beer and a roll and such an artistic, tiny place I never saw. I simply loved it and hated to leave. Had tea in rooms.

Nuremberg. Tuesday, May 7, 1901.

It was a rainy horrid day, but we went around and saw things all the morning going by the Frauenkirche, by the Market, seeing the bagpipe player fountain, and the man with two ducks with water coming out of their bills [Gänsemännchen, Little Goose Man Fountain]. Through the Rathaus into St. Sebaldus [Church], where we saw St. Sebald's monument by Peter Fischer [Peter Vischer, Sculptor 1455-1529] in bronze, which is wonderful. To Dürer's statue and house, which is so picturesque, now owned by a society, but we did not go in.

Came home, had dinner. I did up Longfellow's "Nuremberg", a cunning little booklet with illustrations of the places [poem, "Nuremberg", by Henry Wadsworth Longfellow,1844].

In the afternoon we went to the Museum [Germanic National Museum] and saw the "*Nuremberg Madonna*", which was a green wooden carved statue, pretty good, and lots of illustrations of German life and the miniature house and the regular kitchen was a sight.

We then had coffee and cake and went up to the Berg or Castle [Kaiserberg], begun in the 11th Cent. by Emp. Conrad II. The lime tree planted in1024 by the wife of Emp. Hen. II [Empress Kunigunde] is standing, tho nearly dead. The Iron Virgin [medieval torture device] was awful and the charms we have give a very good idea of it.

Nuremberg - Dresden. Wed, May 8, 1901.

As it was pleasant we walked a while and left at 12:03, had lunch boxes brought onto the train at Bamberg, only three instead of five, but enough with ginger cakes, such a mess! But wine was good. Drank soup out of tin cups, roast veal, beef dropped in liquid spinach, black bread, cherries & wine. Reached Dresden at 11 – came to Weber's. Found Auntie's cheerful letter and Uncle F.'s otherwise [Hotel Card; Weber's Hotel, Ostra-Allée, Dresden].

Dresden. Thursday, May 9, 1901.

"Dresden, the capital of the Kingdom of Saxony, mentioned in history for the first time in 1206, and the residence of the sovereigns since 1485... Population 334,000... The beautiful environs and the magnificent picture-gallery attract numerous visitors, and a considerable English community resides here." Baedeker, *Northern Germany*, 284.

*

We have the luxury again of breakfast in bed and this morning it was brought in by a good looking man who spoke very good English, so it drove my German phrases to the winds. He was such a surprise, and it was most disconcerting.

We got up at ten and went over to The Museum [Picture Gallery, engravings and drawings], which is directly opposite, after Miss Cadwell had been to Frau Dr's and gotten our tickets for the Opera [Frau Doctor Hering; an acquaintance of Miss Cadwell's residing in Dresden]. In the Gallery are some very beautiful pictures among them Correggio's *Holy Night* [Antonio da Corregio, 1494-1534], Hoffman's *Christ Among the Doctors* [*Christ in the Temple*, Heinrich Hofmann, 1824-1911] and then the *Sistine Madonna* [*Madonna di San Sisto*, Raphael], before which we sat and just drank it all in to our hearts content, for it is a gem. The figure [within the *Sistine Madonna*] of Sixtus IV [Pope, 1471-1484] is the grandest figure of all we have seen so far on our trip. His attitude is one of such strength, but simple adoration. The Virgin, I do not care for especially, as her expression to me seems rather affected, but critics say it is simply in awe of her position. The Child is sweet and childlike and St. Barbara is very weak and prim to me. The clouds on which all three rest are so light and fluffy it seems they must be real and the two little angels at the foot are lovely. Without Sixtus IV, I should not care for this picture above many others, but with him, it is superb.

Holbein's *Burgermaster's Family* [Hans Holbein the Younger, 1497-1543; a copy of the original] is most interesting and we did not agree which was the sick child, though I maintained the Virgin holds the Christ Child.

When we went into dinner, we discovered directly back sat Paderewski [Ignacy Jan Paderewski, 1860-1941; Polish pianist and composer] at a table smoking and he seemed to be working at music. His wife finally came in and kissed him on the forehead and then they all ate, another man being with them. It was fine to be so near for we just stared, I know, but he is used to it I am sure. His wife is so sweet looking and it's said she was so devoted to his son whom he has just lost.

We stayed in all the PM and had tea and bread and butter at 5:15, then went to the Opera where we had seats in the top Gallery and which were very good ["Neues Hof-Theatre[3], for operas and important dramas; performances daily..." *Northern Germany*, 282].

The Opera began at six and lasted till 10:30 and I enjoyed every bit of it, which really surprised me, but having just come from Nuremberg, the pleasure was enhanced thereby. *The Meister Singer of Nuremberg* is a splendid Opera and I only wish we could hear it again [*Die Meistersinger von Nürnberg*, Richard Wagner; first performed, 1868].

We had supper after it, but we did not get Munich beer!

Dresden. Friday, May 10, 1901.

The first thing was my little package from Tombini's [of Rome, specializing in cameos; Via Condotti 2] and my surprise is beyond words, for when I opened it after signing the receipt, I only found a little mosaic heart-shaped stickpin, no bigger than a forget-me-not. But still, it's cute and I don't feel so done as perhaps I was, though of course it was a joke on me and if the stupid thing had not put 75 in stamps on the package, I would have gotten something worth speaking of. But anyway, I will keep some of the stamps!

We went to the Garden [Grosse Garten] for the morning which is lovely, then rested in the afternoon and in the eve went to *The Merry Wives of Windsor* [Opera, Carl Otto Nicolai, 1849], which was a pretty and light opera and the setting was very pretty.

Dresden. Saturday, May 11, 1901.

In the morning Miss Cadwell had a lot of errands so we did not get started very early, but when we did go we left Leslie at home and took the train over to the Japanese Garden, which was not as I thought it would be. It is so named because the building on it, which is now a library, used to contain a very fine

Japanese collection. We were a little early in the season for a great many of the flowers were not out yet. The tulips, pansies and wall or jilly flowers were lovely.

In the afternoon, Mary and I went with Miss Cadwell up to her friend's to tea. Frau Doctor Hering, 38 Zellescherstrasse, and we had a very nice time. Then we found our trunks on our arrival at home. Miss Cadwell's box of books did not come. They simply said they didn't know where it was!

Marion and Mary went to Dr. Freischütz. I wrote 42 [?].

Dresden. Sunday, May 12, 1901.

Not an exciting day. Wrote Uncle J. Sherman, Blanche, Fan and Uncle Fred. Received no letter from him.

After dinner with dessert made of sour cream, all put on our new hats and paraded in the girls' room. We all quake at the tho't of launching out tomorrow.

Dresden. Monday, May 13, 1901.

Miss Cadwell and Mary went out early to do some errands and Miss Cadwell's books turned up. I picked off a Molaro label much to my joy, for I had lost mine [from Hotel Molaro in Rome]

We then went to choose table linen and I bought two tablecloths, one to seat eight with eight napkins, and the other for six with six napkins to match. The working is beautiful and I am so glad I have it.

Also bought six fruit knives and two salts and a tea ball all in china, which I am delighted with. Mary got six knives, too.

In the afternoon we took the train at two and went to Cossebaude [small town near Dresden] to see the Baum-Blüte [tree blossoms], but it is too late, as the flowers have fallen, but still the country was lovely and we had a nice climb, coffee and a rest, then went through the most beautiful woods back to the station and home.

Tuesday, May 14, 1901.

I did not go out all day but Miss C. took my ticket for *Carmen* [Opera, George Bizet, 1875] and wanted Frau Dr. to go in my place, but as she was going into the Grosser Garten, she did not promise, so I was ready to go in case she did not come.

I enjoyed it so much and should have been sorry had I missed it, for the music is lovely and Carmen is fascinating. Don José is the tall skinny man who has sat [at the] next table to us and came in for supper after the opera. It was a great surprise. Letter from Auntie - well!

Dresden. Wednesday, May 15, 1901.

In the morning Mary was going to the dentist so we all went to the bank and she and Miss Cadwell left us to go over to the dentist's. Well, Marion, Leslie and I sat there till 11:35, a whole hour & finally a man asked us, very politely, if we wished to be waited on. We could not help feeling it was a hint, but we stayed there and finally Mary and Miss C. came back. Then we went to order Mary's linen and to the china store, but the man was out so we are going again.

The girls and Miss Cadwell and Frau Doctor all went to Bastei and I stayed at home alone [The Bastei; "... 1030 ft. above the sea-level with an Inn on the summit ... the finest point in Saxon Switzerland." *Northern Germany*, 313.]. They expected to get home by eight but did not till nearly nine. Then we all went down for supper. I had had a nap and a great time with the man who came from the cleaners.

Dresden. Thursday, May 16, 1901.

As this is a holiday, being Ascension Day, things are pretty generally closed and all the people are out in their best bib and tucker, so we went over to the [blank] and saw a very good collection of things about the same that we see in the museums generally, but upstairs there is a splendid collection of Japanese and Dresden China and the real Meissen [China] is fine. The swords crossed in the [trade] mark about 1725, crossed with the star is 1775, crossed with the [blank] 1814, and now, simply the plain crossed swords are the present mark.

In the evening we went to the Opera and most of the evening was taken up with such stupid ballet and finally came *Cavalleria Rusticana* [one act Opera by Pietro Mascagni, first performed in 1890], and with the exception of the regular music we know, it was very disappointing and I was so tired & sleepy when it was over.

A Day Trip to Meissen. Friday, May 17, 1901.

Tristan and Isolde [Opera, Richard Wagner] was on for tonight, but as it was a lovely morning Miss Cadwell came in and asked us what we tho't about going out to Meissen instead of going to the Opera. She seemed to think it would be more sensible for us to go out there, so we decided to go, but the Bucks were disappointed they said afterwards.

We left the hotel at ten, took a train out to the new station and took a train at 10:30 going III class and the seats were so cool and comfortable that I wish we could always go in that way ["Meissen, one of the most ancient towns in Saxony, founded about 930 by King Henry I." *Northern Germany*, 327].

We reached Meissen at 11:15 and had a nice walk over the bridge and up to the Burg [Albrechtsburg, erected 1471-1483] and had a nice girl show us through. It is a beautiful castle, having been recently done over and repaired and in the very best of taste. The views from the upper corridors are lovely. From there we went into the church that is close by the Castle & saw the bronze tomb slabs that are said to have been designed by Dürer.

After our dinner at the Burg Keller with fine beer, we walked over to the Meissen Factory, which is so interesting ["The celebrated Royal Porcelain Manufactory... It is shown on week-days 7-12 and 2-6; fee 2 M for 1 pers., or 1 M for each member of a party. The factory was founded in 1710, the year after Böttger had discovered the art of making 'china'." *Northern Germany*, 329]. I had no idea that all the china had to be so carefully done. Of course the process is similar to the Trenton works [Philadelphia, PA], that is in the molds, ovens and firing, but the care in putting on the onion pattern all by hand is wonderful. The workmen have to take a thorough training in the Dresden School before they are allowed in [the Meissen] School at all, I should say factory, and while I do not care especially for the china and bric-a-brac with the garlands, still they are much more wonderful after knowing that every tiny leaf has to be put on by hand and then burned on.

We reached the hotel about five and soon Frau Doctor came and she said she would come and stop for us to go to the Brühl Terrasse [garden and promenade above the Elbe River], so we all went up there and it was very pretty watching the sky as the sun was setting. We had more beer and listened to the music until about ten and then put Frau Doctor on a car and came in and were very thankful to get to sleep.

Dresden. Saturday, May 18, 1901.

Mary stayed in all day and we four went to the Exhibit of Modern Art [Kunstausstellung Dresden, 1901; label in Diary] and of all hideous and fanciful pictures, that collection deserves the medal – it was awful, but the rooms that were furnished were as pretty and sweet as could be and one could easily get nice ideas – the posters are in keeping!

In the afternoon I wrote a nice long letter to Mabel and I do wish I had not waited so long. Now that I know Auntie is settled and comfortable I feel more like sending letters off.

We went to *Mignon* [Ambrose Thomas, 1866] in the evening and it was by far the nicest thing I think we have seen and I described it all to Mary after I got home. Anthes as Wilhelm Meister was fine [Georg Anthes, 1863-1923, a leading tenor of the Dresden Opera] and dear little Frau Wedekind was too lovely for any thing [Erika Wedekind, 1868-1944, celebrated soprano of the Dresden Opera], then Perron as Lothario was fine [Karl Perron, 1858-1928] and I would give anything if we could see it again.

Dresden. Sunday, May 19th, 1901.

We had a nice morning as I got letters from Auntie, Fan and Uncle F. and then wrote Miss Adams.

At the dinner table I managed to place the top slice of pistachio ice cream on the waiter's sleeve and we of course went in fits and Miss C. made the remark we must be careful or we would loose control of ourselves and she then proceeded to burst.

We decided to do the Chateau District in France and return on the *Lucania* the 2nd of Nov. and the Bucks are all excitement over going to Egypt and so staying over, but I think will all return [The intention was to return to the US on the *Lucania*, the same Steamship they had arrived on in October, 1900.].

Dresden. Monday, May 20, 1901.

In the morning we had mail and I had five copies of Life come and it was just lovely to get them, too, and I could hardly wait to read them and also did wish for a letter saying they had been sent.[4]

We all went to the bank and drew, then went to the linen store and paid for our linen. Mine came to 140 Marks and by paying cash down it was 136, so I have the other 4 M for photographs. We just simply did errands the rest of the time and right after dinner Marion and Mary went with Miss Cadwell to the doctor's and Mary had the little thing taken off her chin and she had a bad time and nearly fainted.

We then all went to Blasewitz [a suburb of Dresden], which is the location of the Schiller Garten, and sat by the river watching the ferry and small steamers ply up and down. We were very busy indeed!

Dresden. Tuesday, May 21, 1901.

As the day looked as if it would be a nice one, we took an early start and left the house at nine. At the station we had about given up Frau Doctor when along she came, so we started at 9:45, III class, and rode about an hour and a quarter passing Bastei where I was not able to go with the girls.

I don't remember where we got out, but we took a ferry and crossed the river and then we were in Bohemia, what is called Swiss Saxony, and it is queer and seems different from any of the places we have seen at all. The houses are usually black and white, one half of the ground floor being black logs and all the rest plaster painted in white washes with cross beams of black ["The Meissener Hochland, a very picturesque district, remarkable for its singular rock-formations known for the last century as the Saxon Switzerland." *Northern Germany*, 312].

We soon came to the path that ran along by the water and such a walk as that is. It is for a walk, what Amalfi is for driving. We came to the end, then went in a boat that seemed like a fairyland and had a lunch of ham sandwiches and beer. We walked along and back, getting home a little after six & a lovely day we had [Edmundsklamm, "or Gorge of the Kamnitz... the most remarkable rocky gorge in the entire district. At the narrowest point is a small inn." *Northern Germany*, 316. Postcard in Clarissa's Diary, "Gruss aus der Edmundsklamm!"].

Dresden. Wednesday, May 22, 1901.   Clarissa's Birthday.

To C.S.A. May 22nd 1901
> *As long as you live and until you die*
> *May you never feel like drawing a sigh*
> *And may no teardrop dim your eye.*
> *Nor you do anything to make me sigh.*
> *May you never know what sorrow is;*
> *May you always have to bear with bliss;*
> *May your nights and days be one sweet dream*
> *And all things prove to you as they seem.*
> *And in good time may you return*
> *To those who love you, and who yearn*
> *Now to see and know that you are safe,*
> *And free from danger care and pain*
> *In that old country, full of Dutch,*
> *But we all know that life is such.*

And with our blessing, I will stop
For fear I might hear something drop.
Your foot on the floor, and "Uncle Fred,
Please stop!"

J. Fred Sands

[Poem, written by Clarissa's Uncle and guardian, J. Fred Sands, on her 24th birthday, and saved in her Diary.]

The first thing I fully realized was having an impatient knock at our door, and there was Marion in her wrapper and urging me to please hurry and come to their room to see something from their window. It seems Mary was supposed to try to be very sleepy and finally wake up to the situation, but she was really dead asleep and finally woke up and came over to give me a birthday kiss.

We finally went, and I went first, over towards the window and then I spied Miss Cadwell, squeezed up behind the stove and she came out and kissed me, followed by Leslie, who was crouched down by her trunk and by that time we had a assembled and in front was a table laden with lilacs and the most interesting and mysterious packages at all the corners. Then in front of it was the upholstered armchair with the footstool for me to put my feet on. Marion had made little pen and ink sketches for our breakfast cards and I felt so grand when I sat down. By the side of my plate was one of the illustrated birthday cards as a cover to the adjoining poem and I do think it was so lovely of Miss Cadwell to spend her time writing it for me. By the side of it was Marion's illustration of what we did the day before and it is just like the groups we were in during the day [Drawing on Weber's Hotel stationary, featuring the four girls, Miss C. and Frau Dr. on their outing to the Edmundsklamm as, "The Peterkins".].

We had just gotten nicely eating, when a knock came at the door and the waiter came in with the mail, which consisted of four postcards for me and how in the world those people ever did find just the right things to fit in every instance, for I just think they are the nicest things I ever saw! and we just about went into fits and "Kendrick" is the best thing [postcard], but no one but ourselves appreciated them one third as much.

As soon as breakfast was over they all talked about Ella [a small stuffed elephant] and said Ella wanted to come by me. Then she wanted to get on the table by my gifts, so I finally put her over there and she was so happy and did not trumpet any more. I first opened the package from her and found a lovely box of chocolates, which were delicious. I then opened Miss Cadwell's, which was a beer mug made of birch wood with the bark on it that came from Bastei. The girls gave me the beautiful Sistine Madonna in carbon and I can hardly wait to have it home in a lovely frame. Mary was a dear to give me a hatpin that I can put right in my sailor and wear all the time.

We went over to The Gallery after we dressed and Mary had to go to the dentist's. Frau Doctor said she would come and meet us at the Hotel to go with us for our afternoon's excursion. We hurried through our dinner and she was waiting for us in the hall and handed me a little bunch of lilies-of-the-valley tied to a package that proved to be two cakes of chocolate. But we had to rush, for we took the steamer for Pillnitz [a Royal Chateau of Saxony], about an hour and a half ride and it was a treat and reminded us of the steamer as she puffed out of N.Y. harbor and the people on it were so funny to watch.

We got off at Pillnitz, just beyond the royal residence. As we walked up the winding road we came to the most beautiful display of lilacs with garlands of five-fingered ivy between each of the hundreds of trees, which were simply one mass of blooms.

We then walked along till we came to a most delightfully cool looking "Restauration" where we stopped and Miss Cadwell ordered Maiwine [traditional spring wine, aromatized with the perennial plant, sweet woodruff] and a cup of chocolate for Frau Doctor. Then she asked for her black bag and instead of having her fancy work, she undid the dearest little round birthday cake with a hole in the middle and iced with white and fancy green and white icing. We all ate a lot and the wine was simply splendid with it. All drank to me and I asked that we might drink to Miss Cadwell and Frau Dr.

After we finished, we started for our walk up the hill and through such lovely woods. I wish we had more places fitted up for the public to have a good time when they are off for a feste day. The lights on the trees were such a lovely green and the coo-coos make one realize it isn't America.

We took the boat back a little after seven and reached Dresden at about nine and really, it was so light that one could have read easily and at ten the after glow was still high in the sky.

We had a nice supper and as Miss Cadwell says, "slept without rocking" after one of the loveliest birthdays and to think I am twenty-------! [Clarissa was 24.]

Dresden. Thursday, May 23, 1901.

We went to the Royal Palace and got into see the treasures in the Green Vault and there were some beautiful things there in the way of jewel boxes with the loveliest settings and etched designing on the metal ["The Green Vault, on the ground floor of the palace, contains one of the most valuable existing collections of curiosities, jewels, trinkets, and small works of art, dating chiefly from the late-Renaissance and rococo eras." *Northern Germany*, 288].

I was thunderstruck by seeing a man there who looked enough like Mr. S. to be he and even his voice was like his and he spoke English which made it seem as if it simply must be he. It made me feel most peculiar to say the least.

The clock, which is called The Tower of Babel [1602], is a queer thing, very wonderful of course, but I should think it would drive any one frantic to hear and watch the little ball go round and round till it gets to the foot then whiz back to the top and ring a little bell each minute. The royal jewels are most elaborate and beautiful and some of the stones are of the most gorgeous colors.

After we got through there we went over to the Zoological [and Ethnographical] Museum to see the collection of bird's nests and while I suppose they are wonderful, after seeing all the colors of the collection in London [Gould Collection] these seemed to be rather tame. I suppose because up there we saw only the most rare specimens, while here the rare and somber colored birds were in together. Miss Cadwell and Mary went over to The Gallery and we three finished these and the Gallery was free today so we went over and met them.

In the afternoon Mary went to finish with the dentist, Dr. Jenkins, and I wrote to Auntie and I thought I would never get done, for there was so much to say and I kept thinking of so many important side tho'ts, that before I could finish Mary was back and we had to dress for the Opera.

I must say I think the cast as a whole was very poor but with [Georg] Anthes and Chavanne [Irene von Chavanne, 1868-1938] the thing was kept alive. It didn't begin until 7:30, so we had our tea before we went over and then came directly to our rooms when we returned and what discovery was immediately made, but that Ella had slipped her halter and been lost.

We all felt her loss so deeply that Leslie suggested we should have a wake for her. So Miss Cadwell ordered a bottle of beer for us and Leslie stayed in till Mary and I were ready for it and we all drank, I using my new birch beer mug which is just splendid, for it is sort of varnished on the inside so that nothing soaks in. Marion felt so low over the loss that we could not persuade her to join us, and she went immediately to the privacy of her own chamber. Mary and I fussed around and got to bed about twelve.

Dresden. Friday, May 24, 1901.

I got up at the early hour of 7:30 and finished my letter to Auntie and it was a long one, too, I tell you. Then Miss Cadwell said she was going to take a carriage and go up to Frau Doctor's with our hats and the things we had for her.

Just before Miss Cadwell came in, we had rung for more rolls and Mary took what we hadn't eaten on the sofa by her, so with the hard ones that came from somewhere our room seemed flooded. Miss Cadwell had a letter from Miss Chaffee in which she told about her maid and asking Miss Cadwell if she could suggest a place in Switzerland where her maid and she could be comfortable. Miss Chaffee is going home on the *Commonwealth* the first of October, so she will not be one of us. All the time Miss Cadwell was reading and talking, Mary and I were just about in hysterics.

I hurried and dressed and at 9:45 Marion and I started out for what seemed a most hopeless search after Ella. It did not seem as if we could possibly find her, but we retraced our steps of the night before and what should we see just as we stepped onto the paving in front of the Opera House, but the dear little white elephant, lying out stiff and white on the cold walk between two stores and quite safe. We rushed home and cheers went up for Ella.

When we went out, we brought up at the picture store and they are very expensive ever since we left our beloved Italy. Those we paid 14 for there, are 25 here, so our bills come up very decidedly and the man was so stupid, he only had part [of what] we wanted anyway and so is going to send to the Hotel three of each in the afternoon.

We then went out to the Japanese Garden where the hawthorn trees are just in their prime, the pink and white. As soon as we returned we found Frau Doctor, who had come to say goodbye to us. She brought Miss C. a lovely bunch of lilies-of-the-valley and each of us such an artistic book containing views of Dresden and she was so moved when she said goodbye to us all. She has been so thoughtful for our comfort and so has made our stay more pleasant by her care.

After dinner we began at once to pack, for two trunks are going with us to Berlin and the others follow by freight. Mary and I are going to put our things together and my trunk is simply running over it is so full. When I pack again I can improve on my things and I am thinking strongly of giving my golf cape away, for it is worn quite a good deal and on the steamer I shall have the two rugs, so it really seems as if I would not need it enough to pay for carrying it all the time. So, if I am cramped again for room, I shall simply give it up.

The Opera was not anything to brag of. The music was pretty but the thing put me to sleep and I was so thankful when it was over. We had supper after it then Mary had a lot of things to do and I went to sleep, but she woke me up, for she did not know where to put her beer mug that is like mine. Then she dropped her collar button and while a thing of that sort always is an annoying thing to hunt for in the day, at 12 PM it is especially slippery and I wouldn't have missed the fun for a good deal and I was so glad she woke me up.

Dresden. Saturday, May 25, 1901.

Auntie's Birthday! And for some reason my watch was two hours slow, so I did not get up till the breakfast came and when the man came for the trunks I was so afraid he would take the wardrobe, too, for in my partially clothed state I was forced to take that as my stand. But we got off and left the house at 9:15. The train left at quarter of ten and we reached ...

Berlin. May 25, 1901.

... at 2 o'clock in a pouring rain, thunder and all sorts of things. Mary had a couple of holes stove through the cloth on the bottom of her trunk. Miss C. had to pay the man more than she ought. We came to Wilhelmstrasse 49, and Mrs. Gerling and her sister, Miss Holworthy, are English and such a nice parrot, Jocko, that talks so you can understand him ["Boarding House/ Pensionen, Mrs. Gerling (5-8 M per day), to the South of the Linden." *Northern Germany*, 4].

We went out to so some odds and ends and got caught in the rain again.

Dinner at six and one man in the establishment and he sits by me and opened the conversation.

Tea at nine. Leslie & I stayed in rooms.

Berlin. Sunday, May 26, 1901.

"Berlin, the capital of Prussia, residence of the German Emperor, and the seat of the imperial government... contains 1,676,352 inhabitants, including the garrison of 20,000 soldiers, and thus occupies the third place among the cities of Europe...[Berlin is] perhaps the greatest manufacturing town in central Europe.

In external appearance Berlin is somewhat deficient in interest, its situation is unpicturesque, and it lacks the charm of medieval and historical edifices. There is, however, no want of architectural display and the last 20 years have witnessed the erecting of many handsome buildings in every part of the city... The removal of the town-walls in 1864-66 and the rapid extension of the tramway-system gave a great impulse to the city's new prosperity... Altogether Berlin is now little, if at all, inferior to the older capitals of Europe in the comfort and completeness of its public works, while in such matters

as the cleaning and lighting of the streets it has few equals and no superiors."
Northern Germany, 20-21.

*

Last night we heard Mrs. McKinley[5] was dead from my friend and today that the man who assassinated King Humbert had committed suicide [Gaetano Bresci, Italian American who shot King Umberto I of Italy, July 29, 1900].

A rest day as usual and instead of writing a lot of letters as I ought, I am going to read *The Venetians* [Mary Elizabeth Braddon, 1892]. I think it's terribly trashy, and if I continue to talk with my friend on such deep subjects I must not limit myself to those alone! Whit-Sunday!

Berlin. Monday, May 27, 1901.

It may be Monday, but no one would ever take it to be other than Sunday, for it is a holiday and all the working people are out for a good time. We induced Miss Cadwell to stay in during the morning, for everything is closed that we would care to see. So I wrote to Grace Watson and it is a perfect shame I should have neglected her as I have, for my steamer letter from her was just lovely.

In the afternoon Miss Cadwell read a little to us about the history of Berlin and Prussia but it is so complicated I am afraid I shall have an awful time getting it straight.

We started out about four, went to a shop and had coffee and Bauen-küchen, which is a most peculiar cake. It tastes like sponge, only is very close grain & baked in some sort of a cylinder and as it is shaved down it seems to have a grain that gives it the appearance of wood.

Unter den Linden Strasse[6] is a disappointment, for it does not compare with some of our streets at home - Commonwealth Avenue [Boston] for instance.

The Thiergarten is lovely and seems so wild and cultivated. We walked home through Bellevue St., which has simply sumptuous homes and the shaded street is beautiful. No Parade tickets yet!

Berlin. Tuesday, May 28, 1901.

We had yesterday an inkling that a struggle was before us to get the Kings and Emperors of Germany straight in our minds and so we first went to the Hohenzollern Museum [Royal Family of Prussia, Germany and Romania] where everything is splendidly arranged with a room devoted to each royal person, so by seeing the belongings, it's much easier to fix the people in our minds and from Baedeker I have found the dates to the following:

Frederic William, Great Elector 1640 - 1699
        Queen Sophia Dorothea

(1) King Frederic I, 1701 (Frederic III 1688 - 1713)
        Queen Sophia Charlotte

Frederic the Great 1740 - 1786
        Queen Elizabeth Christine
(2) Frederic William II 1786 - 1797

Frederic William III   1797 - 1840
        Queen Louise

*Frederic William IV 1840 - 1861

*Emperor William 1861 - 1888
        Queen Augusta

Frederic III 1888, 3 months
        Empress Frederic

Emperor William II
        Augusta Victoria

Hohenzollern Family
        (1) Tobacco Parliament
        (2) Brandenburg Thor erected
        * Brothers

In the afternoon we all, excepting Marion, went out to Charlottenburg [suburb of Berlin] where the [Royal] Palace is situated and where Emperor William's [William I, The Great] father, Emperor Frederic III, spent the last ten weeks of his life before he died of cancer of the throat. The beautiful Mausoleum erected by Frederic William III contains the bodies and effigies of Frederic William III, Queen Louise and Emperor William and Queen Augusta and the heart, it's said, of Frederic William IV.

Berlin. Wednesday, May 29, 1901.

Marion did not go with us but we went to the Old Museum and saw a large collection of pictures and as Miss Cadwell says, if one could not go South or to the homes of the painters, a very good idea could be gotten. Murillo's *Adoration of St. Antony* [Bartolomé Estéban Murillo, 1617-1682] is most beautiful and Durér's [*Hieronymus Holzschuher*, 1526] is wonderful, as it should be, for over $100,000 was paid for it.

Our trunks came in the afternoon and I unpacked and how good it did seem to have it again. I returned Marion's Liberty [Liberty Print dress], which she had let me use all during our opera in Dresden and Munich and as a little token of my thanks, I gave her one of the little Dresden salt dishes and she was so pleased.

We went and got Leslie's waist and stocks, then I drew and on the way home Leslie bought the leather case for Marion's birthday, 60 M. I sewed all the evening & Herr Oberst sent to see if we were here [Herr Oberst; a city official of Berlin].

Berlin. Thursday, May 30, 1901.

We went to the New Museum in the morning and saw some lovely modern pictures and at noon when we reached home, we found our ticket to the Parade, so we are at rest now and all that is necessary is fair weather for tomorrow.

We all went out to the Zoo [Zoological Garden, opened in 1844] in the afternoon. Just as we were enjoying the bears and the little cub playing, a man came to demand two kodiacs [?] so Miss Cadwell and Mary took him to the entrance. Not so nice as the one in England, but pretty grounds [Postcard from the Zoo with notation; "It was a boiling hot day and I tho't we would melt when in the sun."].

Berlin - The Review of the Garrison. Friday, May 31, 1901.

"In the Tempelhofer Feld, an open piece of ground extending southwards from the Kreuzberg to the village of Tempelhof, the annual manoeuvres and review of the Berlin Garrison have taken place since the days of Frederick William I (1713-1740)." *Northern Germany*, 68.

"Military Reviews ('Paraden') are held by the Emperor at the end of May... Pedestrians may freely enter the parade-ground, but carriages require a permission from the Polizeipräsidium." *Northern Germany*, 15.

∗

This was a great day for "The Peterkins" and we began it early and were glad to go to bed early, too. We were up at 4:30 AM, and the maid called us a little later. It seemed perfectly ridiculous to dress up in our best bib and tucker at such an unearthly hour, but after we got started it seemed all right. I wore my white ribbon waist and black broadcloth skirt.

We went down to breakfast at half past six and had our coffee and rolls and there were all the rest eating. I, of course, only had my sailor hat, so Miss Cadwell loaned me her white net veil, which she said would make it look "more dressy".

We left the house at seven in a nice looking carriage with our ticket of admission stuck in the driver's hat. Everybody was going and it seemed strange for us to be in the carriage being looked at instead of standing on the curbstone with our toes hanging over the edge.

It was some ways to the Parade Ground. There were policemen standing all along the line and in Berlin the police are fine, for all the men are soldiers who for some reason or other are not able to be in active service.

The Parade Ground is an immense field and we could see the artillery going on from the different sides the men looking like specks. There was a bunch of policemen stationed at the entrance and as we drove along with the crowd. One on a beauty brown horse came up and Miss Cadwell showed him Herr Oberst's card, which we had that wished us a pleasant time. He took it, looked at it, then told us to turn around where we were and get in line. We could see the gate well, but it did not seem to be in the right direction to see the maneuvers, but Miss Cadwell did not seem a bit disturbed.

Finally, the Herr Oberst came in escorted by five or six other mounted police and they are splendid and a sight simply to watch them as they gallop down the lines and over to the Entrance. We fixed, expecting the Herr Oberst would come to us, but he did not.

At last we could see the royal carriages coming through entrance No. 2. The first carriage drawn by six black horses driven by postilions. In it, we could see through the opera glass, sat Queen Wilhelmina [Queen of the Netherlands from 1890 to 1948] in blue with the Empress in pink [die Kaiserin Princess Augusta Viktoria, 1858-1921, last German Empress & Queen of Prussia], both with parasols to match and following them were loads of royalty that no one cared about. They, with the Emperor, mounted, rode the length of the lines and back to their places for The Review [Kaiser Wilhelm II, 1859-1941, Emperor & King, 1888-1918].

Then we all moved forward and it was wonderful the way the Police Corps had each in place so that there was not the least confusion when it came time to go. The nice policeman with the beauty brown-black horse went along by the side of us and we admired his horse, which seemed to please him very much. We drove along slowly and when it didn't seem as if we would ever get to our place, up bobbed "The Peterkins", right in the front row of the whole thing and the carriages were five deep behind. We had a fine view.

First came the Infantry that marched up to the Kaiser, who stood right back of Queen Wilhelmina and saluted each regiment as they went by, each regiment with its band or fife and drum corps following them. After a little halt came the cavalry with the lancers with a little black and white flag flying, their plumes waving with the motion of the horses as they kept step to the music. All the horses in each regiment were of the same color, so of course the effect was very pleasing.

Following these came the Artillery, which went by quickly at first, but the whole thing seemed to go around a second time and when the Emperor came to take the command of his regiment, he passed just by us, so we had a splendid view of him. He then led his regiment back by the Queen and Empress, who stood. The last time the Artillery went by the dust was so thick I thought we never could stand it.

It was so funny to see everyone with their lunch basket opened at nine o'clock [AM] for The Review began at eight. Then the officers and soldiers came up to see their friends and they were given a little wine and a sandwich and some of the carriages were very popular. We had a lunch basket, something like Michaele's in Rome, with nice roll sandwiches and a bottle of wine, but the Herr Oberst did not come to us so we only ate sandwiches.

The Review was over about 10:30 and such sights as we were, I was glad I only had my sailor hat. As we drove home the windows all along the line were filled with people watching and it really seemed queer to be looked at instead of standing on the curbing watching the crowd as we are known to do once in a while.

We heard of a very sad incident of the morning; it seems a man who had just been made commander of his troop was shaking hands with another man when his horse lurched and threw him violently to the ground. He was restored by coffee, but soon after mounting began to ask the meaning of all the crowd and showed his mind was affected with concussion of the brain. It seems so sad!

In the afternoon we went to the Kunst Ausstellung [Art Exhibit], which was similar to the one in Dresden, but infinitely better and we really enjoyed it very much but were dead tired after getting up so early. We took the train and got home in time for dinner.

The Spaniard, who walked into my room by mistake, is horrid and he sits down at our end of the table and simply drives me crazy.

We tried to get some flowers for Herr Oberst Krauser's wife, but could not.

Today is Bob's 18th birthday and I wonder if he has gotten the money I sent in a transfer from Boston. I hope so and am anxious to hear from him.

Berlin. Saturday, June 1, 1901.

In the morning we went to the [Art] Industrial Museum and had a great time guessing the statues of Peter Fisher [Vischer] and Holbein that are at the entrance to the building.

We then walked back [to the Pensionen] and before going in, got a beautiful bunch of red roses to send to Frau Oberst. Then we went back to the Museum and spent the rest of the morning there and my feet do ache and burn so that I just get tired as quickly as I did in the first part of our trip.

In the evening Miss Holworthy and Miss Fletcher joined us & we went out to the Ausstellung where there is an exhibit of all sorts of their most modern and improved fire apparatus, which to us seems very simple and almost primitive by the side of all of our fine engines. So we did not go to see the things, but just sat down to listen to the music. The Strauss who conducted the orchestra [Johann Strauss III, 1866-1939] is the son of the composer of The Blue Danube Waltz. People did not seem to take any interest in the music but simply wandered around and ate as usual.

We had such a nice ride home, for we five came together and happened to get a horse that simply flew all the way taking a step to a block it seemed.

We found a stack of mail waiting for us in Miss Cadwell's room and I had letters from Fan, Auntie, Florence, and Bob, who enclosed a lot of clippings with his picture on them and all sorts of nice things said about him.

Mrs. Groling had sent up to the rooms soda water and wafers.

Berlin. Sunday, June 2, 1901.

The first thing after breakfast we all had a conflab and talked over the trip to Egypt, which sounds so lovely. We thought Mary would decide to go but she thinks she had better not, so Miss Cadwell will go home with us two, leaving the Bucks in Leamington probably and we hope to sail on the 9th on the *Campania*, getting home about the 26th of October.

I tried to settle down to writing letters, but it was hard work, but I did finally write Uncle Fred, Fan and Florence - no Nellie - in the evening.

Berlin. Monday, June 3, 1901.

It was not quite so hot this morning but the girls had on their white summer waists and we had a great time going to the Arsenal [Military Museum] and

I did get so tired of looking at war guns and costumes. It's simply because my feet hurt so that I did not take more interest in things.

In the afternoon we went out to do errands and shopping. Marion got her pretty lavender skirt and ties. Then we went to the Bank where Marie Cruikshank and her mother are registered, some weeks ago, though. Mary sent her cable and I bought a nice Journal [Heinlein & Richter, Oberwallstrasse 5, Berlin] and I am sorry it is not a little larger, but still it will do very well indeed. Miss C. & I went up a moving staircase [escalator]. At dinner the young man that sits by Mary spilled his lamb on the table and we had such hard times not disgracing ourselves.

When we bought our Opera tickets, which came to 52 M, we saw the officer who had the pretty horse that pawed so at the Parade and he knew us as old friends apparently.

We had beer and crackers in the girls' room at 9:30.

Berlin. Thursday, June 4, 1901.

In the morning we all went to the Old Museum and finished the statuary there and "the twins" followed, or rather they went too and when they were not here for lunch we thought we had surely left them there, lost to the world, but they turned up for dinner.

In the afternoon I accomplished more than I have since I left home, for I had a shampoo and also made a pair of hook-on elastics, which is a big piece of work to get done. I hope these will last me until I go home but I think the elastic is poor so I shall probably have to do it again soon.

We of course stayed in all the afternoon as we are going out to the Opera. We did not need to have an early dinner as the Opera did not begin until 7:30, so we all wore scarves over our heads and took a carriage and the girls said when we got home that we caused the greatest excitement all along the Leipsiger Strasse and two people almost were run over because they were simply transfixed. We had very nice seats on the floor and it was as cool as could be [New Royal Opera Theatre, redeveloped from the Kroll Opera House, opened in 1895]. We were directly under the Royal Box, but I don't think there was anyone special in it [*L'Elisire d'Amore (The Elixer of Love)* by Gaetano Donizetti, 1832. Program in Diary in German: *Die Liebestrank*, starring Marcella Sembrich, Polish-born Opera Diva.].

It was Mdm. Sembrich's last performance here, so she was very warmly received and Sig. Constantino was simply fine. He did not have an especially full voice but his notes were perfectly beautiful and his love song was superb and he repeated it. Then an immense wreath of green foliage was presented to him and when the applause was almost deafening, he broke off a sprig and tossed it over to the orchestra leader, who of course in a measure was responsible for the success of his song.

When we got home we went in the girls' room and had soda water and biscuits [cookies], which were very nice indeed.

A Day Trip - Potsdam. Wednesday, June 5, 1901.

When I went to the table I found Nellie's letter telling me of her engagement to Harry Richmond, and I must say, while I was surprised at hearing it so soon, still I thought it would end in that way. I must say from a selfish point of view, it seems as if I was losing her and all our plans for being so much together in years to come had all gone to the winds. But I think from what I know of him that she is fortunate and I know he is!

We started on the 10:05 train for Potsdam [location of the Residences of the Prussian Kings] not knowing what might turn out in the way of weather, but it proved a lovely day.

We first took a carriage and went to The Palace, which is in the town in front of which is the tree [where people used to gather] to make their requests of Frederick the Great [1712-1786]. The interior is not so very elaborate at first, but then we came to the solid silver balustrade, which was in his bedroom with the library adjoining, which is the room where the table stands [dining table] which could be let down through a trap door so that no one could hear their conversation. There was an inclined plane instead of a staircase where the Emperor could be wheeled down when he had the gout. Queen Elizabeth Christine was his wife.

We then went to the Garrison Church, which contains the simplest form of a sarcophagus containing the remains of Frederick the Great and his father, Frederic William I.

From there we drove some ways to Babelsberg [Chateau] where Emperor William II lived. This is beautiful and so unique in its furnishings, and the grounds & English lawn, with the view over the water, are lovely.

We then went to the Marble Palace, which was begun by Fred. William II and completed by Frederick William IV and it was there we first saw the funny felt slippers which are worn to protect the floors, but we simply went in fits. The deformed woman really looked the best in them [Large, soft, felt slippers; a person slips the entire foot, with shoe, into while touring fine buildings so as not to scratch fragile flooring; still in use, 2009.].

We then went to Sanssouci [Palace], which means "without care", built by Frederick The Great. We saw the clock, which he always wound and is said to have run down just as he died. The pictures that we see of him there are very little like the others. In going there we passed the windmill, which he tried to buy but could not compel the owners to give up. The gardens of Sanssouci are so large and are wonderfully laid out.

We then went to the Orangery, which is a large building, and where we had to wear the slippers again in going around to see the china. The officer looked so funny with his spurs sticking out behind.

After, going for coffee at a little outdoor restaurant where there were soldiers eating at a table. We had our own lunch after we came out from Babelsberg and with the sandwiches, which Mrs. Gerling put up, and the apples, we had delicious Munich Beer, and it never tasted better.

We just caught the 5:09 train and reached Berlin in time to dress for dinner. Then after dinner, I wrote a long private newsy-letter to Auntie, going in later to the girls' room, where we had soda water and biscuits.

My yellow silk waist came home in the morning from Spindlers [?] and looked like new and only cost 50 cents.

Berlin. Thursday, June 6, 1901.

In the morning we went to the P.O. first and mailed our packages that have been collecting for some time including my Baedekers.

We then went to the Old Museum and walked through the rooms of casts first, then going into the Egyptian sections where we saw about the same things that were in London and other places.

Leslie did not go out all day, but in the afternoon, we went shopping and first bought leather goods, which are lovely, and I should like to get more, too. I bought a clock for Leslie with an alarm for four marks and she was so delighted with it and we all had fun watching the thing arranged. Mrs. Groling left for her summer in England, also Miss Fletcher with her. Mrs. G. says she will send us some of Jocko's feathers.

Berlin. Friday, June 7, 1901.

In the first place I had a great time hunting for my umbrella, which I distinctly remember bringing home from Potsdam, but I simply could not find it anywhere in my room or in the others. So we started to go through the Palaces [in Berlin].

We first went to Vantines [?] and Miss Cadwell bought a little pillow and I the album containing the views of Berlin. From there we took the tram and went to the Schloss [Palace of the Empress Victoria] where the Kaiser lives in winter. We had to go through with a large party and wear the felt slippers again, which were so big they nearly engulfed us. The palace is rather nice and the white chamber where the ghost appears when any member of the royal family is to die is quite elaborate and it's there that the large functions of any sort are held. There was a school of nice looking English girls there and a queer woman who tried to talk to us all in tune ["The white lady who haunts the palaces of Baireuth (Bavaria) & Berlin and periodically appears to portend the death of a member of the royal house of Hohenzollern." *Northern Germany*, 34].

We next went to the Old Kaiser's Palace [Palace of the Emperor William I, 1836], which is very simply furnished compared to most. We had to wait such a long time before starting to go through and then the woman guide was so slow. The old Kaiser's work room and desk that stands by the window under which people used to stand waiting for him to come to bow to them everyday at just noon.

Mary and I bought the little work boxes, which were so cunning, and in the afternoon we started out to get shampoos and as I had had one, the others could have them. Then I came home and suddenly remembered I had left my umbrella in the leather store, so found it there. In the evening we went out to get ice on the Leipsiger Strasse.

Plans for *Campania* [Ship] came and ordered no. [blank] to be saved.

Berlin. Saturday, June 8, 1901.

In the morning we went to get our pictures first and Miss Cadwell left us, going to see about our tickets for Holland. We could not find what we wanted, that is not the ones we really needed, and we understood her to say for us to stay there until she came back for us, which we did, but evidently it was quite wrong, for Miss C. expected to find us home. She and Marion came over for us and then such a time as we had going to the other store, and with all our round packages we had a great time getting home.

In the afternoon we started out right after lunch and went first to the Ethnographical Museum, which is of the different races [of man] and especially the Schliemann Collection, which are various treasures that have been recently found in Troy and, of course, are very valuable.[7]

We then went to the Industrial Museum and did the Jewelry, which we had not time for the other day. After seeing those things we went over and saw the exterior of the Parliament Building, which is beautiful. Then we walked around to the side of it and the back or front, whichever it is, is in Italian Renaissance style [Reichstag-Gebäude; completed in 1894. The latest reconstruction was in 1999, after the reunification of Germany.].

In front of the West Façade is the statue of Prince Bismarck, which is to be unveiled on the 16th of June [Otto von Bismarck, 1815-1898, the first

German Chancellor. The statue was moved in 1938, by Adolf Hitler, to the Tiergarten.].

A little way from this is the Siegesaule or Monument of Victory [1873]. From this leads the Sieges-Allee, down which we walked to the beer garden at the end, where Leslie and I had some of the best coffee we have had for a long time. It began to rain while we were there, but the awning was let down so we had a cozy time.

On our way home we stopped at Ubertheines [?] and while there got a weigh by sitting in a chair while the man adjusted the weights. Mary was 56.5, Marion 58.5, Leslie 60 and I, 54.8, which is Kilos and in lbs it is 1.5 pounds to a kilo [Clarissa is mistaken. There are 2.2 pounds in a kilo.].

In the evening I marked and made a list of my pictures and after our soda and cookies, Marion brought her Journal and read to me, so I could catch up in my line-a-day book the three weeks that I didn't keep track of while in Florence.

Berlin. Sunday, June 9, 1901.

This is called a rest day but as usual it is a busy one, for we are packing to send our trunks to Vitznau to be there when we reach Switzerland in July, and I am so glad I have so nearly finished this book. It didn't seem as if I ever would when I bo't it.

Finis.   [The End of Clarissa's 1st Journal]

Hildesheim and Hanover. June 10, 1901.

Yesterday we were busy all day getting all packed and ready to leave Berlin and we went downstairs to say goodbye to Miss Halworthy who gave us some of Jocko's feathers. The one above came out of his tail someplace, for just his tail is red and the rest of him grey and a lovely color too. He is so cunning when he says, "Danke. Was wilst dü haben? Hurrah Bobs! Good morning!" and his cough is one of the funniest things he does.

We had to get up at six and be ready for our breakfast at quarter of seven, which was brought to our rooms. We only had our hold-alls, for our trunks started to Vitznau [Switzerland] yesterday, so at 7:10 Marion and I started off in our carriage. The train left at 7:45 and we reached Lehrte [Germany] at 11:50. There we went into the little private dining room to eat a ham sandwich and Munich beer, but the beer tasted sort of sour, but the ham and bread were just fine. We had to rush though to catch the train for Heidelberg, which left at 12:25 and reach H. [Hildesheim] at 12:55.

Hildesheim, Germany.

"... an ancient town with 39,000 inhabitants ... has retained many medieval characteristics." *Northern Germany*, 141. The architecture there is perfectly fascinating as much so as Nuremberg and we were so glad we went. First we walked along by some of the queer houses and crooked streets till we came to the Rathaus in the Alstädter Markt, which is the square around which stands the Knochenhauer Amtshaus, which was the guild house of the butchers and is said to be the most perfect example of its kind in northern Germany. Built in 1529 and with its tier upon tier of windows, between which are carved panels and carved masks. Above the ground floor are frescoes in a long row, which are seen in some of the other houses but not so elaborate.

Across the way is the Rathaus. The large hall upstairs is a symphony of colors for even the stained glass windows are in the very best of taste.

To the left of this building is the Templer-Haus, late Gothic style with a beautiful oriel [window] and two corner turrets. Then comes the Wedekind Haus, beautifully carved and decorated. The Roland Hospital and Kaiser Haus are beauties. The later being so named because the medallions in the front are of various kings and emperors.

The St. Michael's Church is very interesting, being a good basilica and used to belong to the St. Benectines & was founded by Bishop Bernward [Bishop of Hildesheim, 993-1022], who did so much in the way of art for Hildesheim. It is said to be the finest in the decoration of the ceiling north of the Alps, which are of the 12th cent. Part of the church is Protestant and the Crypt belongs to the Roman Catholics.

We then went to the Cathedral and as it's Christ's or God's birthday there was a service, so we came back later. This contains the brass doors made by Bishop Bernward [1015] and the Font of the 13th Cent.

Out in the Cloisters we saw the old rose bush, which is said to be 1000 years old and is connected with Louis the Pious and the founding of Hildesheim. The large candelabra is very elaborate, being a large circular one with figures of walls & gates of Heaven.

St. Godehard's Church is nothing special. A queer old duffer without any teeth told us about it.

We then had cold chocolate, bo't pictures, left at six, waited an hour in Lehrte and reached Hanover at eight. Had a nice supper and soon after went to bed. Mary and I are together [Grand Hotel Hartman, Hanover].

Hanover - Amsterdam. Tuesday, June 11, 1901.

The first thing we went in the train out to the [Schloss] Herrenhauser, which is the old royal residence of the Kings of Hanover during the 18th century and the garden there is simply beautiful, especially the open air theatre, of which the above is a picture [postcard], adorned with the bronze statues and the flies bring off a thick growth of foliage.

On the way out we passed what used to be the Palace of the Geulph Party, now a Polytechnic Institute. We looked into the windows, went by the Opera House, which used to have the best Operas in Germany, bought sour cherries and then went back to the Grand Hotel for our luggage and the lunch, which they put up for us.

The train left at 12:40 and we had a nice compartment to ourselves with a table in it for our luncheon. We tho't we were to go through to Amsterdam without changing but had to get into another carriage. The guard was very nice to us and simply turned some people out of the compartment, for he told them we were Americans and must have what we wanted. The examination of our luggage at the Frontier amounted to nothing, so we had a most comfortable trip getting here at a little after 8 PM.

The scenery is lovely with the fields of high grass sprinkled with the cornflower or bachelor buttons and in places scarlet with wild single poppies. The cotton grass in the swampy meadows is lovely. The windmills are, some of them, perfect beauties and the huge wooden shoes and lace caps that the peasants wear are sights. I am glad to see thatched roofs again and on some of these the thatching almost comes down to the ground.

We saw storks all along now and then and in one settlement a stork was standing on the nest, which was built on the top of the house chimney. This is considered a very good omen. The town clocks seem to have chimes, which ring every quarter of an hour a few notes to the air.

We are at The Victoria Hotel [Amsterdam] and it seems very nice indeed. And the first thing we saw was a drunken [?] and kisses [?] as the bridge is crossed.

The Netherlands - Amsterdam. June, 1901.

"Expenses. Living in Holland is not cheap… the Dutch seaside resorts… have the reputation of being expensive. Passports may be dispensed with in Holland.

Hotels. The hotels at the principal towns and tourist resorts are generally clean and comfortable, but inferior to those of Belgium and Germany. In some respects they resemble the hotels in England.

Cafés. As in Belgium are frequented usually after midday. The Milk Shops, which are found in larger towns, are recommended; They supply tea, coffee, lemonade, eggs, etc. as well as milk.

Language: A slight acquaintance with the Dutch language contributes greatly to the instruction and enjoyment afforded by a tour in Holland. German, however, is very generally understood." Baedeker, *Belgium and Holland*, xxiii-xxiv.

"Amsterdam, the commercial capital of Holland… originated at the beginning of the 13th century… The real importance and prosperity of Amsterdam date from the close of the 16th century, when the Spanish war had ruined Antwerp, and numbers of enterprising merchants and skilful manufacturers, and distinguished artists were compelled to quit Spanish Netherlands.

Amsterdam is the chief money-market in Holland, the seat of the Bank of the Netherlands (one of the leading financial establishments of Europe), and the headquarters of the large shipping companies." *Belgium and Holland*, 328-329.

*

A Day Trip to Marken. Wednesday, June 12, 1901

We all slept beautifully and got up, as Fred would say, "looking as charming as ever" and had to hurry off at the last minute in order to catch the steamer, for the local time and railroad time differ twenty minutes, which makes a big bother often and lots of confusion, but as usual "The Peterkins" didn't get left. The passengers were all either English or American so we had a fine time watching them and now and then saying a word. There were two girls traveling together and they must have such good times and just the same good times that Fan and I will have when we come abroad together one of these days.

We first got off at Broek [6 miles from Amsterdam] and all followed the first mate along, who looked so much like Mr. Beatty. We went along the little narrow paved street, which showed very plainly the evidence of cows having passed along earlier. The wooden shoes were left at many of the doors, all turned on their side so that it would not rain in them.

This is the place, I suppose, where the famous Broek cheese is made and we went into a cheese-making house and while it was, of course, all in spick-span order to show off. The old lady was all dressed up with a white cap and her side hair in front was twisted up as if on a hairpin with big locket looking things to hold it, or for an ornament. We went into the living room and the beds were built right into the walls with little snowy white curtains before them hung on a brass rod.

We then went out through the little entryway to the big rooms in the rear and that is where the cows are all kept in winter up on the raised platform next the wall, which has a trough for feed and a trough on the level back of the cows. Then the platform is partitioned off and arranged for two cows, the ropes are at the side and when the cows lie down, their tails are tied up. The cheese was being made, some in the brine where it has to soak for three days and then is put in a press under weights. When it is done, it is put in a crocheted bag like our tennis ball bag and this is what makes the marks on the pineapple cheese.

We then went along to an old church and it was so queer, but just like what we would fancy. For instance the contribution plates are little black bags hung on the end of a stick like insect nets, with a little bell at the bottom to jingle. The chairs are wooden and the women have feather cushions to sit on and under each chair is a box about the size of a starch box with holes bored in it, then inside is put a little bowl of coals for a foot warmer.

We took the boat again and went down into the cabin and ate our lunch, which they put up for us at the hotel. We reached Marken [11 miles from Amsterdam] and all went ashore. There the people were sights, for all are in the killing costumes that they used to wear years ago. The boys and girls are dressed the same till they are six years old and the boys have little round patches on the back of their caps so they can be told apart. The women wear a long lank curl each side of their face, which comes down from under their cap in the funniest way. The bangs are about to their nose and then turn up out of their eyes. Until sixteen the girls wear their hair down and then it's put up.

We went into some of the houses and they are all dark and horrid I think. The drain water runs along in the street and why they don't have worse looking faces I can't understand. All the rooms are decorated with china and brass plates and some have very nice carved furniture that has been handed down for generations.

We had an awfully cold sail coming home but were so amused at the English woman who tried to light her alcohol lamp and then boil her tea kettle out on the deck where there was a perfect gale blowing and the kettle tumbled off and they had a great time.

We reached home about five and on the way home I thought I saw Bishop Doane on the street.

Amsterdam. June 13, 1901.

We went and took the tram to the Ryks Museum, and there we saw such lovely pictures by Dutch artists that we had never heard of before ["The Ryks Museum; an imposing building covering nearly 3 acres of ground, was erected 1877-1885... the collections are open to the public daily, free." *Belgium*, 339].

The nicest were Rembrandt's *Night Watch* painted in 1642, which is his largest and most celebrated work. It represents Capt. Frans Banning Cocq's company as [they are] coming out of their guild house. The lights in this picture are simply wonderful and it seems as if the Capt. and his Leut. could walk right out of the foreground. Each Guild member paid 100 florins for his portrait and there are sixteen [Harmensz van Ryn Rembrandt, 1606-1669].

Frans Hals [1580-1666] and his wife in the garden are fine [*Married Couple in a Garden*, 1622]. Melchior d'Hondecoeter's [1636-1695] of the pelican, duck and peacock group is wonderful, with the feather painted as floating on the water [*The Floating Feather*, 1680]. Bol's, the *Managers* and *Manageresses* of the Leper's Hospital [Ferdinand Bol, 1611-1680; 2 large paintings, *The Governors* and The *Patronesses* of the Hospital]. Maes', *Grace before Meat, Old Woman Spinning* and *The Dreamer* are lovely, but in places are so dark that the photographs are very unsatisfactory [Nicolaes Maes, 1632-1693]. Flinck's, *Arquebusiers of Amsterdam*, celebrating the Peace of Westphalia, painted in 1648, is his best [Govert Flinck, 1615-1660]. This shows all coming out of their Guild House.

To the left of the *Night Watch* is Van der Helst's, *Banquet of Arquebusiers* [*The Banquet of the Amsterdam Civic Guard in Celebration of the Peace of Münster*, Bartholomeus Van der Helst, 1613-1670] and opposite it is Van der Helst's, *Comp. of Capt. Roelof Bicker*, but the first is the better and Rembrandt's, *Portrait of Elizabeth Bas* is his best portrait and she is a splendid old woman with her white Dutch cap and brown fur.[8] Also, his *Director's of the Guild of Cloth Makers* [*The Syndics of the Cloth Makers Guild*] of the four sitting and one partly standing figure are the best sort of realistic faces.

In the afternoon we left at 2:20 and weathered the gale and probable storm and took the boat going as far as Wormerveer, then coming back to Zaandam where we got off and saw the hut of Peter the Great [Peter I, Tsar of Russia, 1682-1725] where he lived for one week in 1697 while he worked at the trade of ship's carpenter in disguise, but was discovered and left. It is now the property of the Czar of Russia and there is a fine brick building built about it to protect the hut.

Before we reached there, we all went down for chocolate and it was boiling hot and we tried to hurry for we tho't the man called out Zaandam. Of course we tried to drink it, but tears came to our eyes, for it was so hot and two men who were there nearly rolled off their chairs laughing and we found it wasn't time to get off at all.

All the way coming home it poured and we sat under our umbrellas, which sheltered us from the wind.

We tried to get labels [to stick onto their trunks for souvenirs], but only got tags, besides having heart failure in the effort.

Amsterdam - The Hague. Friday, June 14, 1901.

We had to begin with a time getting our wash straightened out and everything seems high priced, for I only had seven simple pieces and it came to fifty cents. I think our stay in Holland and Belgium is going to be plenty long enough for it is very expensive. I think I should have gotten more pictures, but the silver prints are forty cents a piece, so I am very well satisfied with a few.

We started out about ten so we could get an idea of the town and where the nicest houses along the Kaissersgracht and Herrengracht are. We first went across the bridge in front of our hotel over to see Admiral de Ruyter's House, then around through the Fish Market, which smelled like the dickens and all this time it was simply pouring and my shoes got so wet that the water oozed through the tops. But we said let's go on as long as we were wet, so we went to the New Church [Nieuwe Kerk], where a young man who looked like Harold showed us around. This was interesting because the little queen was crowned there [Queen Wilhelmina of the Netherlands, who began her reign in 1898 at age 18.].

We then went across the street into the Royal Palace, which is a big barn of a place. It is so long since any one has lived there that it is not kept up to date at all and the man who took us through was horrid and officious. Mary met the Lowes as we were going in.

We asked for labels and got some beauty ones. As our train leaves at four, we had a nap, reading, then went to the station. The men carried our hold-alls and put them in a compartment by ourselves as usual, but the guard was so very angry and said the English always took up the whole compartment. We decided he was a Boer [South African Dutch] man, and so had an ill feeling toward us, but the hotel man was fine and told us to stay just as we were for he had been and told the head of the station about it.

We whizzed along and passed Haarlem, where Frans Hals was born and all along the way there were such fields of flowers in blossom for the bulbs.

We reached here about five and came to The Toelast [Hotel, Groenmarkt, The Hague]. As dinner is at 5:30 we did not go out before. Such a big dinner I never saw and so much meat was not appetizing at all.

We went out after dinner and got an idea of the city, going by the Royal Palace, which is small and plain to say the least.

The Hague. Saturday, June 15, 1901.

We went the first thing to The [Picture] Gallery and first saw lots of our countrymen. We saw Rubens' portrait of his confessor [*Michael Ophovius, Bishop of Bois-le-Duc*] and no end of portraits by Ravesteyn [Jan Van Ravesteyn, 1572-1657], all of which are just in the same position and might be good if there weren't so many. Ruysdael's [Jacob Van Ruysdael, 1628-1682] *Distant View of Haarlem* and it is a lovely picture with the lights and shades. Before the little cottages linen was bleaching on the grass.

Rembrandt's *School of Anatomy* is simply wonderful and I shall never forget the earnest, thoughtful faces of those seven men in front of Tulp [Anatomist, Nicolas Tulp] and over the body. This was done in 1632 and was done to adorn the dissecting room of the School of Surgeons in Amsterdam. Adriaen van Ostade [1610-1685] *The Fiddler* is good and the group about the Dutch doorway is so natural after having seen these during the week. Rembrandt's *Presentation* [*Simeon in the Temple*] is fine, and with the shine on the robe of the high priest is splendid. Paul Potter's [1625-1654] *Bull* [*The Young Bull*] is here and with the group of friendly sheep, cow and man, makes a queer combination. The bull is the only very excellent feature. Jan Steen's [1626-1679] picture of himself and family is rather good and his *Poultry Yard* [*Menagerie*] isn't bad.

After we finished there, we went into the Municipal Museum, which was nothing special.

In the afternoon we went out to the Park to the Huis ten Bosch House, the House in the Woods, where the Peace Conference of 1899 was held and in it are some beautiful rooms furnished in Japanese and Chinese [style]. The house was built in 1647 for Princess Aurelia, widow of Prince Frederick Henry of Orange.[9]

We then got Marion's presents and looked out at the people after dinner.

("Regent" and "Doelen" pictures; peculiar to the Dutch. 'Regents' = presidents, placed in Guild Halls, and shooting galleries. 'Doelen' portraits are of groups of the various guilds.)[10]

The Hague. Sunday, June 16, 1901.

I stayed in bed the forenoon, getting up in time for luncheon and then in the afternoon I wrote Fan, Aunt Libbie, and Uncle Saunders and Mr. F. We three felt sort of done up and are terribly afraid Marion's birthday will not be as nice as we hoped to have it. Marion drew the picture and brought it in to me of my ice cream accident in Dresden and it was so funny that we never will forget it I am sure.

The Hague. Monday, June 17, 1901.

Marion's Birthday and Bunker Hill Day! Her 22nd Birthday.

I was awake early and got up about 7:30, for as the birthday breakfast was to come off in my room, I could not be up too early for it was a great event. Miss Cadwell had the maid come in and do my work and then the waiter set the table and put the nice dish of strawberries in the center and the table looked so pretty, for Mary brought her flag in and put it under Marion's plate, then tied little bows of red, white and blue on the fork handles. We put the little boxes on the plate at Marion's place and I then knocked at the girls' door and asked if she wouldn't come in a minute, then she walked in and was so surprised she could hardly speak.

She opened all the things; the little Delft pin tray from Mary; Miss Cadwell's present, a button pin; and the cuff links I gave her, which matched the pin. Leslie had given her the lovely writing tablet, which was too nice to bring in the hold-all. And there was the one little box left, which we all wondered what it could contain & what should it prove to be but my little Tombini box of powder, which Miss Cadwell thought was meant to be put on for her, as my present was on it. It relieved the stiffness, but was one on me. We had a nice breakfast, sitting an hour over our strawberries, coffee and rolls.

It was rainy, so Mary and I stayed in and I wrote Edna, Eugenia and Florence. In the afternoon we all went out and bought pictures first, then the girls bo't Delft tiles, then we went to a private Picture Gallery with irises and coffee in Miss Cadwell's room and after we left, Miss C. wrote the poem to be sent to Auropt [?] and asked my advice about sending it.

Scheveningen, The Netherlands. A Day Trip from The Hague. June 18, 1901.

"Scheveningen, a clean fishing-village with 21,000 inhabitants, visited as a bathing-resort since 1818, has now become the most fashionable watering-place in Holland. Bathing is permitted daily from 7 AM till sunset… There are three bathing-places, one for ladies, one for gentlemen, and one where ladies and gentlemen bathe together in the French style." *Belgium and Holland*, 306-308.

*

It was so stormy we could not go out yesterday, so we started early this morning in the tram. Leslie, Marion and I rode on top and such a lovely ride through the long lines of trees on each side of the track. It was rather cold, so we did not stay long, but it was nice to have seen it and the bath chairs are so funny. We stopped and got charms and postcards, then hurried for the tram and just caught it.

We looked for charms and Miss C. did not feel well. Went through the Prison [The Gevangenpoort] and saw instruments of torture at the time of the Inquisition.[11] Marion broke her hold-all strap & had to rush out for a new one.

The Hague - Antwerp.

Start at 3:05 for Antwerp, which is a two hour ride and I hope Mary and I will room together for it's great fun and we manage to have lots of sport. We left as we had planned and the ride was a very uncomfortable one, for the train jolted terribly and no one could get comfortable. The ride lasted two hours and a quarter and 20 minutes before we got there the guard came to the door and said "Good bye, ladies. I leave you here." And we nearly convulsed at his attention.

We had to get out at a little branch station and then we found our carriage and after lifting all our luggage out ourselves, we finally were squeezed into and onto one carriage and got here safely (Pension Kern-Loos, Longue Rue d'Herenthal 35, Antwerp). Mary and I have rooms opening off of each other.

We found mail here from Brussels and I had letters from Uncle Fred, Fan, Rob, Mrs. C. and a postal from Eugenia. Mary and I talked till 10:30 about Egypt and I do want her to go and am so anxious she should go.

Antwerp, Belgium. June 19.

"Belgium. The works of the painter and the architect are Belgium's great attractions… *The Handbook* (Baedeker's, *Belgium and Holland*) renders the services of commissionaires and guides entirely superfluous, and the traveler is particularly cautioned against employing those of an inferior class by who he is importuned in the streets.

Money. The Monetary System of France was introduced in Belgium in 1833.

Expenses. Most travelers should be prepared for a daily expenditure of at least 25-30 Fr. each. Passports are now dispensed with in Belgium.

Language. The population of Belgium is mainly divided between two chief races; the Walloons... and the Flemings... The Walloon language, which resembles a very corrupt dialect of French... The Flemish language differs slightly from the Dutch, both being branches of the lower German language... a slight knowledge of French will enable the traveler in Belgium to converse with everyone with whom he is likely to come in contact." *Belgium and Holland*, x-xv.

*

We are all dead broke, so the first thing we did was to go to the bank and they were so slow we thought we never would [get] away from there. Everything is French and the money and language are both in it.

We then walked over to the Bourse [Exchange, 1872], which is rather new but a perfect stunner and the Coats of Arms are so ornamental. Then we went along and looked at the Cathedral [Notre Dame] and the old well made by Quintin Matsys [1460-1530], who is said to have been an ironworker but in order to marry some girl so to please her father, he became an artist. On the top of the well canopy is a statue in iron of Salvius Brabo, the mythical hero who defeated and cut off the hand of the giant Antigonus. The giant used to exact a heavy toll from vessels landing in the Scheldt [River] and used to cut off and throw into the river the hands of those merchants who refused to pay. Thus the two hands are the Coat of Arms [of Antwerp].

Then we saw the Guild Houses, the [Hall of the] Carpenters and the [House of the] Clothiers being the most elaborate. The Hotel de Ville or Town Hall is a most beautifully decorated building and the frescoes are the best modern ones we have seen I think by Leys [Hendrik Leys, 1815-1869]. Such a little mite of a girl showed us through and used such good English, which she learned in school.

We then walked down by the Steen [Castle], which was originally part of the Castle of Antwerp built in the 10th cent. and the seat of the Spanish Inquisition in the 16th cent.

The docks are so interesting and busy. Then we had a glass of beer among us and sat by the water to drink it. Rode home and wrote in the afternoon.

Antwerp. Thursday, June 20, 1901.

We first went to the Cathedral and as everything seems to be free today we shall just coin money. Usually it is a mark or franc to open the pictures.

We first looked at Rubens' *Descent from the Cross*, which is a wonderful picture and considered so because of the use and treatment of the white sheet at the back, which is said to have been tho't of after one of the Italian painters use of it. The Christ figure looks perfectly dead and limp and the three Marys are good. It is said that during the absence of Rubens, the picture fell from the easel and Van Dyke [Anthonie van Dyke, 1599-1641] was chosen as the best man to repair [it], which, when the master saw it, declared it to be better than his own. The parts Van Dyke did are said to be the face of the Virgin and arm of the Magdalene. On the other side wall corresponding to the descent, is the *Raising of the Cross*, which to me is almost repulsive, for while it shows Rubens' skill in the anatomy, it seems to me an unfit subject to choose in order to show that skill.

We then went to the Museum [Museé Royal des Beaux-Arts], which was also free. We saw Quintin Matsys' *Entombment of Christ* done in 1588, which is fine. Rubens' *Communion of St. Francis* and Roger van der Weyden's [1400-1464] *Sacrament of the Eucharist* with six other scenes representing the scene in a church and very fine. Rubens' *Christ á la Paille*, the body of Christ resting on a stone bench covered with straw. Rubens' *Christ Crucified Between Two Thieves*, with the mounted nobleman piercing the side. The thieves are very real and the agony depicted is dreadful. One has pulled his foot loose from the nail. Rubens' *Adoration of the Magi* painted in 1624, which is said to have been painted in 14 days and I guess it's so. A lovely Memling [Hans Memling. c. 1430-1494] with such delicate work, Frans Hals' *Fisher Boy* and Rembrandts' *Burgermeister*, which is fine.

In the afternoon we went to the Museé Plantin Moretus, which is in the house of a printer by that name who had his printing house in Antwerp in 1549. We went through it and it looks just as if he had only left it and everything was tied up and put on shelves. It has such a lovely court to it and the vines looked so pretty up the stonewalls.

We then went to the jeweler's and the girls got some lovely little pieces of real Flemish enamel for little stickpins and to be set in rings. They are lovely and I don't know but I shall get some when Marion goes.

All but the English lady have gone and she is so funny and she and Miss C. almost come to blows at each meal. Miss Cadwell has scared her now by telling her the hotels in Bruges are dreadful and the old lady is all worked up over it for she is "very particular".

We went out to the pretty little garden after supper and it was just fine to get out without gloves and veils for a few minutes. We have to get up so early that we are going to bed right away.

A Day Trip to Ghent. Friday, June 21, 1901.

We had to get up at seven and then left the house in time to get the 9:05 train. We tried a new way to get to the station and if it had not been for the man who happened to be going our way, I am sure we would have been dropped on some corner and left. He got off down by the wharf and began to run, and at that, we five struck into a trot and all the natives on the sidewalks stepped on one side and a little tiny yellow dog ran out at Mary, but we finally all got on the boat and crossed the river and there were such loads of peasants on.

We went through the loveliest part of country. The grain, poppies, and cornflowers were prettier than we have seen any time. We reached Ghent in 1½ hours and went to the Cathedral first [Cathedral of St. Bavon] and saw the Van Eyck piece [brothers, Jan 1380-1440, and Hubert 1366-1426, Van Eyck], which is the original altarpiece, and is the original center part to the four wings we saw in Berlin and I think it comes next to Fra Angelico. There are a number of other pictures but none amount to much, only the *Adoration of the Immaculate Lamb* in the altarpiece. Baedeker gives a fine description of it [Baedeker, *Belgium & Holland*, 50].

The Belfry is historically connected with the city of Ghent. It was begun in the 12th Cent.

We then walked around and saw the Hotel de Ville, then the Market Place - Marché du Vendredi - the old cannon - Mad Meg, dating from the 14th cent., by which Marion took Leslie's & my picture.

We had luncheon at the Hotel de l'Etoile [Rue de l'Etoile, near the Marché aux Grains] then took a carriage and went to the small Béguinage, which is a convent that dates back to the 13th century and is a little village [unto] itself, walled in and two to three sisters live in each cottage. Then there is a large house where they live before they go into the little ones [Convent de St-Joseph, Petite Béguinage Notre Dame, Belgique: "There are at present about twenty Béguinages in Belgium with about 1300 members...The members of the Béguinages are unmarried women or widows of unblemished character ..." *Belgium and Holland*, 65]. We were taken all over it and the sisters are so sweet looking. There are 80 cottages and about three hundred live there. When we came downstairs after going to some of the rooms, we found the table in the reception room covered with lace that has been made there. I bought some Val. lace that will be dear on corset covers; 11 yds. for 7.50 or $1.60 and I am glad I got it .

Then we went right to the station and got back to Antwerp about four, stopped and got some Augustiner Brau for it was awfully hot all day and by the time we got back here we were pretty nearly roasted.

Had tea and [?] milk, sent up a big tray of bread and some butter.

I carried my two postals for Mr. B. and Eugenia around with me all day and could not find a place to mail them till we got home.

All but Mary went to walk in the park before tea.

Antwerp – Brussels. Saturday, June 22, 1901.

Marion and Mary played on the piano and then after Miss Cadwell came back from her errands we all went out and stopped at the jeweler's and I got two of the little Flemish enameled pieces to be set in a ring and one for a pin. They are over one hundred years old and while they are imitated, Miss Cadwell knows of no other place in Europe. They are beautiful and I am so glad I have them.

We then went to the Cathedral and looked it over for the morning. We saw the Rubens' [*Descent from the Cross*, 1612], but we did not have time to take in the whole.

From there we went to the St. Jacques [Church], where the inside has a very pretty light from the stained glass windows and the altarpiece is splendid by Rubens. It is an *Adoration*, which shows his father as Joseph, he himself as the knight, St. George, and his wives, Isabelle Brandt and Helena Fourment, are two of the three Marys. I like this the best of any of Rubens'. The colors and groupings are lovely.

We left Antwerp at 4:20 and almost didn't get our hold-alls, for the man didn't bring them up, but Miss Cadwell got there just in time.

We reached Brussels about 5:30 and Marion and I had such a poor old lame horse, it was simply a sin to let him live. It is perfectly lovely here and is where ministers and things live and we shall just enjoy it as much as we did Molaros [Rome].

S. Bernard Private Hotel, 48 & 50 Rue Belliard (Quartier Léopold) Bruxelles ["Fashionable, largely patronized by British travelers."].

I found my shoes with eight francs to pay on them that had just come today, six duty and one franc for delivery, a lovely letter from Auntie, with one from Fan in it, also one that did my heart good from Mr. F. and were just all I wanted.

Our rooms are lovely and homelike and the table just like home with our little dining room and salon to our selves. We feel like company.

Brussels. Sunday, June 23, 1901.

"Brussels, the capital of Belgium, the residence of the royal family, and the seat of government, is situated in the centre of the Kingdom. In 1899 the population… including the ten self-governing provinces is about 570,000." *Brussels and Holland*, 82.

*

We have big tubs for coffee and they seem as if they would simply drown us, but they are fine.

We did nothing special and in the afternoon I wrote Uncle Fred and Fan and Mary decided to go to Egypt and I will make plans to return with Miss Chaffee and go to Boston, which I think will be fine, and I can hardly wait for the plans to be made for I have been anxious to land in Boston.

We had a lovely dinner and I never saw such beautiful white chicken in my life. Well everything is perfect. Mary was struck dumb at dinner and rushed upstairs right after. We went in the Salon and talked over all the plans and about our shopping up in Paris next August. We then had coffee and did not come upstairs until nearly eleven and Mary had been weeping all the time and rushed in to tell Miss Cadwell she would not go [to Egypt with Leslie and Marion], for she had just thought of her teeth. Of course Miss Cadwell was awfully tried, for she had written Mr. Keppir that the going home was indefinitely postponed. I think this matter will be a lesson to the rest of us, but it is rather hard on Miss Cadwell. She tore up the letter before Mary came out.

Brussels. Monday, June 24, 1901.

We started out on errands but, when we got our bills, I didn't have quite enough to pay with before drawing, so Marion loaned me 50Fr. so that she and I could draw together next week. We then went to the bank, going through the park out at the end of our street. Mary was going to send a cable home after she decided to go, but of course now she won't.

We tried to find Dents' gloves [English glove manufacturers since 1777] but didn't succeed, but the shops are lovely here and all look very Frenchy and as nice as in Paris, I think.

There are simply packs of green Americans who have lately landed and I am beginning to feel quite blasé in my shabby clothes and do not mind. Leslie did a number of errands and Marion was not out. The *Maasdam* [Ship of the Dutch American Steamship Company], on which Miss Crepo-Smith is coming, has not landed.

In the afternoon we went for a car ride after getting our things ready for the cleaners. And I had a time changing my seat in the car for there were too many on the seat. We changed and got into such a funny buss-looking tram [buss; refers to an electric bus]. Then when we got out we saw the funny soda fountain on the man's back with bells around the top and carrying the glasses in his hand.

We then went to the Botanical Garden, which we passed coming from the station and in a glass building [greenhouse] was a Victoria Regia, which is like a pond lily, only the leaves are large enough for a boy to sit on and the blossom in proportion of a pink hen. The gardens are not kept very fine.

Then we saw the house where the Ball was held [15 June, 1815, by the Duchess of Richmond] where the men had to rush off to the Battle of Waterloo and where the screw is laid in Becky Sharp [Heroine, *Vanity Fair*, by William Thackery].

We got a nice view of the tops of the houses from the Column of Congress [erected in 1859 to commemorate the establishment of the Constitution in 1831]. Then went to the Park and watched the fountain and children play.

Went to bed early. Leslie tried on her new shirts.

Brussels. Tuesday, June 25, 1901.

We first went to the Palace de Justice, which is the most handsome building we have seen, in Greek-Roman style. It is larger than St. Peter's and took fifteen years to build but it is a beauty and a sight to go through it. A lot of the Appellate Courts were in session. There is a room for each of the provinces of Belgium [Palace de Justice; largest architectural work of the 19th c.].

We then walked along to the Monuments of Counts Egmont and Hoorn [executed in 1568 for resisting the Spanish Inquisition], which is in a square park adorned with flowerbeds and statues and on the iron fence posts are statues in bronze representing the trades of the 16th cent.

We then went into the Picture Gallery of the Duc d'Arenberg, where we saw some good Teniers [David Teniers, 1610-1690], Steens, fairly good Van Dyck portraits and Cuyp [Albert or Jacob], Terburg [Gerard Terburg, 1617-1681] and Ruysdael. Also some interesting church books.

We stepped in Notre Dame du Victoires a second, but it was time to close at noon so we hurried out [founded in 1604 by the Guild of the Crossbowmen]. A poor old lame Baron with a Sister and man were also rushed out.

On our way home we passed thro' the gate to the Royal Library and Modern Art Museum.

Then came by the dirty looking palace [Palais du Roi] of the present King, Leopold II [King of Belgium, 1865-1909], and everything looks so shabby.

The new American women sit at the table with us, Mrs. Ross & [blank]. They are from Chicago and seem very nice after you know them.

We started about three and took an open car for what was a ¾ of an hour ride. I think the trees around Brussels are the nicest we have seen anywhere, unless it is England.

We went in through the public gates to the Café, where we had coffee on the terrace and bread and butter with raisins in the bread. A woman played a mandolin and why she did it I don't know, for none of us wanted to hear her I am sure, but then after she finished she passed a hat so we had to give her a little.

We strolled through the woods down to the Fountain, which is surrounded with the most exquisite roses on bushes and the dear trees. They were in their prime and with the afternoon lights on them they made a stunning sight, all colors imaginable from white to almost an orange and the Swiss variety of white with the outer petals of pink. Coming back in the car there were lots of people's hats to watch blow off and we were beautifully entertained.

A Day Trip to Waterloo. Wednesday, June 26, 1901.

"Battlefield of Waterloo; the final battle of the French Emperor Napoleon Bonaparte, who was defeated by the English, under Field Marshall, the Duke of Wellington, and the Prussian armies, commanded by Gebhard Leberecht von Blücher.

A detailed history of the momentous events of 18th June, 1815, would be beyond the scope of a guidebook, but a brief and impartial outline, based upon the most trustworthy sources, may be acceptable to those who visit this memorable spot." *Brussels and Holland,* 127.

*

We got up rather early and started at 9:40, reaching Braine L'Alleud at about 10:30 and as we got out of the train, the same man who pounced on us when we reached the Brussels' station, rushed up for us to take his carry-all out to the Battlefield, but the man at the railroad bars told us a tram would be right along. It had evidently just left, so rather than ride with that man, we all said we would much rather walk, which we did.

The Mound [of the Belgian Lion] was about a mile and a half from the station and we enjoyed [the walk] thoroughly and it was so nice to be near the poppies and daisies & cornflowers.

We went into the Museum, which adjoined Mrs. Brown's Hotel [Hotel du Musée]. Then we went up the 245 steps to the top of the Mound, which was erected on the site where the Prince of Orange was injured [King William II of The Netherlands]. It is 200 feet high and the Lion on the top is made of the metal from cannons captured by the Duke of Wellington. The old man, who was a strong large soldier from the Scotch army, Private Thomas Little, made the description very interesting and as the day was nice, we enjoyed it very much.

We then came down, had our usual simple lunch of omelets, salad, ginger ale, bread and butter with cheese. Having finished we bought charms and the little photos, the above picture showing the Obelisk erected to the memory of the Hanoverian Officers of the German Legions and the Pillar to the memory of Col. Gordon [family erected monument to Officer Gordon, who died during the battle]. At our left from the Mound we saw the farm of La Haye Sainte, which protected the center of the Allies and where the German Legion fought to defend it [Three small photos are in the Diary; the two mentioned above and a small photographic copy of a painting of Napoleon Bonaparte.].

After our luncheon we walked through the fields about half a mile to the farm of Hougomont and the brick wall which encloses it shows many big bullet holes and Miss Cadwell and I had a great time getting by the young bulls. Then we went around the wall and went in the gate to the farmhouse where we saw the well where the men were thrown in and the Chapel was decorated in memory of the event of June 18th, 1815.

We then walked back to the station and I must say, I felt as if five pounds of flesh had been walked off, but the trouble is as soon as I get back from such days out, I am so hungry that I eat so much and that spoils it all.

Miss Halworthy sent us some feathers. Had a shampoo and wrote Auntie in the evening.

Brussels. Thursday, June 27, 1901.

In the morning we went to the Picture Gallery and saw a good collection of the Dutch and Flemish Masters and had just time to go through the modern paintings.

In the afternoon we went first over to the Wiertz Musée and the pictures are the worst I ever saw [studio and residence of artist Anton Joseph Wiertz, 1806-1865]. His scope was wonderful but must have resulted in an unbalanced mind.

We then went into a greenhouse and saw a most beautiful display of orchids and I never saw anything like them before.

Then taking a car we went for tea and after hearing the music in the park, Marion and I came home while the rest went for shampoos. We got here and enjoyed the treat.

Heard that Auntie was sick again and, of course, wish I knew more, but must wait I know and they would let me know were she not improving.

A Day Trip to Bruges. Friday, June 28, 1901.

"Bruges, with its picturesque streets and low gabled houses, has best preserved its medieval characteristics… The population, which was at one time 200,000, is now only about 55,000, and of these 11,000 are said to be paupers.

In the 13th and following century Bruges and Venice were the great commercial centres of Europe. Bruges attained the culminating point of its prosperity during the first half of the 15th century… During this period a brilliant colony of artists was retained at Bruges in busy employment, and their works still shed a luster on the name of the city. The gradual silting up of the harbors on the adjacent coast [among other factors] by the latter half of the 16th century, completed the commercial ruin of Bruges." *Brussels and Holland*, 20-21.

*

Had letters from Uncle John and Nellie. Both were dear and a Latin School Register from Bobbi. The copy was very artistic and Bob's picture isn't at all bad [in the Diary]. I took Nellie's all the way to Bruges, but did not have the least chance to read it and was crazy for so many men were with us in the train. Took two hours to get there.

We first went to the Cathedral [Sint Salvator], which amounted to nothing. Then up to the St. John's Hospital. In the Museum [of the Hospital] we saw the lovely Memling, *The Reliquary of St. Ursula*, done in 1489, a [*Mystic*] *Marriage of St. Catherine* possibly by Memling, *Adoration* and *Presentation* [Memling] and two portraits.

We then had luncheon, looked at The Belfry [Tower in the Grand Place or Market-Place], went to the Hotel de Ville and Chapel of the Holy Blood [Saint Sang; built to house drops of holy blood brought from the Holy Land in 1149 and presented to the City. *Belgium and Holland*, 32.], [Church of] Notre Dame and coffee, then charms and back at six.

Brussels. Saturday, June 29, 1901.

Our waists and things came home last night and it was only .25 cents [each] and done so nicely. I put my blue one on with my black skirt and felt so very dressy.

We went through the Royal Lace Factory and saw the work being done; one piece required two thousand bobbins. We also saw the pattern for two royal veils with the Coat of Arms woven in. I did not buy any, only Mary invested in two ties [Brussels Lace; "About 130,000 woman are employed in this manufacture in Belgium." *Belgium and Holland,* 78].

We then went into the Cathedral, but it is only a good gothic church, very large, with some fairly good stained glass.

Then we went down to the Grand Place, around which are the Guild Houses and the Hotel de Ville, which are fine examples of those things. We went through the Hotel de Ville, but it's about like all the rest we have seen.

Then we went around by the Mannikin Fountain, which is simply disgusting for the common people worship it about as they do the Bambinoni in Rome and I think it must be an improvement when it is dressed [From 1619; "He is a great favorite with the lower classes, and is invariably attired in gala-costume on all great occasions." *Belgium and Holland,* 112].

In the afternoon we went out and did errands, getting pictures. Then we four girls went for a drive to the Bois de la Cambre [Park and Promenade in S.E. Brussels] going up the Avenue Louise where we saw loads of lovely turnouts and no end of automobiles scooting around in every direction. The grounds are lovely and the Laiterie [Restaurant] is the swell place to go in the season for a glass of milk. We had a swell turnout with rubber tires and a bell attachment. The lights were simply lovely for we did not start till five o'clock and got back at 6:30.

In the evening I read the first volume of *Don Orsino,* by [Francis] Marion Crawford [American novelist, 1854-1909. *Don Orsino* is the third novel in his Saracinesca series.].

Brussels. Sunday, June 30, 1901

Finished *Don Orsino* and wrote Fan, Uncle Fred two letters and did all I had planned to during the day except write 42 [?].

Brussels - Cologne, Germany. Monday, July 1, 1901.

"Cologne, the largest town in the Rhenish Province of Prussia, the residence of the archbishop, and one of the most important places in Germany... with 300,000 inhabitants... It lies on the left bank of the Rhine." *The Rhine,* 50.

*

It sprinkled when we first got up, but not so very hard. Had breakfast at quarter of nine and left at 9:15, Marion and I in a closed carriage by our selves. The train left at 9:45 and we saw more Americans than ever before.

We changed cars at [Blank] and on the Frontier had our lunch interrupted by having to get out to have our luggage examined, which really did not amount to anything. They put up such a nice lunch for us at Bernard [Hotel in Brussels] with grapes and cherries for dessert.

We reached Cologne about 4:30 and went by the Cathedral to the Dom Hotel and we all had single rooms along in a row, just like nuns, overlooking the entrance to the N. Transept [Hotel du Dome, near the Cathedral].

We went out at once and got some raspberry sherbet then went inside the Cathedral to look around and it is simply a lovely spot ["The Cathedral, or Dom, which justly excites the admiration of every beholder, and is probably the most magnificent Gothic edifice in the world, stands on a slight eminence about 60 ft. above the Rhine, partly composed of Roman remains…". Baedeker, *The Rhine*, 31].

We then took the little steamer and went to Flora [Flora Garden Restaurant, adjoining the Zoological Gardens] where we had the best German supper of ham on bread, which we ate with a knife and fork, potato salad with French dressing and lots of fine onions and Munich Beer. We sat and ate like old stagers at it, ate all up clean and then asked for more salad, etc. The grounds, in front of us as we sat on the terrace listening to the music, were beautiful, a perfect mass of geraniums and other plants.

We got to the hotel about nine, then Miss Cadwell read about what we had seen, then we finished our fruit and went to bed and it was real cozy and my bed was so hard I had a time getting and keeping settled.

Cologne - Bonn. Tuesday, July 2, 1901.

We first went over to the Cathedral and sat quietly on a pew to listen to the music and they had a lot of incense, but unless they used "Triple Extract" the people in the nave could not get a whiff of it and so we never got a sniff. Then we went to the Bank and Marion and I drew. The girls gave French paper in to be changed and as usual Marion didn't get hers and after a rumpus I found it in with mine.

We then went to St. Ursula Church and saw the bones and thorns and our money's worth generally [Dedicated to St. Ursula, who according to legend, was murdered at Cologne with 11,000 virgin attendants. *The Rhine*, 50].

Then we went to the [Municipal] Museum and saw the famous Queen Louise [Louise Augusta, Queen of Prussia], which isn't she at all, but really the portrait of the wife of a man Miss Cadwell knows, but it's lovely anyway [Gustav Richter, 1823-1884, in 1879; most sources say the model for the painting is not known.].

Also saw some 14th century by Meister Wilhelm [of Cologne, 1378] and [blank].

Then we walked around by the Rathhaus, which has a beautiful old façade. On our way back we four girls went up to the roof of the Cathedral and had a lovely view.

After dinner we went to the Apostles' Church with nothing special in it, then over to St. Gereon Church, which is queer and only because it is odd is it interesting, with a circular Nave.

We then took a car and went around the Ring or outside row of houses about the city ["The most striking feature in the new town is the wide and handsome Ring-Strasse… 3½ M long, which completely encircles the old town, and occupies the site of the old fortifications…" *The Rhine*, 50].

When we came home, we went out and bought cologne and Leslie's present, a souvenir spoon and my little bottle charm ["Eau de Cologne… This celebrated perfume first brought to Germany in 1690." *The Rhine*, 28].

We started at 6:05 and reached Bonn at 6:45. Came to the Rheinecke, which is right over the water and the view is beautiful [Hotel Rheinecke, "… at the pier, second-class, with terrace."].

Tomorrow is Leslie's birthday and she will be 18.

A Day on The Rhine. Bonn - Maynce [Mainz]. Wednesday, July 3, 1901.

"Steamboats on the Rhine: Travelers for pleasure should undoubtedly select the Rhine steamers between Maynce and Cologne … Regular service above Cologne was instituted in 1827…The ordinary steamers stop at numerous small places where passengers are landed in boats. The charge for landing and embarking, including 100 lbs. of luggage, is 10 pf.

The fares are moderate… refreshments are provided on board the steamers, in the style of the larger hotels. Table d'hote on the German steamers at 1 o'clock, 3M. The wines are made a special feature in the commissariat… Travellers starting at an early hour will find breakfast on board pleasanter than a hurried meal before leaving their hotel. The waiters occasionally offer worthless books, maps, and panoramas for sale at exorbitant prices." *The Rhine*, xvi-xvii.

*

We had a great time getting to sleep last night, even after we thought we were all quiet and had hung out the window watching the boats come by the house, for we were on the very shore and it was perfectly lovely. So after we ate a little chocolate and Mary had dropped hers out of the window down on the tin roof, we at last settled down.

We were awake early and had it all planned to go in Miss Cadwell's room for breakfast and presents. It was quite like the others only a rainy morning. Leslie seemed delighted with everything. Marion gave her a beauty necklace; Miss Cadwell, a Brussel's net veil; Mary the silver pencil and slot; then I gave her the Cologne spoon and chunk of pumice stone. Miss. C.'s poem that she wrote was one of her best.

It looked as if it might clear, so we went down to the boat to go as far as Coblenz anyway then see how the day turned out.

The Rhine is just as picturesque as I had imagined and the soft mist really added to the beauty of it and the legends connected with all the castles are a study in themselves. Miss C. says *Legends of the Rhine* [Wilhelm Ruland, 1869-1927] is no use and poorly written.

The Castle of Drachenfels, erected in 12th cent., and in the cavern in front and below housed the dragon slain by Siegfried, the hero from the Low Countries who became invulnerable after bathing in the dragon's blood. Wine made here is called "Drachenblut" or Dragon's Blood.

Roland's Arch is all that remains of the Castle of Rolandseck and is mentioned in 1045. The brave knight Roland, who was the Paladin of Charlemagne, while searching the Rhine for treasures along its valley, found himself the guest of Count Heribert, Lord of the Seven Mountains [and of the Castle Drachenburg]. The daughter, Hildegunde, offered him food. Of course he fell in love with her, but he was called to the Crusades. She, supposing him killed, took orders in the Kloster of Nonnenworth, and was lost to him on his return to the Castle of Drachenburg. So, he built his castle and watched her as she went to the little chapel. Finally she died and Roland never spoke again, but after a wretched existence he was found dead with his glassy eyes turned towards the chapel.

Castle of Stolzenfels restored by Emp. Fred. William IV and the Old Kaiser used to spend some time there

Sterrenberg and Liebenstein [Castles], or The Two Brothers, have a beautiful situation on the left bank. The two brothers, Conrad and Heinrich, loved their foster sister, Hildegarde. But Heinrich tore himself away and went to the Crusades. Then Conrad was to marry her. In order that they should be near, the old knight, Bayer von Boppard, built Sterrensberg for them, but he died before they were married, so the wedding was put off. Then Conrad, envious of his brother's honors in the wars, left [to join the Crusades] and Hildegarde retired to Liebenstein, weeping lest Conrad should not return. Finally, Conrad returned with a Grecian bride, then Heinrich, hearing of his sister's wrongs, returned late at night to the castle and challenged [Conrad] to fight, but Hildegarde interposed and then Conrad's bride left him. He found reconciliation in his brother's friendship. Hildegarde had gone to a convent and finally the brothers lived together peacefully. These are the most interesting ruins that we have come to so far.

The Lurlei, 430 ft. above the Rhine on the rocks. The nymph [the Rhine Maiden of the legend] is said to have lived there years ago and enticed sailors and fishermen to their destruction on the rocks.

The Nibelungen Treasure is said to lie hidden beneath the Lurlenberg.[12]

The rocks known as the "Seven Virgins" lie opposite, and when the river is low may be seen and used to be seven fair maidens who were condemned by the river god.

The Mouse Tower, which is now a signal station, and the legend is that Archbishop Hatto compared the poor people to mice who ate the corn during a famine & ordered them burned in a barn. He was then attacked by mice and they followed him to the island where the tower is built and there ate him.

The Fortress of Ehrenbreitstein is a beautiful spot, just before we reached Coblenz.

We had such a nice time on the boat, although it rained a good share of the time, and after we left Bingen it began to rain harder, but we did not get cold much and considered ourselves awfully fortunate that it was not too hazy to see the shore well. We had a nice dinner on the boat then coffee on deck and about seven had chocolate and brötchen on deck.

Reached Maynce [Mainz] about nine and had just a little to eat out in their summer dining room. It was so funny, but awfully nice. We went to Stadt-Coblenz Hotel [Rhein-Strasse 49] and Miss C., Mary and I were together.

Maynce - Heidelberg. Thursday, July 4, 1901.

We were pleased to see a lot of American flags up on the hotels, but I suppose it's done to attract customers.

Leslie stayed in, but we went to the Cathedral, which is queer and rather good. Has altars at both ends and a gallery on each side of the choir; cloisters are pretty.

Gutenberg's statue we saw. He is said to have invented printing [Johannes Gutenberg, c. 1400-1468, introduced movable type printing to Europe, 1439.].

Got sour cherries, "Schwarzwald", and enjoyed those after we got to the hotel.

Left for Heidelberg at 1 PM and got there about four. Went to Darmstädter Hof [near the station] and first thing saw the "Eagles", then we started right off for Heidelberg Castle.

"Few towns can vie with Heidelberg in the beauty of its environs and its historical interest. Conrad of Hohenstaufen, who became Count Palatine of the Rhine in 1155, selected the old castle as his principal residence... Since 1802 Heidelberg has belonged to the grand-duchy of Baden. The town now contains 35,000 inhab." *The Rhine*, 26.

*

We took the cog railroad up to the Castle. Then walked around thro the grounds and a "nice kit" took us around. Then we went down to the big cask that holds 50,000 gallons ["The Heidelberg Tun, a monster cask capable of holding 49,000 gallons. The present Tun, was constructed in 1751 ... as the successor to three others." *The Rhine*, 266] and by it stands the court-jester [Pecheo] and Mary pulled the ring to make the clock at his side work and the door sprang open and the tail almost hit her in the face and then we had a good laugh.

We had a nice German supper at the restaurant between the castle and the terrace [Schloss Restaurant]. After that we went out on the terrace, built in 1610, and had a lovely view down the valley of the Neckar [River]. We got back to the hotel about 9:30.

Heidelberg - Baden. Friday, July 5, 1901.

After buying cherries we had our first mountain climbing. Took the car up as far as the Castle then by a winding path went 1200 feet to the Konigs Table from which we had a lovely view and sat in the grass to eat our cherries.

Left at 3:45 for Baden [Baden-Baden, Germany] and such a time as we had getting seats. We had to go into a 1st Class compartment in a vestibule car where they would not let the "Gepäckträger" [porter] come, so our hold-alls had to be brought in through the window. Leslie, Mary and I were with such a nice German lady and her son, about twenty, and a little boy with dimples. They were so nice and could not do enough for us. Even got cherries and offered some to us, then the big boy tried to take the hold-alls away from our feet and upset the paper plate of cherries and mashed two. Then the ashes from a tray blew all over him and Mary and we had our succession of mishaps. Mary gave the little boy one of her charms when we left and such a time as we had getting the baggage out.

We changed at Oos, which is very near Baden-Baden, and we got here about five-thirty and felt so dirty and black after our ride, but we were sorry to leave the nice people.

Stayed here – Hotel Müller, Baden-Baden [Langestrasse 26, "... pensionen from 6M, well-spoken of."].

We all washed and dressed for a 7:15 supper, which was awfully good, then went over to the Casino to hear the music and watch the people who have come for the cure. It reminded me a little of Saratoga [Saratoga Springs, N.Y.] but without the style. The Conversationhaus used to be for gaming as Monte Carlo is now. We sat in the front row of chairs and enjoyed it. The band played Carmen so we have that tune in our heads for the next few days.

Mary and I room together and have a nice front room. We are all settled to stay any length of time.

Baden-Baden. Saturday, July 6, 1901.

"Baden, or Baden-Baden, lies at the entrance of the Black Forest, among picturesque, well-wooded hills, in the delightful valley of the Oos-Bach... It is one of the most popular watering-places of Europe... The population is 15,000 and the number of visitors is about 60,000 annually.

Baden has the reputation of being an expensive watering-place, and probably it is to those who live at the first-class hotels, attend all the numerous concerts, and liberally patronize the shops and bazaars; but many of the advantages of the place may be enjoyed without very serious inroad on the finances by visitors who are content to put up at the less pretending hotels... The season proper lasts from May 1st to Oct. 31st." *The Rhine*, 36.

*

We got up at half past six and were ready to go over to the Trinkhalle at quarter after 7 ["...most frequented from 7 to 8 in the morning, when the band plays and the waters are drunk." *The Rhine*, 361]. The water is from a hot spring & at first does not seem to have much taste. Then it is sort of flat but we had two glasses apiece. Had coffee and rolls after we heard the music at the Grounds.

We then took a nice two-horse carriage and drove up to the Alte Schloss and is one of the prettiest ruins we have seen. The Rittersaal [Knight's Hall] is over grown with vines and has Aeolian harps in the windows that make it seem as if it must be back ages but it is said to date from the 14th century and that's doing pretty well. We went to the top of the tower and it was great to feel we were in and looking down into the Black Forest.

Then we drove over to Ebersteinburg, which is a lovely old ruins and also dates from the 14th cent. I really liked it better than the other for the view was superb. Marion took me sitting in the old windows fringed with vines.

After dinner we all took "forty winks" and went to the afternoon concert. Then looked in the summer shop windows and after took a walk and it is so pretty here.

Saw the big Alsatian bows on the women [an immense bow or headpiece, worn as part of the women's traditional dress of the Alsace Region of France, which in 1901 belonged to Germany.].

The shower stopped, so we went to the concert in the evening.

Baden-Baden. Sunday, July 7, 1901.

We got up early again and all drank the water. Then went to the concert after which we had a nice breakfast. The honey is simply fine here and I am as usual eating away as fast and as much as usual.

We waited until 10:30, then Miss C., Marion and I went to the Kaiserin Augusta-Bad ["Reserved for Ladies"] and had a Turkish Bath and it was such fun and I am sorry we can't take another someplace. We first went into a tiny room, undressed and put on a linen shirt thing. Then lay down in a room that was heated up to 140 for twenty minutes. From there we got under a spray, then lay on a bed made of slats and the attendant scrubbed me in soap suds with a brush, and such a scrubbing, every inch was gone over. Another spray, then we all went into a steam room and stood at two hot water fountains from which the steam rose and it seemed as if it must be fine for our faces. Then we went & paddled around in three tanks of water at different temp. Then put on a sheet & on over our heads a sort of towel, linen slippers and took a nap for 15 minutes. It took nearly 2½ hours & was fifty cents.

The envelope below is as my name was in the paper here. Leslie = Cesse, Mary J. & Miss Chadwell. [Envelope addressed to: "Miss *Clarine* S. Arnold", containing a message to consult for cabins that can be had for all lines for the return trip to America.]

Baden-Baden - Vitznau, Switzerland. July 9, 1901.

We got up at 6:15 as we had our hold-alls packed and Mary and I went with Miss C. to the Trinkhalle and had the last of the water.

We reached Oos where we had to change cars and were prepared to manage our own hold-alls but the man brought them into the car, which was a corridor train. For a while Miss C., Leslie and I sat in a compartment with a man, then we finally all got in together with another man.

At Basle [Switzerland] we had to change again, reaching there about two and Lucerne [Switzerland] about 3:30. There was a shooting feste on in Lucerne and the boat was packed with people coming to go up to the Rigi [Mt. Rigi], for Vitznau is at the very foot of the Rigi. The Hotel du Parc is about ten minutes walk from the station and the situation is perfectly grand, for it is right on the water's edge with the loveliest trees and shrubs including fig trees and along the road the pear and apricots are growing along on trellises on the side of the houses. We watched a lovely sunset from the cozy corner at the edge of the path. Mary & I are in single rooms. The picture [in Diary] is of the Alpine Rose ["Hotel - Pension du Parc, with baths and extensive grounds, pens. 7-10 fr." Baedeker, *Switzerland*, 94.].

Part V * Switzerland

"Expenses. The cost of a tour in Switzerland depends of course upon the habits and tastes of the traveler...

Money. The Swiss monetary system was assimilated to that of France in 1851...

Hotels. Switzerland is famous for its hotels. The large modern establishments... are models of organization; the smaller hotels are often equally well conducted...

Passports. In Switzerland passports must be shown in order to obtain delivery of registered letters and are sometimes of service in proving the traveler's identity...

Walking Tours. In a mountainous country like Switzerland it is to pedestrians alone that many of the finest points are accessible...

Disposition of Time. The first golden rule for the walker is to start early. If strength permits, and a suitable halting-place is to be met with, a walk of one or two hours may be accomplished before breakfast. At noon, a moderate luncheon is preferable to a table-d'hote dinner. Rest should be taken during the hottest hours and the journey then continued till 5 or 6 pm when a substantial meal may be partaken of.

Equipment. A superabundance of luggage infallibly increases the delays, annoyances, and expenses of travel. To be provided with enough and no more, may be considered the second golden rule for the traveler... A pocket knife with a corkscrew, a leathern drinking-cup, a spirit flask, stout gloves, and a piece of green crepe or coloured spectacles to protect the eyes from the glare of the snow, should not be forgotten... an opera glass or small telescope, a supply of strong cord, sticking plaster, a small compass a pocket lantern, a thermometer, and an aneroid barometer. Special attention should be paid to the boots...

The mountaineer should have a well-tried Alpenstock of seasoned ash, 5-6' long, shod with a steel point...

To prevent the feet from blistering during a protracted walking tour, they may be rubbed morning and evening with brandy and tallow... Soaping the insides of the stockings is another well-known safeguard against abrasion of the skin." *Switzerland*, xvii-xxi.

*

Vitznau. Tuesday, July 10, 1901.

We are simply to rest today, so did not have breakfast until eight out on the open porch of honey, rolls and coffee and all were so good that I think I shall pick up a bit of flesh possibly.

We went down to the landing and spent a good share of our morning watching the people land and take the cog railroad for the Rigi Kulm. When we came back we strolled out in the woods back of the vegetable garden up to the cascade where it was so cool. Mary and Leslie left with Miss C. to come down to look at the pictures but Marion & I stayed.

We wrote down by the water's edge on the tables. At 4:30 we walked to Weggis, the next town, & back getting coffee & beer there. It's four miles there & back. Marion got so hot.

Vitznau. Wednesday, July 11, 1901.

We got up at quarter after five and took the half past six boat, going over to Gersau and then walking home from there, which took us about as long as it did to walk to Weggis. On the way home I found three four-leaf clovers and I was delighted for I have been on the lookout for them ever since we got in Europe and these are the first I have found. We got to the hotel at 9:30, then went down to the water's edge and Miss Cadwell read to us from Mark Twain about his climb up to see the Rigi sunrise and it is so funny! [*A Tramp Abroad*, 1880].

Leslie and I then went up to explore the woods back of the house. After we had strayed off a little bit on a narrow steep path, we saw two men picking cherries and I offered him the fifty centimes they would not take at Cook's, so we dived down and each took a handful. Then such a time as we had getting up the hill again! But they were fine to tide us over after our early breakfast.

In the afternoon we started about 2:40 for the boat into Lucerne.

"Steamboat 6-7 times daily between Lucerne and Flüelen, 2 ¾ hrs." Flüelen is the furthest point on the lake from Lucerne. "Vitznau, 1 hr... Soon after leaving Lucerne, the steamer affords a strikingly picturesque view of the town, with its tower and battlements. To the left rises the Rigi, to the right, [Mt.] Pilatus, and facing us, the Bürgenstock." *Switzerland*, 77.

On the way in, the man next me made the remark, "It's a poor day to view the mountains." Of course I did not notice in the least.

We hurried around and did errands, got tea at a swell place. I bought a scarab ring, which I shall have made smaller and keep for myself. We got home just in time for supper, then went at our cash account and had a fit not getting it straight.

Vitznau. Thursday, July 12, 1901.

We had a 7:15 breakfast and as Mary saw Mrs. Lou and family as we were taking the boat yesterday, she went into town early to meet them and we followed. Then after doing the polite, the old man, Zimmerman, whose family keeps a store, came up to the little side landing and we got in and had a lovely ride, sitting in state under the canopy. His face when Miss C. described the *Lucania* to him was rich.

Marion played a while and so the morning went with nothing in particular happening and I worked on my hem-stitching that's got to be done.

We took the little steamer at 3:15 and went over to Bürgenstock. We took the funiculare and then walked up to the top of the mountain & the view on all sides was simply wonderful and the pictures Marion took were great & I am crazy to see them. It took us ¾ of an hour on a steady climb to get up there, but we all felt it was a conquest to have done it ["A good path … ascends through the woods to the NE to the Hammetschwand (3713'), the summit of the Bürgenstock… striking view of the greater part of the lake." *Switzerland*, 107].

Had Munich beer when we came down at the landing. I bo't some Alpine Roses and they are so lovely.

Vitznau. July 12, 1901.

We got up at 5:15 taking the first boat at 6:30 and going to Gersau about ¾ of an hour. There we got off and walked to Brunnen. On the way we passed the little chapel which is known as "Kindel-maud" or Child-murder, for the story goes that once a fiddler returning from Treib after his evening's performance and feeling that he had not the money to support his child, dashed it to pieces on the rocks and threw it into the water. A black-iron cross stands by the rock, which is said to mark the spot.

We reached Brunnen at 8:55, so it took us an hour and a half to walk the four miles and a half. I ordered four handkerchiefs for presents. We took the boat home.

As my clock had to go back, we bought chocolate at a little store in the village. Then L. and I went up into the woods and found the benches we wanted full, so we went from place to place to get a nice place to sit down, which we finally found by the rocks where the spray from the cascade every little while touched us and we had a fine time with the chocolate, which is by far the best of any we have ever had. I am thinking of getting some to take to Auntie, for I am sure she would love to have some again. It's the same kind she gave us all when she was at the Villa Natalia in Florence and also the kind Mrs. Philadelphia gave us the name of. It is so very cheap because it is made here, I suppose.

My new clock works fine and I think it will make a dear little gift for someone. I wrote Fan and answered Mr. Nelson's letter in the afternoon.

Vitznau. Saturday, July 13, 1901.

We four girls started to go down to town after we did some little odd jobs, but Miss C. said she would rather we did not, so we took books, work, pictures and chocolate. Then Leslie and I took them to the nice path we found the other day from which the view of the lake and mountains is superb. Leslie and I looked at the pictures and enjoyed it so much. It took us just about two hrs.

Finally Mary asked the man who was picking cherries to "Yodel, Bitte." and of course he did not understand what she said, but jumped down from his ladder in the tree and brought us at least two quarts of black and red cherries emptying them there all on the grass and I gave him twenty centimes. Then he poured out yards of Swiss [words] to us but finally went and we had a feast – so sick we could hardly see. By the time we were through it was dinner time and we had to come down and be hungry.

In the afternoon I read *Kenilworth* [Sir Walter Scott, 1821] and at 4:30 we all had tea on the path by the water and heard some "Mark" [Twain].

Vitznau. Sunday, July 14, 1901.

We have had the most glorious weather everyday, so after breakfast I wrote Auntie and read awhile then fussed around and dressed.

Found at my place letters from Uncle Fred, Fan and Mr. F. and I don't ever remember such a long hour and a half before I could read them. They were all nice ones, and in the PM I wrote Mr. F. and also Miss Childs who is up in London taking singing.

Mary and I had a long musing talk after we both finished and it is awfully nice to be so quiet and not rush. This is really an ideal spot for a summer.

Watched a storm come over Mt. Pilatus [across Lake Lucerne from Vitznau] but we did not get much.

Vitznau. Monday, July 15, 1901.

We were all prepared for a rainy day but it was just as bright and lovely as before. So we started off for the wharf to see the people come in to go up to the Rigi. I bought a peach at the stand and it was fine to be sure. It tasted of money, for it was eight cents.

We had great fun watching the steamers let the passengers off, for there seemed to be more than usual this morning. They fairly came off in droves and were armed with every sort of a thing from wet lunch bags to their alpine-stocks and one man, who seemed to be carrying everything the law allowed, stumbled and went down full length.

We came home about 11:30 and I stayed in the rest of the day, but L. & M. fished. Then in the afternoon Miss C. went into Lucerne to call on a friend and the girls walked along to the boat, buying chocolate on the way home.

What is it that can't go up a chimney up or down a chimney up, but can go up a chimney down or down a chimney down?

Vitznau. Tuesday, July 16, 1901.

I stayed with Miss Cadwell on the path and worked, then she had a telephone from Miss Chaffee saying she was in Lucerne at Pension Tivoli and had just gotten Miss C.'s letter sent to Zurich. We did not know whether to expect Beatrice or not, but Miss Chaffee came alone on the three o'clock boat and brought her maid with her, who is French and very nice looking. We drove out in the bus and then Miss C. told the maid she could go up into the woods if she wished, so she got Miss Chaffee all settled down in the garden. Then we had a nice visit and talked all about the old places and gossip. Miss C. [Chaffee] goes home the 10th of Oct. on the *Commonwealth* and said she would love to have me go with her, but the plans seem too mature for me to interrupt them now.

At 4:30 Leslie and Marion came down to the garden and we all had tea & cakes. Then at 5:50 we rode to the landing and took the boat with Miss Chaffee, going as far as Hertenstein with her. She kissed us all around when she left and it embarrassed the girls to have it done before so many people, but if she wanted to do it, I am sure I did not mind.

We know she had a fine time and wants to come out and be with us for the rest of the time and she is to let us know as soon as she can decide about it.

We walked back to Weggis just in time to get the boat home and it was such a pretty walk, about the nicest one we have had, for the lights were so lovely on the mountains.

Vitznau. Wednesday, July 17, 1901.

I did very little during the day to report. Sat with Marion all the morning and worked on my gnomes [needlework piece purchased in Belgium]. Then we had tea in the garden and Miss Cadwell began reading Napoleon [?] to us, but the first isn't very interesting to us, simply seems to pick to pieces what everyone else had said about him, but she turned over to the personal chapter and I am sure it will be very nice now. It's the book Auntie & I gave her for Christmas.

I did the last gnome and now am ready to start in on the foliage of the edge and I expect to have a great time getting it.

Mary and I had a great evening watching the two Frenchmen [employees of the hotel] doing the Russian bride and groom on the piazza below us with their tea and finally champagne. Then they, with the other Russian, went for a walk at 11 and we had to know they got in at 11:45.

Vitznau. Thursday, July 18, 1901.

We had a busy, but not such a very exciting time watching the boats come in and the Rigi-Bahn start up ["The Mountain Railways, which ascend the Rigi from Vitznau and Arth, are now used by the vast majority of travelers who visit this justly famous and most admirable point of view... Each train on the Vitznau line consists of one carriage only, with 54 seats, not divided into classes." *Switzerland*, 84].

I began the foliage part of my gnomes & it really is too much fun for anything. I can hardly let it alone long enough to eat and now if it is possible, I am going to finish it before I leave here.

In the afternoon we all took the boat at three, going to Brunnen to get our handkerchiefs and I dreaded to see mine, I was so afraid some of the marking would be wrong, but instead it was fine. Coming back on the boat, the young man drew the girl with the big white veil.

Mary and I had beer for tea.

Then we went out to our little point of land and saw the most beautiful sunset of all. Marion mused over the old chieftains who used to watch such sunsets years ago but without the little twinkling lights on the hotel piazza below its horizon. My dreams went into the future and I wondered if my chieftain would ever be in this spot to watch another such sunset with me!

The Russian "bride and groom" have been off all day and we heard them come home late in the evening.

I wish I were strong minded enough not to keep nibbling on chocolate for it upsets me every time that I have a time eating it. I suppose if I would only eat it moderately I might feel better by doing so, but I eat it by the whole sale and then always feel horrid the next day for it.

When I went to bed the thought of getting up at five o'clock didn't seem worthwhile but I hope it will wear off before morning.

Vitznau. Friday, July 19, 1901.

I did wake up at five and just Miss C., L. & I went for the walk. We left on the 6:30 boat which should have gotten to Beckenried at 7:05, but it did not reach there till 7:10, so it made too short an hour and we were just about a five minutes walk from Buochs when the boat passed us and we had to wait two entire hours for the next steamer [Bechenried and Buochs are villages across the lake from Vitznau.].

We did the tour in great style, what there was to do, and did see some lovely potted plants in the windows. The above house [picture] is there, but we did not see it. Then we watched an old man fish, children play, etc.; old fishing man, with turned-up trousers, waded into the water with his boots on; rode on a baggage truck that was on tracks; drew beautiful kitten of stone pigments; Miss C. fixed "natural coral" for Mary and at 10:10 the boat came.

When we got here I bought a ripe fig, which was rather good, very sweet and tasty.

We hung around and read and worked in the afternoon having our tea down on the garden terrace. In the evening the awful Greek played while we were at dinner, but it was so hot in the dining room that when tea was over everybody got up and left when he had only played the first half of his program. He was furious and simply glared as the people were leaving. Mary and I stayed till everyone was gone.

After supper we went in the garden and as at dinner, a paper was passed around for fireworks and an illumination in the evening. Lanterns were hung all around the garden paths, then the "bride-groom" party saw the fireworks. The Frenchmen went out onto the lake to set them off and it was very pretty to watch.

Later we went into the girls' room to watch the last ones go off from the fountain. The colored lights were lovely and it must have looked dear from the mountains and other houses. We had a time deciding whether to order beer, but did not.

A Day Trip up the Rigi. Saturday, July 20, 1901.

"The Rigi (5,905' above Lake Lucerne) a mountain group about 25 M. in circuit, lying between the Lakes of Lucerne, Zug, and Lowerz... Owing to its isolation, the Rigi commands a panorama 300 M. in circumference, unsurpassed for beauty in Switzerland. The mountain was known to a few travelers in the 18th cent., but it was not till after the peace of 1815 that it became a resort of tourists." *Switzerland*, 101.

*

We left the hotel about 9:40 for an all day excursion up the Rigi. By going early we got good seats in the Rigi-Bahn, but had to wait until 10:20 before starting up it and the ascent is perfectly fine. We went as far as the station Kaltbad, then got out, taking another train over to the Rigi-First Hotel, which is kept by Herr Bonn's brother. We reached there about quarter of twelve and found dinner wasn't until one o'clock, so we wandered around, but as usual by not following Miss Cadwell, we missed the excitement of the day, for she went in the hotel a minute and right by the side of her a woman fell down the stairs and we heard afterward her arm was broken.

We kept our Capri hats on for dinner and had one of the center tables. The man that sat next me had such a breath I thought at first I could not stand it, but he finally kept quiet.

After dinner a woman came to Miss Cadwell and asked if we were English and said she wanted to thank us for the pleasure we had given them all by wearing our bright pretty hats into dinner. We had a good laugh over it afterwards and Mary said if we gave them such a good time we might have made some money by passing the hat.

By the long dinner and the various excitements, we missed our train that connected with the one that went up to the Rigi-Kulm, so we started and walked across the mountain over to the station, which was a lovely walk and we were sorry when we got to the station. We stopped at a number of little bazaars and looked over all the things as usual and the girls bought some awfully pretty blue silk handkerchiefs with the coats-of-arms of all the cantons [regions] of Switzerland. Then there were some pretty little stickpins and I bought one, thinking it was Lucerne, but it proved to be Zurich, but there is hardly any difference so it doesn't matter any.

Miss Cadwell suggested that she, Leslie and I should walk up to the top instead of waiting for the train, so we started and it was the hardest climb I have tried. I did think several times I could never do it, for I lost my breath and everything happened, so I fell behind and did the best I could and I was so glad when Miss C. stopped to ask where the kennels of the St. Bernards were. We found them just below and back of the Staffel Station.

We first raved over the first two we came to that were six weeks old, then the cunning mites that were but six days old were really the sweetest little things. They were so much like David, only dark, and we had such a good time holding them for they were so dear to cuddle and had one corner of each eye open and we could have held them for hours. We walked along and looked at the rest, for there were about fifty altogether.

We walked along to the Kulm [Summit, 5905'] and got there as the girls came up. It took us just about an hour to do it and I was thankful to see the top. We had absolutely no view whatever but had a nice time poking around at the different bazaars that were under the big white umbrellas, and we saw the fine old St. Bernard Mentor who belongs to the funny old Swiss, Pius Rickenbach. The girls took pictures of him and he was lovely.

We had coffee at the terrace of the Rigi Kulm and then hung around at the top and tried to get a view. We didn't go up on the Belvedere for it wasn't worthwhile and our skirts were too short.

We had an awfully nice ride down the railroad and the Swiss cows were so pretty with the cowbells around their necks.

We left at 7:35 and got down at 8:30. I found letters from Auntie, Nellie, Eugenia & Mr. F., all fine ones. Auntie told me of her brother's sickness and I shall cable her to have him come [to Unadilla].

Vitznau. Sunday, July 21, 1901.

In the morning I wrote to Aunt Belle, a long letter and one that I should have done long ago. Then Mary and I had fine shampoos, for the water is simply fine and it did it just fine.

We then wrote some more, I to Auntie and Uncle Fred, and tomorrow I shall send a cable, for I know today the office wouldn't be open at home so probably she wouldn't get it.

Before and after supper we went down and sat in the little arbor and Miss Cadwell read to us from the London paper about some of Steyn's letters that had been lately found [Martinus Theunis Steyn, 1857-1916; Statesman and last President of the Orange Free State of South Africa].

Vitznau. Monday, July 22, 1901.

We were going to get up at 5:15 and take the boat to Brunnen then walk to Tells Platte [location of a story from the life of William Tell, the legendary Swiss marksman from the 14th c.], but it sprinkled a little so we gave up and decided to go to Lucerne and do that.

We left on the 8:10 boat and got there a little after nine and first went to the bank to draw, then to the Capell Bridge [Käpellbrücke] built in 1303 over the River Reuss and has such queer old paintings on the roof. We passed the tower, which was once a light house, and gave the name to the town (Lucerne). We then walked to the Mühlen Bridge [Brücke], which has pictures all through it of the Dance of Death. Then we walked around and saw some old houses and fine tafeens [elaborate hanging signs] hanging by doorways.

Mary stopped and got her little Swiss-house music box, which is as cunning as can be. It plays four tunes and is simply complete, just like the little houses we see all the time, hitched to the side of the mountains with the roof held down to earth to keep them from blowing off.

Then after buying my peasant handkerchief we went to see the Lion of Lucerne, carved by Thorvaldsen [Bertel Thorvaldsen, 1770-1844], 28 feet long and carved in a high cliff commemorating the 800 soldiers of the Swiss Guard who died in the defense of the Tuileries [Palace, Paris] in 1792 against the French [Revolutionary mob]. We then went through the Glacier Garden and it's well worth seeing, for it is the most wonderful construction of the sort in the world and is fine. We took a carriage and just caught the boat by my waving my umbrella.

In the afternoon I sent my cable to Auntie. Then I slept two hours and worked on my gnome piece while Miss Cadwell read to us.

Vitznau. Tuesday, July 23, 1901.

We wanted to go to Brunnen today but we are having our first rainy day since we came here and there is a lot to do. Mary got her music box after breakfast for it was sent. Then we listened to that awhile. After, Mary and I put on a lot of labels on our trunks and they look fine, too. I don't think they possibly can come off, still there is no telling.

Herr Bonn sent up word they could not find the place my cable was sent to, so Miss C. and I went down between the showers and they showed us the message and it was no more Unadilla but I suppose I am to blame, but if the first letter was a U the rest might have been anything so all there is to do is to correct it and send it on again, which makes it pretty expensive for, 'Hurd. Unadilla, New York. Entertain Brother. Arnold.', and it will be 19.50 f. or nearly four dollars, but it may make a big difference to Auntie, so I shall by all means send it. I had to pay nine francs to send it again. We cut out one word by saying "Entertain brother" [Clarissa was sending a telegram to Auntie in Unadilla, suggesting that she ask her brother, who was ill, to stay.].

In the eve we had a fine time playing 'Consequences' and it did not seem as if we could make anything so funny, for we just put down in most cases what and who we have seen during the year abroad. We played until half past ten and then were sorry to have to stop [the 'Consequences' are in the Diary].

Mary found a darning needle [dragon fly] in her room on her tassel, and we had such a time, for Marion came in and Mary took her fish pole and got tangled up in the hook, but finally we got him in a towel. I say we, I only stood and peeked through the door and then when he flew, I shut the door but I gave directions at times, none of which were carried out, but that didn't matter. Mary came and got in bed with me awhile. Then at 1:30 the Whistlers had a general move but I didn't hear it.

Vitznau. Wednesday, July 24, 1901.

In the morning we went down and saw four steamers come in and on two there were big parties of Cook's, but some very good Americans were among them and the best we have seen any time so far. But from now on we probably will see them all the time. Of course we got them started up the Rigi. I bought "[?]" and "[?]" and the mucilage [adhesive] had two flies in it that will stay until time immemorial.

Miss Cadwell had a "phone" from Miss Chaffee asking if we couldn't come into Lucerne to see her in the afternoon. Then she wanted to know if we were going to be home but we had to say, no, we were going to Tell's Chapel.

So we left the dinner table early and got the 1:50 boat and got to Tell's Platte at 3:50. Lots of people got off there and it is a most picturesque place and commemorates the place where William Tell and two other men took the oath to support Switzerland. The fourth side is simply grating [open-weave iron fencing] so one can look in at the frescoes, which show incidents at that time in his career.

We then walked up miles of steps and came to the road finally [the Axenstrasse, "scenery very striking"]. Then started to walk to Flüelen, which is the town at the very end of the lake and it was about the prettiest walk we have taken so far for it's right up above the water, which was a most glorious green. One place it was especially pretty where we went in the tunnel and could look through the arches that are cut out solid rock and make a perfectly stunning frame for the snow topped peaks beyond us.

We bought some of the nice black cherries off a woman along the road. Then when we got to Flüelen we went to one of the hotels and as usual, Mary and I and also Marion had beer.

We went at once to the boat, which left at five. The man who has been on before was also there with his beautiful French poodle.

We had a lovely trip home for the lights at that time are simply beyond words, they are so lovely on the peaks, green slopes and the water takes on such lovely colors.

Vitznau. Thursday, July 25, 1901

It simply spilled all day, so in the morning I wrote and wrote, getting letters written to Fan, Rob, Olive and Mrs. C. All the last three should have been done long ago, but I did the very best I could and hope that will make up for their being left until now to be written.

In the afternoon we wrote until we were tired then started out to walk to Weggis, but it looked so much like rain that we turned around getting our umbrellas and Herr Bonn handed my letter to me from Miss Childs. She is in Bayreuth for the Opera, sails for home Aug. 8th [Bayreuth, Germany; site of the annual Opera Festival of the works of Richard Wagner since 1876.].

We went "to town" and bought photographs, getting back in time to see the rainbow, which made a complete circle from the side hill by us into the water and the reflection was superb. The newcomer next to me snores awfully!

Vitznau. Friday, July 26, 1901.

It poured all day and we just decided to stay around and do odd jobs so we were, as usual, busy all the morning.

In the afternoon we did more odds and ends and then about four we walked down to Weggis ["...thriving village in a very sheltered situation, frequented as a health resort." *Switzerland,* 94] and just as we reached the terrace at the hotel for coffee, it began to pour and kept it up for an hour. Then Miss C. read to us from Mark Twain so we had a nice time and got home about seven.

On the way back there was another beautiful rainbow just like the one of the night before and I never saw more beautiful ones than these have been. Monsieur Martin and his "accomplice" have gone and it's restful to say the least. The "Geheimrat" has been complained of on account of their insisting on the dining room being so shut up at mealtime [Geheimrat; high official of the German Court].

Vitznau. Saturday, July 27, 1901.

We wanted terribly to get up early to walk from Tell's Platte to Brunnen so as to have done the length of the lake on foot, but it was too dubious to start, neither was it a good day to go up to the Seelisberg.

So, we took the 8:45 boat and went to Brunnen and I first got six bears @ 50 centimes a piece. They are dear and will be nice to hand people that I don't want to give much. The white one with a "pouch" I shall never part with.

I then went over to the handkerchief store where Miss Cadwell and Mary had gone first and there the woman said she had some of the batiste handkerchiefs that I had asked for the time before when I was up to get my others. She brought them out and they were just what I want exactly, so I gave her an order.

4 A.M.K. @ 1 f marking .40 = 5.60
3 H.B.M. @ 1 f marking .30 = 3.90
2 F.C.E. @ 1 f marking .30 = 2.60
6 C.L.S. @ 1 f marking .30 = 7.80
3 N.E.Y. @ 2 f marking .90 = 8.70
2 J.M.M. @ 2 f marking .90 = 5.80

I paid her and she is going to send them on the 5th of August to Grindelwald. I think they are lovely and I hope Fan will let me give them to the people for it will save my getting more and I hope she won't mind.

We came home and got here just in time for dinner and found a letter from Auntie with one enclosed from Fan. She says Auntie isn't quite so well as when she first got home, but I am trying not to worry for it will not help matters a bit and I can't get home any sooner.

Another shower in PM. Went down to Zimmermann's and got last things.

The house is full for Sunday.

Vitznau. Sunday, July 28, 1901.

In the morning it looked as if it would be a rainy day, so I wrote Auntie a long letter after getting nice ones from Auntie, Fan and Uncle Fred the day before.

Then I got upset [?] and mended, took out spots etc. with benzene. Gave away my brown poplin waist and a lot of other things.

After dinner and Asti, Mary and Marion took the little Russian boy's picture and we are fazed as to who he belongs to of "the Whistlers".

Miss Cadwell and I went to the three o'clock boat to meet Miss Chaffee, but she did not come and found over the telephone that she is sick and would send Francine to the station with a note in the morning to us. We are so sorry to leave here and my trunk is not nearly full for I have given loads of things away and have just what I need to last.

Vitznau to the Berner-Oberland. Monday, July 29, 1901.

Today our travels begin again and we were up at six with out dear hold-alls packed and ready for breakfast at 7:15 and leaving the boat landing at 8:20.

We were so pleased to think that old Herr Zimmermann came down to see us off. We got to Lucerne and saw nothing of Francine [Miss Chaffee's maid] in the station, which is a big one and loads of Americans hurrying around.

Our train was great with the aisle on the side so we could stand out and get the stunning scenery. We had a fine time. After Brünig [Brünig Pass] we had new engines and two cars to each then began to climb, climb, climb till it seemed as if the train must get tired for we were so high and as we got up we could see the [Engelhörner and Faulhorn Mts.] and we reached at the end Meiringen.

We had such stupid men to get the hold-alls out and we had to help but we took pains to have them no heavier than necessary. We went over to the Hotel Brünig and had Belegtes Brötchen [sandwiches] and Munich Beer. Miss Cadwell, Mary and I started on ahead to walk to the Aareschlucht [Gorge of the Aare River], which is about a mile and a quarter out of the village. We made good time and had to wait about five minutes before the girls came, then we went in and it is more wonderful than the picture shows [in Diary], for the height adds so much to the grandeur. Last year the balcony, as the path along the side is called, has been made on the principle of the one beyond Tell's Platte, with arches, and at night the whole place is lighted up with electric lights and must be lovely.

We took about two hours to do it all and then had coffee when we got back to the hotel. Had a little while to wait, then took the train for Brienz. We had to get our hold-alls in through the windows. It was only a short ride to the lake [Lake of Brienz] where we took the steamer to Giessbach. There we had a glimpse of the falls, but just the part where it went into the lake ["The Giessbach is one of the prettiest and most popular spots in the Bernese Oberland." *Switzerland*, 193].

We took the funicular up to "The Giessbach" Hotel ["Tramway to the Hotel, 6 mins., 300 ft. above the lake."]. Mary and I had the room next to Miss Cadwell right by the falls, but they made such a noise I tho't I would go crazy. We sat opposite five Americans at table and when we were walking after dinner, we were stopped by four out in the covered promenade. They were so funny and when we run across such people it is simply a good thing, for it makes us realize what a chance we are having.

We had a great time keeping awake till the illumination at 9:30, but when it did come we felt amply repaid, for it was the most exquisite thing I ever expect to see, for all the seven falls were at the same moment thrown into one blaze of light from points at the side of the bank. The white lights lasted just a few minutes then were blended with red and finally faded ["Illumination of the Falls, with Bengal lights every evening from the first of June till 30th

Sept. (inmates of the hotel 1 fr. each for the first evening only; other persons 1½ fr.)." *Switzerland*, 170].

We went to bed immediately and I was almost sick with a headache the same as I had after our long day at Hildesheim, but Mary gave me her smelling salts and not withstanding all the noise, I went right to sleep, but I made the remark that I did not see how anyone could get any rest amid such continuous roaring.

Giessbach - Interlaken - Grindelwald. Tuesday, July 30, 1901.

But we proved it most satisfactorily, that it is possible to sleep in Giessbach, for Miss Cadwell came in all dressed for breakfast and a walk at 9 o'clock and both of us were like logs. But we hurried and had good luck so we managed to get down to breakfast not so very late.

Soon after it we went up to the lookout place and got the view of the surrounding mountains and lake. Then came down and went up to the falls, walking under one of the huge cataracts on the dripping rustic bridge.

We left at 12:40 and coming down the funicular took the steamer to Interlaken ['Between the Lakes' of Brienz and Thun]. We got there at two and went over to the garden of the Hotel du Lac and had a nice dinner of cold meat, potato salad and bread. We then walked through the town & saw the big hotels, but while it is more attractive to me than Lucerne, I am glad we are not to stay there.

We had coffee at the same hotel and then took a two horse Victoria with bells and set off for Grindelwald. Leslie sat up with the driver and I had my ideas fulfilled of driving through the Alps. The roads are as smooth as can be and the scenery simply superb and those great huge mountains looming up on every side is impressive. We drove along by the Lütscheine River all the way, starting at 4:35 and got to Grindelwald at about seven. On the way we passed a man blowing his head off on an Alpine Horn. From the distance it was very pretty but close to it was terrible to say the least. The girls saw a young chamois at the place where the horses were watered.

We came to the Burgener and the mountains are simply glorious. We heard the Italians singing [Hotel-Pension Burgener].

Grindelwald. Wednesday, July 31, 1901.

"Grindelwald (3415' at the station; pop. 3087), a large village in a sheltered and healthy situation, almost entirely rebuilt since the fire of 1892, is an excellent starting-point for excursions, and a favorite summer resort. Three gigantic mountains bound the valley on the S., the Eiger (13,040') the Mettenberg and the beautiful three-peaked Wetterhorn (12,150'), the characteristic feature of the entire landscape." *Switzerland*, 185.

*

We decided to have breakfast at eight so sat on the piazza with the superb view of the Wetterhorn, Mettenberg, Finsterhorn, Eiger & the Mannlichen with the sound of the rush of the Lütschine at the foot and the Upper and Lower Grindelwald Glacier. We went for a walk after the shower around and across the river and home by the [Bär] Bear Hotel.

In the afternoon we started out at five to walk to the Abbach Falls, but it began to rain so we just went a little beyond and then turned and came back in the rain but we have gotten so that we do not mind the rain at all.

We sit next three Australian ladies at table.

In the evening we saw signaling from the climbers on the Wetterhorn to their friends down here in the village.

Grindelwald. Thursday, Aug. 1, 1901.

Miss Cadwell told me of the letter from Auntie in reply to her's asking if she were willing that I should return with someone else so she need not put us to the expense and the trip of crossing with us and so I telegraphed to Barings to know if they had Miss Adams' address, for I think I can without doubt go with her and shall try to [Clarissa has decided to return to Unadilla in early Autumn, ahead of the rest of the party, due to the ill health of "Auntie". She is trying to get in contact with a Miss A. L. Adams to see if she would be willing to be her companion and chaperone on the return voyage.].

We then walked to the Abbach Falls and were gone two hours and a half. I got another top with a decent tassel on it for my white hat and found the letter from Uncle Fred.

In the afternoon it rained so we were in the girls' room and Miss C. read *Victor Emmanuel* [Edward Dicey, 1882] and I did a lot on gnomes.

About 3:30 telegram came [Telegram from Baring Brothers informing Clarissa that they have no address for Miss Adams.].

Grindelwald. Friday, Aug. 2, 1901.

It poured all day long so we began *The Gadfly* [Ethel Lillian Voynich, 1897] and it's exciting from beginning to end and a very strong book. We could hardly let it alone to go to luncheon. Mary finished her Florentine work, so began to read for the first time and is in for it now, for she reads well and rapidly.

We took a nap in the afternoon, I on my bed with the washbowl at the foot to catch the drips from the ceiling and my grip under my pillow to make it a little higher. We then went in the girls' room, had tea, worked and Mary read to us some more. I had to move out for the night as my bed was wet and it kept on leaking as long as the rain kept up. I went in the corner room and took my cowbell along in case I needed to give alarm, but when I got to sleep it was all right.

Grindelwald. Saturday, Aug. 3, 1901.

In the morning we went out after the rain of yesterday and bought things at all the stores in the line of loose bears, cork bears, pins, etc. [the Bear is the mascot of the Berner-Oberland]. Then we came home and on the way Marion dropped her package of bears in the puddle and her belt had a time coming off.

We walked up the road a ways but it was getting warm, so we sat in the garden and read. Finished *The Gadfly* after dinner and then when it began to get cool and we had had our tea in the garden, we walked up to the Lower Glacier, but did not go in, but the Gorge of the Lütscheine is very pretty as it came out between the huge rocks with a cold blast with it. It was a very nice walk up there and I used the alpine stock [hiking staff] for the first time. The other girls have bought their own, but if I go to Boston, I think I should get pretty sick of carrying it before home. We came back by The Bear.

Kleine Scheidegg. Sunday, Aug. 4, 1901.

We have had so many rainy days lately that we decided if it cleared, to walk up to the Kleine Scheidegg, so we were up at five and ready to start at six thirty. Everything was shut up and it seemed as if it must be the middle of the night. We went past The Bear and over the river then began a long steady pull. The girls laughed because I wore gloves and no collar just a handkerchief around my neck, but it was so comfortable and my hands did not blister ["Walkers from Grindelwald to the Little Scheidegg cross the Lütshine above the station of Grund… to Alpiglen 2 hrs., thence to the Scheidegg 1½ hr." *Switzerland,* 185].

On the Trail to the Kleine Scheidegg

The path was great and pretty steep in places for it reminded me of the Bürgenstock walk toward the top. On the way I saw some alpine roses and went down the bank to get a big bunch, which I tied on my stock with a hdkf. We met lots of peasants all dressed up in their best things with vests made of a cross-stitch pattern [Kleine Scheidegg Routenkarte in Diary]. The herds of cattle on the hill, each with a bell on her neck and a different tinkle to it, is one of the things I like best in Switzerland for they do blend with the country just fine. There are lots of goats also on the hills, but not so many at a time. We had to go through brooks and water for all the streams are full from the recent rain and lastly we had a herd of cattle to go through, which really was as bad as water, but Miss Cadwell hates them, so that it makes one quite brave.

We got up to the Bellevue [Hotel Bellevue, The Kleine Scheidegg; built in 1854] at just ten, so it took us exactly the three hours and a half that Baedeker said. We were up above everything but grass, though they had little evergreens in tubs setting around and umbrellas for shade. The view of the mountains was superb and prettier than the panorama seems ["The summit of the pass (6788') affords a striking view of Grindelwald, bounded on the N. by the mountains which separate it form the Lake of Brienz. On the S. fine views of the Mönch, Eiger and Jungfrau (13,670')." *Switzerland,* 159-160].

We had coffee first then took our lunch down to the station restaurant where we had Munich Beer that was simply fine.

We took the 1:10 train down and got here at 2:30.[1] Miss C. thought we stood the walking so well that it would be better not to overdo the matter. Leslie and I wanted to walk back, but I guess it was just as well we did not for we were not tired in the least.

Mary and I went to sleep about as soon as we got in the house and did not wake up till six, so missed our tea.

Some English people sit opposite to us, a lady and two daughters and Miss Burrows and her father, Loftus, sits next to me, but Loftus is quite above speaking to us but talks a blue streak to the ones opposite. In the hotel across the street to our left we see the singing artist and I hope he does not think we try to get his attention but he is in the window as much as we are.

Fireworks from Eiger & Bear but we went to bed.

A Night at the Schynige Platte. Monday, Aug. 5, 1901.

We got up at six this morning and at 7:30 started for the Glacier and it was a lovely walk up there, but really is further than it looks as if it would be, because it is such a big affair that one is not expecting so long a walk. But it was a beauty. Miss Cadwell did not think it best for her to go in with us so we went along with the guide. It was exactly like winter and outside the men had a rack of shawls and capes for people to put on if they were not prepared for the change after the warm walk. The ice was so clear and the light a lovely blue, just like the light in the Blue Grotto. The Grotto [artificially hewn] took us about three minutes to walk through, then we came out at the same place we started from. Then we took the new narrow path up the mountain and came home by way of the Chalet Milchbach, which is through the woods and then came over the river and on to the main road just above the house.

It began to look cloudy but Herr Bücher said it would be nice for the Schynige Platte [6790'], so at 2:33 we packed our "mighty-coats" and started. Got to Wilderswyl and took the 4:21 train and got there at 5:40 ["The Schynige Platte, one of the finest points of view in the Bernese Oberland..." *Switzerland*, 173].

The ride up was just superb for we sat in the front end of the train so got a nice view [Rack and Pinion Railway, began service in 1893]. We could easily see Brienzer See with Interlaken & Lake Thun. The fields looked like a patchwork quilt and I must find out just how high the summit is [6,893']. I liked it better than the Rigi Bahn for the view of the Grindelwald Valley with the river and road that we drove over from Interlaken.

The hotel at the top is very nice, simple, but everything is as it should be [Hotel Restaurant Schynige Platte; "A first class mountain hotel. Newly built in 1898, Kitchen and wines excellent. Prices moderate." Brochure in Diary]. We went to our rooms first and then we (Mary just brought in her stick that had been marked with all the places we have been and in my excitement my pen got loose and ran all over the pages) went up to the pyramid of stones at the summit. It was awfully high and a cloud came pouring in, so we got down the path again. Miss Cadwell went in the house soon because of her tooth but we hung our feet off "An Alp" and watched the big herd of cattle below us.

At table we were with English and the lady next to me spoke and the man across the table, too, when we were laughing at Marion because she did not see the rain. We stayed in the Salon a while, but it was so cold we went to bed at 8:30 so as to be ready for the 4:30 sunrise. The beds were fine but the water dreadful, so we drank Neuchatel Wine [wine from the Neuchatel Region of Switzerland].

At an unearthly hour the gong rang, but it was cloudy so we did not get up.

Had breakfast at eight and we were just enveloped in a fog. Couldn't see a blessed thing till after nine, then we had a glimpse of the Jungfrau etc. Left at 9:33, got to Grindelwald at one and Loftus deigned to speak and talked to me "a considerable".

We wrote after luncheon then went in for tea and Miss C. read about Pauline Bonaparte sister of Napoleon from *Roman Gossip* [Francis Elliott, 1894].

Miss Burrows talked a lot at dinner and is nice.

We were awfully cold when we went to bed and could almost see our breath as we could easily last night.

Grindelwald. Tuesday PM, Aug. 6, 1901.

No mail when we got down here and I was just low for I don't care to spend a lot for the cable if the letter is on the way with the address [of Miss Adams].

We went out alone after tea for Miss Cadwell sent her shoes to be tapped and we went down by the river path, had a fine treat with strawberries and cream, nice field berries at 30 centimes a dish. She only had three and we thought we must go without because there were not four, but someone rose to the occasion and we divided them. Then we picked a nice lot in the woods and by the time we were through it was time to come back and dress for dinner.

There was a slight alpine glow and we had coffee out on the terrace but under cover so Miss C.'s tooth would not feel it. We decided there would be no view from S. P. tonight either.

Grindelwald. Wednesday, Aug. 7, 1901.

It was a rainy morning and we did not go out but I did a lot of writing and did not seem to do much that counted. I did get a letter off to Auntie though, but did not feel in the spirit of enlarging on what we did.

It was this afternoon we went down and got berries that were so nice. No mail yet, and I am getting crazy!

Grindelwald. Thursday, Aug. 8, 1901.

We got up at 5:15 and left for Bäregg [Chalet Bäregg, 5410'] at 6:30 and it was just a fine walk. It was long, but I think the views of the valley were the nicest ones we have had at anytime. It took us two solid hours to get up there and we pegged along every minute. We had just fine views down onto the Glacier and the avalanches were tumbling down all around but just out of sight.

When we got up there we had some Dézaley Wine [wine from the Canton of Vaud, on Lake Geneva's north shore] to refresh ourselves and Mary took a picture of the little fox terrier that was in the shanty.

We got down feeling as fresh and nice as could be, met the Looper girls all rigged up in veils and gloves on the way up in the hot sun. I don't think enough stress can be laid upon an early start for there is nothing like it.

In the afternoon we four went out and after shopping we walked down toward the waterfall but stopped on the way & had a nice time in the grass and taking pictures. Sent cable in eve, "Send Adams address to G. C."

Grindelwald. Friday, Aug. 9, 1901.

Our last day here! but we four girls had seven o'clock breakfast and started for the Lower Gletcher. We had bad luck for we paid our money and went to the Gorge [Gorge of the Lütschine] instead of using our sense. Then the result was 50 cts. more, but it was the principle that made us so simply disgusted, but we got up to the Grotto finally and it was nice with an altar inside and we had a good time after all [230 foot long grotto hewn into the ice]. I got more things of bears and Mary lost her pear out of the window when I told her to be careful.

On the Road. Saturday, Aug. 10, 1901.

We got up early, about 6:15, and did a lot to get ready to start. Then we had breakfast at 7:15 in the dining room and at eight the carriage was at the door for us. Miss Burroughs said she would be down to see us off and we had about given her up when along she came after we were all fixed. Marion sat up on the seat with the driver all the way and when we stopped for water the flies were so thick that the horses could not drink.

We got to Interlaken about ten, left on the boat at 10:35, got to Thun at twelve. Then we had a great time with our luggage, for the train was packed. We had to take them in through the windows. There were four Americans and the man, Mr. Matteson, from Cambridge - at least his hat said so - seemed very sick and weak. Leslie and I changed places so they could eat together and after he had drunk a good share of the quart of Rhine Wine, he became very talkative and it was disgusting. We got to Bern at 1:15. There we had a mouthful of Belegtes Brötchen and Münchener Bier, which was fine.

We left about 1:45 and had a great time getting seats. We were not together any during the day, for the cars had isles and doors between every two seats. Miss C. and I sat in the seats with what should have been the 3rd class passengers. The man and woman, who seemed to be on their wedding trip, had their heads out the window and her hat blew off, but it did not seem to matter much even if it was lost. Then he got angry and set Miss C.'s bag on the floor. I was afraid of him he was so horrid. We got to Lausanne about 4:45 and had to wait some little time in the train and it was so hot I thought I would melt.

We finally got to Montreux [Switzerland] at 6:15. There was a nice bus at the station to meet us and it was about a mile up to the Breuer Hotel, where they are repairing and it must be very nice in the season, which is in September, for the Grape Cure. We had a delicious dinner and only one man in the dining room besides ourselves, but everything was so nice [Hotel-Pension Breuer, Montreux BonPort, with gardens on the lake. "The Grape Cure begins towards the end of September and lasts about a month." *Switzerland*, 225].

Montreux. Sunday, Aug. 11, 1901.

"The Lake of Geneva… 45 miles long… For centuries it has been a favorite theme with writers of every nationality. On the N. side it is bounded by gently sloping hills, richly clothed with vineyards and orchards, and enlivened with smiling villages… the town of Montreux-Vernez, on the lake, with railway-station and pier, quays with gardens, a large covered market on the lake… and a Cursaal, with pleasant grounds." *Switzerland*, 254.

*

First thing after our nice breakfast we went down to the garden and my cable came, forwarded from Grindelwald for we had them send it on. I wrote at once and then to Uncle Fred, 16 pages [cable containing the address of Miss Adams in Diary]. After tea I cleaned Miss C.'s, Mary's & my spoons and Marion's bracelet with silver cream.

Montreux. Monday, Aug. 12, 1901.

It poured in the morning but Miss Cadwell thought it would be better to send a telegram on to Miss Adams, so we went out against my will, for she had a bad night with the tooth and I wanted her to stay in, but she wouldn't stay and so we said, "Wire me your address. Letter for you at Harjes." [Bank; Morgan, Harjes & Co.]. Then we came back after going to Cook's, where the man didn't seem to know a thing about trains, etc. [The rough draft of Clarissa's letter to Miss Adams is in her Diary. She explains her reasons for needing to return to Unadilla ahead of schedule, and asks if she could join Miss Adams on the voyage home, sharing a stateroom or reserving one near. She apologizes for the urgency of her letter, but explains that the movements of the rest of her Party are being held up until she, Clarissa, can arrange her return.]

We read and worked and had a nice morning. Then after dinner, or luncheon I should say, we fussed around some more and the workmen made a good deal of noise for the entire house is torn up and everything is simply topsy-turvy with it all. We are about the only people here and I don't see how they can give us such very dainty things and so well cooked and everything is served in the nicest way.

We had tea and then some nice plum cake that Miss Cadwell and I bought this morning, after which we all, except Marion, started out to go to Castle Chillon, which is beyond the station Territet-Glion ["... stands on an isolated rock 22 yds. from the bank, with which it is connected by a bridge... The interior has been lately thoroughly restored." *Switzerland*, 256].

We were ambling along and looking in the windows of the tea rooms, which are only a little beyond here, when who should come out of one but Mrs. Waite and Mrs. Morrison with Miss Emily Waite. Of course we were really awfully glad to see them and we all stood and talked for the longest time until finally we had to move on. We asked them to come the next day to the Tea Rooms to tea with us. Marion had to guess who it was we saw and she "guessed right the very etc.".

Montreux. Tuesday, Aug. 13, 1901.

We first thing after breakfast started out and walked up to the Gorge du Chauderon ["From the bridge of Montreux to the head of the Gorge, and back, 1 hr." *Switzerland*, 255]. We went up the road and over the track thro some real Italian looking streets that had little dark rooms opening off of them with the real southern odors and poor thin spotted cats wandering around in the same aimless fashion. The acres and acres of grape vines grew in the same way only were trained far different, for in Switzerland they climb a stick not more than three feel high. I think maybe ours would do better if the vines were pruned more.

The path went through the Gorge and at the entrance a woman had a stand of lovely looking fruit. All bought but I, for some unknown reason, and I was sorry after we moved along that I didn't.

We had a nice climb through real dark and mossy places. There were so many benches along the route but none of them were aimed toward the pretty places.

We went into the grounds of the Grand Hotel [de Caux] and had the most superb view of the Lake of Geneva and if I can only find a Liberty [fabric] in those shades, I shall be perfectly delighted.

We rested in the afternoon then all dressed up in our best hold-all things and went with Mrs. & Miss Waite and Mrs. Morrison up to the Tea Rooms and had a real nice time ["At Home Ladies Tea Rooms; English Cakes & Biscuits, Wines, Spirits, wholesale & retail. Montreux Bon-port. Prop. E. Basil Green"; Establishment's card in Diary]. It was a splendid review for us and after we finished the tea and cakes we came up to our garden, but it was so upset I am sure they couldn't have been very much impressed by it. We were sorry to have them invite us for tomorrow to the same place, but they insisted upon it.

In the evening we all went out so Mary could send her telegram to the Lowes, who sail in the morning. The P.O. was closed so we went to the Territet [Post] Office, which was open.

When we got back to the hotel we decided not to go to the Kursaal [Casino-Kursall de Montreux, opened in 1881 to entertain the guests staying in the hotels of Montreux.]. I put on all the different coats and hats and it was so funny.

The swells with maid, valet and parrot are in the next hotel and are pretty rapid style. [Menu in Diary: Hotel Breuer, Montreux – Bouchées Mariniére – Cotelettes de Veau Maître d'hotel – Pommes Sautées – Volaille en Mayonnaise – Compote de Rines Claudes]

Montreux. Wednesday, Aug. 14, 1901.

Our plans for coming here are not coming out as planned, but it can't be helped and no news from Miss Adams. I am sure it is too late now for me to arrange to go with her, but I am going to leave a blank line to fill in when we know for sure.

We walked to the end of the town and looked in the windows and so killed time in that way and Mary bought a lovely Roman silk table cover at the Italian Store. We came back for Marion, then went down to the Kursaal and sat an hour but the music was simply awful - ladies orchestra.

At luncheon there was a lady and her son at table with us but we don't know their nationality.

We drew lots to see who would go to tea and Marion and I stay at home.

The girls went to tea and had a spread really and flowers and they did the thing up just the very nicest that they knew how and they were so sorry we couldn't come and even wanted to send the tea over to the hotel for us first but did not, but sent the roses and edelweiss, which are just lovely.

Montreux - Geneva. Thursday, August 15, 1901.

In the morning Miss C., Leslie and Marion went up to the Castle Chillon, but M. & I stayed in the hotel and had a fine time watching the woman with the maid have her breakfast out on the balcony. Evidently the man did not get up, for the maid fixed an egg all nice and took it in to him, then the valet came out and showed her his arms that were burned from some trip they took the day before. The evening before we had a great time watching the man sitting alone and he looked so dejected.

It began to rain but not much. Then when it was time for us to leave at three, we walked to the boat and got some crescent teacakes and nice citron loaf [From Montreux to Geneva, "Steamboats preferable to the railway..."].

We all went up on deck the first thing and got settled and the roses looked so pretty that Mrs. Waite gave us but we hadn't been there long when the wind began to blow and the waves were higher then we had on the *Lucania*, so after a while we had to go down into the cabin and had nice coffee with our cakes. After we finished, I began to feel queer and asked for Mary's salts. Then Miss Cadwell and Leslie went on deck with me, but finally, I went down to the ladies room and was so thankful to see the Cook's woman get through so I could have my turn. Then I threw up a lot and felt better. After awhile I went on deck and it all cleared off and the trip and lights on the lake and mountains were lovely.

We got to Geneva about 8:30 and went to the Hotel de la Poste, but they said they had had no orders to save rooms, which we know was not so, and everything was full, but Miss Cadwell and I went out as Leslie said "into the night" and after hunting finally brought up at the Pension Richardet and got rooms here [Rue de Montblanc, 6 Fr.]. It's perfectly horrid, but still might work, I suppose. I have a single room and so have Mary and Miss Cadwell. The landlady expected ten Americans who didn't come, so we really were in luck.

Geneva. Friday, Aug. 16, 1901.

"Geneva, population 86,535, including the suburbs… capital of the [second] smallest canton, lies on the S. end of the lake [of Geneva], where the swift blue waters of the Rhone emerge from it." *Switzerland*, 235.

*

The first thing, we went to the bank and inquired for Miss Adams, of whom they knew nothing, but the man said a Miss Arnold was asked for a little while before and the note, on the other page, left. [Finally, Clarissa has a letter from Miss Adams. Miss Adams' letter contained the information that she would be sailing from Antwerp, Belgium, on the Steamer *Zeeland*, of the Red Star American Line, Sept. 7th. That Clarissa would be welcome to travel with her, but she is all ready sharing a stateroom with another traveling companion. Miss Adams would be at the Hotel Metropole (by the English Garden) in Geneva, until Aug. 20.]

Miss Cadwell and I went to the hotel where they were very uncivil, so I waited until 12:15 for her and in the meantime Miss Cadwell had been to Cook's and they had telegraphed for a stateroom.

In the afternoon we went to Château Rothschild [Pavillon de Pregny, near Geneva; the Chateau of Baroness Adolphe Rothschild] where we ran into all the fifty "cookies & jumbles" including my sick friend and conducted by the Genoa man.

We then went to Cook's at six and they had stateroom 288 for me 500 francs, so I wrote a note and took it to Miss A. in the morning for Miss C.'s tooth hurt her so that she didn't feel she could go to the Kursaal and we were so glad she could stay in.

It was great luck to get a stateroom for the man told Miss C. that two weeks before there was but one vacant.

Geneva. Saturday, Aug. 17, 1901.

We went to the Royal Tiger Fur Store and I selected my sable fox, which is a beauty. Marion got one but cheaper and Mary ordered a neck-piece and a muff made of Alaska sable to be sent to London. Then we took our enamels to a jeweler, but I was the only one who left mine, for I want it when I sail for home and I also left my scarab to be made smaller. He is going to rush it so I can have it Monday at 6:30. I am not setting my heart on it.

Miss Cadwell had to come home, for the medicine the dentist gave her to put in her ear, which I dropped in, has upset her and she is so, so sick to her stomach. She kept quiet all the PM and we went out shopping for things and got some sour glacé and graham bread and butter, so we made sandwiches for her for she ate no dinner. By evening she felt better.

Geneva. Sunday, Aug. 18, 1901.

Mary went with her to the dentist's office and the doctor said he would put in something to kill the nerve, but it didn't pain her as he said it would.

In the PM, Mrs. & Miss Frothingham from Columbia Heights, Brooklyn, came to see Mary and we made tea and took it in, for I went in Marion's room.

Then, just before supper, Miss C. came in and told us to hurry for there was a fine view of Mt. Blanc and we could see the Napoleon head perfectly [The likeness of Napoleon was said to be visible on Mont Blanc, Europe's tallest mountain, in this view from Geneva.].

Geneva. Monday, Aug. 19, 1901.

The girls went with Miss Cadwell to the dentist's and he is going to let her tooth stay as it is and be finished in Paris.

Mary got me the pretty wooden fan with the dress and coat-of-arms of the Cantons of Switzerland.

The man came into my room to fix the blind and I was frightened most to death.

Got up for dinner and the girls went to Ariana [Musée de l'Ariana]. I packed, etc.

Geneva - Paris. Tuesday, Aug. 20, 1901.

We got up at six and left at 7:15 for Paris. We had to change at Mâcon and Dijon and had such a hot ride, for we did not get here until quarter of seven. Then came to Hotel Lord Byron, No. 16 rue Lord Byron, just off the Champs Elysees. It is fine here and the air is lovely and cool. We had a fine dinner and were glad to get to bed.

Part VI * Return to Paris & Home

Paris. Wednesday, August 12, 1901.

Miss Cadwell had to get up early and went to see about the trunks, taking the keys. Also brought us a nice bundle of mail and I was glad to hear from Auntie and got the check from Uncle Fred.

We all went out about ten over to the milliners and got very pretty hats. Mine is red straw and I hope the people at home will like it.

In the afternoon we went to the Louvre [Grands Magasins du Lourve] and I got a corset and had it fitted there, but it wasn't at all what I wanted when I got home and tried it on in the evening. I went in to see Mary and she said it would not do either, so I made up my mind then and there to get the Leoty like hers [Maison Leoty; famous Parisian Corset Designer, 8 Place de la Madeleine, Paris]. I stayed in there a long time and finally had to come into my little single room because I was so sleepy and she was too. [During this time in Paris, the four girls are consumed with acquiring Parisian fashionable attire; hats, dresses, suits, corsets. All custom made to order.[1]]

Paris - September, 1901

Paris. Thursday, Aug. 22, 1901.

In the morning we all went over to the milliners and the girls tried on their hats, which were as pretty as could be.

Then Marion and Leslie came home and we three went to the banks, drawing and getting mail at Perier's [Bank], then looking in the registers to see if there were any others to try to have Mary go with, but we found no one.

We then went to see Miss Cadwell's dressmaker but she was out of town and will have to be written to.

In the afternoon we went to the Bon Marché [Parisian Grands Magasin, Department Store] and I got my cotton figured skirt and yellow silk one, ordered the corset covers for Nellie and half a dozen handkerchiefs marked for Uncle John.

The afternoon before we went to Mamby and Saddler's [?], but could not find anything in a suit that I really wanted, so was a little low over it all.

Paris. Friday, August 23, 1901.

Leslie, Miss C. and I started very early and I wore my grey skirt, white-ribbon waist and red hat. We first tried to find a skirt for Leslie, for the waitress in the tearoom spilled cream all in her lap the day before, but we could not find anything that would do at all.

Then we went to a swell tailor-dressmaker in the Place Vendome and such a show as it was. The models were all on girls who were powdered, laced, painted and dyed hair, who came in and looked around and walked up to the people who were sitting around the room. I chose a lovely grey rough goods that is a perfect stunner and will be a perfect dear. I never was bowed around to such an extent in my life. We three went in another room and my measure was taken. Everyone in the place was beautifully dressed and it was just the sort of place I have wanted to go to for something, so I am delighted with it all.

After leaving there, Miss C. said my corset must be attended to, so we found the Leoty place and I went through the same performance there as in the Louvre, but I am sure I will be pleased with the corset, but never expect to get another. It had to be fixed over the hips and under the arm, so it is to be done in the evening and I only hope it will be, for I need it to be fitted over tomorrow.

In the afternoon we three went to the Louvre while Miss C. and Leslie went to the shop hunting for a skirt. We did it pretty well and were rather tired so went to the Rubens' room being attracted by the inviting looking seats. The others tho't it a good joke.

We had tea in the tearooms then all came home and late in the eve my corset came and I was so glad for it's very nice and gives me a figure.

Paris. Saturday, August 24, 1901.

We had to hurry but got ready finally and all started out, Miss C. and I only going to the Modists [designer of fashionable gowns].

We were ushered into a little room, one of a lot just such, filled with mirrors and electric light fixtures. I got all I could off, for my grey skirt is so tight over my new corset I nearly died getting it together in my room, so I was glad to have it undone before anyone came. Finally, a girl came and unhooked my waist taking off the rest of my things. Then, the one who came for my measure the day before brought in a long piece of unbleached muslin putting one corner at the bottom of my skirt, then she fitted it to me perfectly. Another one brought in the waist lining of the same and fitted that.

I was then dressed and we went out, having to run the gauntlet of all the people sitting around looking at the models, but we got out all right and whizzed down to the street in the modern elevator that was just like New York.

We were so thirsty that we went in a place and got some horrid sweet syrup and fizz. Then met the girls in the Louvre where they were turned loose to wait for us.

In the afternoon we went out to the Jardin something and saw sights. Everything seemed to be devoted to love making. Loads of brides and grooms around. The brides seemed to be trying to see how dirty they could get their new white bridal gowns and did it successfully. Then, there were no end of love birds cuddled up together. We went in the little tram with the seats like the tops of the busses and were so funny.

I am upset from something & ate no luncheon or much dinner.

Paris. Sunday, August 25, 1901.

Got up and had a good bath and fussed around then wrote Miss Jeyes, Miss Adams and Miss Chaffee. I do wish Miss Linderfelt had not written me, for goodness knows, she is the last person in the world I want to see [Miss Linderfelt, a friend of Joshua Sweet, the young man who Clarissa sent away, disappointed, when they were in Munich in April.].

I then wrote Auntie a long letter about clothes etc.

We had coffee after dinner so I wasn't sleepy and did not go to bed till after twelve, but wrote another letter and then a little in my Journal.

Paris. Monday, August 26, 1901.

In the morning Miss C., Mary and Marion went out for corsets. Mary got Leoty and had a great time being waited on and getting what she wanted.

Marion went to Mmd. Augustine Thomas, rue Tailbout, where they make to order and had fine ones, but they are expensive, being sixteen dollars a pair, but are nice enough to make up for it.

In the afternoon we all went to the Trocadéro [Parc], where we wanted to see the Aquarium, but it was closed so we could not get into it. Then it began to rain but we took refuge in a doorway, so did not get very damp.

We walked along the Avenue Henri Martin past the Hot Spring [Artesian Well of Passy] to the Muette Grounds [La Muette, former Royal Hunting Lodge]. It is said, a very wealthy man owned the grounds and had them fitted up for his daughter who was a mute. She could be seen wandering around the grounds always dressed in white.

We stopped at one of the sidewalk places and got beer and waited there for a hard shower to be over which came up suddenly.

Miss C. and I went to the milliners & I picked out a big black hat and ordered another winter one which she will make for me.

Paris. Tuesday, August 27, 1901.

Miss Cadwell and I went to the dressmakers and I tried on my suit, the waist and skirt and I am sure I will like it very much indeed.

The girls shopped in the rue de la Paix, then I got two sweet little Jap. fans. From there we went to the Bank Monsieurs Perier & [?], 58 rue de Province. I drew a lot.

In the afternoon we went to the Bon Marché and I got candlesticks, ties, handkerchiefs, pins and a lot of nice little things.

Then Miss C. and I took a bus home and dressed just in time for dinner.

There is a raft of noisy Americans up on our floor and they are so annoying to us.

Paris. Wednesday, August 28, 1901.

Marion and Miss C. waited for Marion's corsets while Leslie and I waited at the bank for them and while we were waiting I drew some more money.

We all went to Pingrin's, and I am going to have a light silk dress, a pongee [soft fabric of thin silk] made to fit me that was a copy of a Pack and Gown [?], a blue waist that goes with it, a carnelian [reddish-brown] silk waist, a pale green tucked unlined silk waist and a narrow grey stripped silk waist. She is going to have them all done for me in time [Maison Pingrin, 39, Rue Lafitte, Paris].

In the afternoon we took a train and went out to St. Denis [town where the Kings of France are buried, 4½ miles from Paris]. It was a long ride and we got back just in time for Miss C. and I to go to the milliners. I did not like any of the hats so very well and so she is going to fix some more for us to see tomorrow or next day. I should like to get Fan one, but there are no shapes I think she would like.

Paris. Thursday, August 29th, 1901.

Miss Cadwell and I went to the dressmakers and the suit is getting along nicely. Then we went to Pingrin, where we met the girls, who drove, for Marion's corsets came and so she had to get into them properly. Pingrin had silks and I selected one for my church dress, but I am afraid it won't be just what I shall care for. The pongee I know is going to be sweet.

Miss Cadwell went out with Mary and Marion to see about dresses for Mary. They first went to Callot Soeurs [Fashion Design House, opened in 1895], then to Raudnitz [Maison Raudnitz, 21 Place Vendôme] where she ordered a black velvet suit.

Paris. Friday, August 30th, 1901.

I went first with Mary to see about her dress, but the air is entirely different than my place and they are both on the Place Vendome. She then went over with me and I was in hopes she would get something there, but she didn't. Mmd Des [blank] is too sweet for anything. I have it on for the last time and it is dear. I am so glad Miss Cadwell likes it so much. She couldn't have taken more interest in it as well as in all of my things.

In the afternoon we went to the Bastille [Place de la Bastille; site of the Bastille St. Antoine, the castle that was a state prison for persons of rank during the French Revolution. Destroyed on 14 July, 1789.] then out to the Père Lachaise ["…largest and most interesting of the Parisian burial grounds." *Paris,* 180.] where we saw the graves of Abelard & Heloise (12 cent.), [Luigu] Cherubini & [Frédéric] Chopin. It was great, for we rode out on the top of the bus and had a good idea of the rush and bustle of "Gay Paris" and the people did look as if they were having such a good time drinking & smoking at the tables that lined the sidewalks.

A Day Trip - Versailles. Saturday, August 31, 1901.

"After the year 1682, Versailles became the permanent headquarters of the court, and is therefore intimately associated with the history of that period. It witnessed the zenith and the decadence of the prosperity of Louis XIV...to whom the Palace owes its present extent almost wholly...

The accounts handed down to us regarding the erection of this sumptuous palace and the laying out of its grounds almost border on the fabulous. Thus no fewer than 36,000 men and 6,000 horses are said to have been employed at one time in forming the terraces of the garden, leveling the park, and constructing a road to it from Paris..." *Paris,* 309-310.

*

We started at quarter of ten for the station and got out to Versailles after three quarters of an hours ride [utilizing train or tramway from Paris] at half past eleven. Then we had our light luncheon in a very musty garden, of omelet, cold meat, salad and what we thought was going to be Munich beer, but it was so poor we couldn't drink it.

We then went to the Palace grounds, in by the big fountain that costs fifty dollars every time they play it. Just as we got in the grounds, Miss C. lost her glasses, so Mary and I said we would go back and hunt for them for we thought they were just a little way back, but found that they were under the table we had been sitting at. When Miss C. started to take them out, she found they were broken.

We walked up to the Palace and out to where we could see the grounds as laid out in flowerbeds and fountains. Then we went to the Palace around by the Louis XIV Statue, who built the wings, the center by Louis XIII. The other parts and the theatre were built by Louis XV.

We went around inside the chapel [Salon de la Chapelle], etc. and saw no end of Crusader pictures. The Galerie des Glaces of Louis XIV was where King William of Prussia was made Emperor [of the German Empire, 1871].

We went to the Grand Trianon [Villa, Louis XIV for Madame de Maintenon, his second wife] then to the Petit Trianon [Villa, Louis XVI for Marie Antoinette]. We sat on the grass and had such a good time before train time, then we went into Paris and got tea ready and that's all.

I had a note from Miss Linderfelt and she invited me to come to dinner, but I wrote for her to come to see me instead Sunday afternoon, then I shall have a good visit.

I have given Marion ten dollars to get in London two pairs dog skin or reindeer gloves in men's 8½, four pairs boys' 8½ or 6¾ in regular size, the balance to spend for me in boys' sizes. She has given me $2.00 to get her a moneybag in New York to be sent to her in London.

Paris. Sunday, September 1, 1901.

I stayed in bed a long time but finally got up and in the afternoon Miss Linderfelt called and I was so glad and enjoyed the call more than I had any idea I would. She is really a lovely girl and very bright. Leslie brought in tea to us.

I wore my swell suit down for dinner and it is a beauty. Just the sort of a suit I wanted.

Paris. Monday, September 2, 1901.

I had a hard cold come on. It began out at Versailles and has kept getting worse all the time until last night I fell down sick with it. So they made me some whiskey-toddy to go to bed on and it was fine, but I didn't sleep at all well and got so tired thinking.

In the morning Miss C. and Mary went out and they went to the Red Star Office and the headman knows a Mr. de Young who is going on the *Zeeland* and he thinks I can perhaps go to Antwerp with his family. He is going to see about it.

In the afternoon we went to the Pingrin's and I tried on everything. I wish I had gotten one waist at [blank] instead of two from her, but I shall profit by this years experience for next time.

Mary has her passage on the *New England* for Oct. 24th with the Cotton Party.

Paris. September 3, 1901.

We went out at 9:30 to [blank] with Mary and she ordered a long coat of black, lined with lavender or cream brocade satin. Miss Cadwell went to see if Mr. de Young had been heard of, but he hadn't been found, so then we went to Liberty's, where I got three scarves and table covers for gifts.

We then went to the bank and Mr. [blank] cashed my check for £15 from home and I drew £40 more, which I hope will last me.

I wish I could hear from Miss Adams.

We drove to Pingrin's, stopping to see if Mr. de Young was on deck yet, but they hadn't seen him. He is from San Francisco and is the headman of the "San Francisco Chronicle" [founder of the newspaper, Charles or Michael de Young].

If I can't go with him I shall probably get someone to take me, for she can get back at eleven at night, so it will be possible if nothing else can be arranged.

[Maison] Pingrin sent home all the things in the evening, and they are ever so pretty. The pongee suit and blue silk waist, green silk shirt waist, grey silk waist, carnelian evening waist and the yellow whole dress, which is very pretty indeed and with my hats, I have some sweet pretty things, though I am very sorry that I have not a swell expensive dress waist besides my suit. [The carnelian evening waist and the yellow dress were kept by Clarissa and are in the possession of her family. The workmanship is exquisite on both garments, 'Maison Pingrin' being clearly labeled. Pinned to the carnelian waist is a note written by Clarissa; "Waist that I wore with a lovely brown traveling suit when I was married, Dec 31, 1902."]

Yesterday I had such a dear note from Miss Linderfelt written after she got home from her call and I think it was so nice of her to write it, but it was much more than I deserve in any way, but I shall answer it just before I leave for America. Josh sailed on Saturday.

Paris. Wednesday, September 4, 1901.

In the morning Miss Cadwell went out with me and did a lot of shopping and we accomplished loads of things. We went to the Louvre then took a carriage and went around to the swell places. I got my cut steel white belt and it is a stunner! Mr. de Young has not been heard from, so I shall plan to go with someone else.

In the afternoon we went out to the Sèvres China Factory and Museum and Marion broke the cup that the show man passed around. Then we went to Saint Cloud where the lovely museum used to be – I mean Chateau [Chateau Saint Cloud, destroyed by fire in 1870].

In the evening we all had ginger ale in my room. It was great fun and the girls all drank to me and a safe voyage. We put the tray on my stool and sat around it, the three girls on my trunk and I on the floor at their feet. I was going in to visit Mary, but it was rather late, so I did not.

Paris. Thursday, September 5, 1901.

Miss Cadwell went with me to the bank and then on the way to it I ordered my coffin hatbox. When we got back, Miss C. and the girls went to the milliners but Mary and I stayed in. I got to thinking about the hatbox and decided I couldn't stand it, so she conceded and went down and told them I wanted another, so I got my black one, which is fine! I stayed in during the afternoon and packed, so I got along fine with Mary's and Leslie's help.

We had tea and I finished my packing.

Then after dinner we took the bus and went down the Champs-Élysses to the tea room that we went to in the fall, but it was closed, so we took a carriage and drove to the hotel and it was a sight to see all the cafés and gardens lighted up and it was a nice way to spend my last night with the girls.

Paris - Antwerp, Belgium. Friday, Sept. 6, 1901.

We had an alarm to get up at six and my maid came and went in the bus with us. The train went at 8:25 and all the girls went with me to the station, each carrying some of my belongings. Marion gave me a lovely undressed kid pocket book, Mary a silk pillow, Leslie, Scribner's *Perseus* and *The Tragedy of the Korosko* by Hall Caine [Sir Arthur Conan Doyle], and letters from all. Miss Cadwell gave me a little box and note to be opened before lunch.

Two priests, a queer man and a sleepy woman were in the compartment with me. We had to get out at Custom House and at Brussels. One priest got left. The girls put in plums, a big peach, and little cakes with chocolates for my lunch.

I went to the St. Antoine [St. Antoine Hotel, Place Verte 40, Antwerp, Belgium] and then dismissed my maid, found Miss A. [Adams], who had not gotten my letter.

We went out shopping and got some pretty brass things, then we had a nice dinner, went out again to take my windmill back and I then wrote Auntie, Miss Cadwell and Miss Linderfelt. I was going to bed early, but it was rather late.

Antwerp - *The S.S. Zeeland.* Saturday, Sept. 7, 1901.

Belgian Royal and U.S. Mail Steamship "Zeeland" of the Red Star Line.[2]
Sailing from ANTWERP for NEW YORK, Saturday, 7 September 1901.
Captain: John A. Broomhead.
Surgeon: Dr. M.J. O'Neill;
Purser: I. Dubois;
Chief Steward: G. W. Campbell.
[Passenger List Brochure for this sailing.]

*

I was awake at 5:30, got up a little after six and attended to my bill and fees. I ordered a carriage, but it was a little late in getting there and then was an open one and Miss Adams took her trunks with us and they almost fell off three or four times. I finally called a boy to hold them on, so we got to the dock in fine shape.

My stateroom is fine and with Mrs. Chapman. I had my steamer chair places engaged, but when I went to look, they had been moved and I was furious, so I attacked Mr. [blank] who was fine even though he had his places engaged since last July, but he was so gentlemanly and moved his two out to the row in front of us, for they were two deep.

We met Mr. and Mrs. Flag and three children who sit next Mr. Davenport and at the table it is simply fine. Three fine young men sit opposite the father of one, Mr. Coy (Hotchkins), who is a professor and a man on Miss A.'s left and one on my right.

The steamer letters are fine. My bib and poem especially nice and very appropriate, for this morning I dropped some coffee on the front of my waist.

Just before leaving Antwerp we heard Mr. McKinley had been shot.[3] My man, Mr. [blank] announced at the luncheon table it was not fatal. He talked a lot and is awfully interesting.

Zeeland. Sunday, Sept. 8, 1901. Day 2 at Sea

I got up as fine as a fiddle about eight, got my shoes and stockings on then relapsed into silence after two or three eruptions. Every time I tried to get up I was so sick that there was no use of it. I slept a good deal and about six got up on deck, but I had to lie down between everything I put on, so it was hard work. Judge Davenport came to me as soon as he saw me and sat down. Then I gave the seaman five francs and he called the steward and I ordered beef, potato and bread, but I couldn't eat. So then he brought me some nice tea with lemon in it and bread, which I thoroughly enjoyed.

Miss Adams was not up all day, so I sat out till about ten and the Judge sat with me all the time and he is so entertaining. I think we were in great luck to be with the party.

Zeeland. Monday, Sept. 9, 1901. Day 3 at Sea

Oh, but I felt perfectly horrid and did not get up till late. Then I did not get anything to eat for breakfast, but Miss A. had just finished and it didn't look so very inviting.

I had luncheon on deck and gave the steward 10 francs, which I think was rash for I am not going to be sick enough to get my money's worth, but I must try my best. In the afternoon, I tried to read and write and do all sorts of things but didn't feel real [well] and I had my dinner out here, too, but I was not very happy and sat out, but not so very late, with Mr. Davenport.

Days run 384 miles.

Zeeland. Tuesday, Sept. 10, 1901. Day 4 at Sea

Went into breakfast and had oatmeal, coffee, rolls and marmalade, but young Mr. Coy simply would not bow to me, where all the others were so nice. I felt real chipper and even went and wrote the girls - that is Mary - a real nice letter and gave them all the particulars of the trip up to the time of writing and such a lot I had to write that I was quite exhausted, so had to rest and read some, but I had a great time getting interested in, *The Battle of the Strong* [Gilbert Parker, 1862-1932].

Miss Adams has a horrid cold and I am so sorry, for it makes it very unpleasant for her. The wind blew awfully hard in the afternoon, but I walk quite a good deal and as the deck is so narrow I am rather glad that there is no one that I care especially to be with. The young people are rather nice, but I hope, even though it is stupid, that there will be no games started.

Days run 384 miles!

Zeeland. Wednesday, Sept. 11, 1901. Day 5 at Sea

Nothing special happened. All day it was blowing and in the afternoon it was cold and Miss Adams sat inside most of the time.

At dinner we got in conversation with Prof Coy and his son about our travels and we four were the last in the dining room. Then we came out and Miss Adams and young Mr. C. came up while I went in to get my wrap, and when I came up they were talking in the hall. Mr. C. asked me if I wanted to walk and we had a number of brisk turns and then sat down in our places and talked till I went in. He graduated from Yale last June and is one of the great football players. He is a splendid looking fellow but is not an especially good talker. I wish Dr. Reed, who is an instructor in Yale, would visit!

Days run 376 miles.

Zeeland. Thursday, Sept. 12, 1901. Day 6 at Sea

Miss Adams did not go out to breakfast, so I had to face the assembled multitude all by myself and I must say I wasn't sorry when I was through, for

I did feel uncertain to say the least. I found Miss Adams in the hall eating her poor breakfast a little at a time, but she said it was nice because it was not in one of the horrid old baskets but was on a tray. She had a fine time talking to Mrs. Erben and then we saw a whale and passed the *Campania* on her way to Liverpool.

I finished, *The Battle of the Strong*, but do not think much of it.

It was not pleasant so we did not come out again after dinner. Wrote the Bucks [Marion & Leslie].

Days run 356 miles, 1465 from home.

S.S. *Zeeland*. Friday, September 13, 1901. Day 7 at Sea

We have given up all hopes of getting in Sunday evening as we hoped to do as our time for the runs are not up to time. There are 1695 on board. 1st Cabin 226, 2nd Cabin 195, Steerage 988, Crew 285. The pitching of the steamer has caused the propellers to race and then we have lost time, verbatim from the Judge.

Leslie gave me a Cassell's Mag. [Cassell's Family Magazine, published 1867-1932] to open for today and it has been perfectly fine to have things to look at each day and it is so nice.

An Afterword...

The Diary ends with Clarissa's entry on the 13th of September. The *SS Zeeland* arrived in New York City on September 16, 1901, after nine days at sea. Clarissa does not comment on the last two days at sea, her arrival in New York Harbor, or her homecoming in Unadilla. The last items included in the journal of her eleven months abroad are; "A Passenger List" from the *Zeeland*, three pictures of the Steamship cut from postal cards, and a rough draft of a poem Clarissa had written to one of the Four Girls, Mary Sawyer:

To Mary, from a sympathetic "pal",

The first day called up gravest fears
That made me nervous hearted,
The next day called up memories,
Of friends from whom I'd parted.
The third day called up tho'ts of Land.
The fourth day called up everything,
I'd eaten since I started!
Oh Mary, write me all about it, for I must know the particulars.
Claire

Finis!

*

A Brief Biography

*

Clarissa Sands Arnold

Clarissa was born on May 22, 1877, in Unadilla, New York, a small town resting quietly on the banks of the Susquehanna River in Otsego County.

Clarissa's parents, Clarissa Mygatt Sands and Frank B. Arnold, were married in 1873 and lived in the center of the village at 62 Main Street in the grey stone house that had been the Sands' family home since 1857.

Clarissa's Home, 62 Main Street, Unadilla, Constructed - 1837

The elder Clarissa, Clarissa Mygatt Sands Arnold, was twenty-eight when she and Frank married and thirty-two when young Clarissa was born. She died in 1881 following the difficult birth of a son, who was to die shortly after his mother.

Clarissa Mygatt Sands Arnold, 1845-1881

Frank Arnold was born in 1839 in County Clare, Ireland. He immigrated to the United States in the 1840's with his family, settling near West Hartford, Connecticut. Named Michael Edwards at birth, he changed his name to Benjamin Franklin Arnold and at age twelve, left the family home and moved to New York State, where he lived with the Charles Root family in Gilbertsville, a village not far from Unadilla. In the next few years, he rearranged his name to Frank B. Arnold, graduated from Gilbertsville Academy and continued his education at Hamilton College in Utica, New York, paying his tuition by teaching part-time at a private secondary school in Unadilla (The Unadilla Academy, founded in 1851).

Frank B. Arnold, 1839-1890

After his graduation from Hamilton College, Frank continued to teach at the Unadilla Academy, where he also served as Principal for a time. While teaching, he began to "read the law" and on admittance to the Bar, worked for a firm in Binghamton, New York. In 1867, he moved to Omaha, Nebraska, returning to Unadilla two years later where he married, became a father, continued to practice law and eventually became involved in local and state politics. He served as an Otsego County Supervisor for six terms, followed by three terms in the State Assembly and then was a State Senator for the 1888 and 1889 terms. In 1890, he unsuccessfully ran for a seat in the US Congress. Depressed, he tragically took his own life on December 11, 1890, leaving Clarissa an orphan at thirteen.

Clarissa continued to live in the family home cared for by long-time Arnold family housekeeper, Mrs. Charlotte Elizabeth Hurd (Auntie), and her maternal Uncle, J. Fred Sands, her guardian and advisor who lived next door at 64 Main Street.

Clarissa and Mrs. Hurd on the Porch of The Unadilla House.

At seventeen, in 1894, Clarissa graduated from Unadilla Academy, and in September of that year began a two-year program of study at Lasell Female Seminary in Newton, Massachusetts (Lasell College, founded in 1851). She studied Algebra, History, English, German and Voice her first year and Solid Geometry and Trigonometry, History, Art, German and Voice the second. She graduated on June 10th, 1896.

Clarissa at Seventeen

In 1900, when Clarissa embarked on her European Tour, she was twenty-three. During the time between graduation from Lasell at nineteen and sailing for England on the *RMS Lucania*, she had continued her life in Unadilla under the watchful eyes of Mrs. Hurd and her Uncle. In her diary one can sense a yearning for purpose and meaning, and there are references to the turmoil of the recent past, especially in a letter from her Uncle Fred that Clarissa saved in her scrapbook. The letter was to be read on the voyage across the Atlantic and he wanted her to reflect on the pain she had caused the previous summer to those who loved her and who wanted only what was best for her. So there is a mystery, but she chooses not to divulge her thoughts, hopes, or perhaps regrets, on what had taken place.

In September, 1901, Clarissa returned to Unadilla after her year abroad and on December 31st, 1902, married William Becker Stewart of Oneonta, New York. They were both twenty-five, and William was in the process of completing his studies in medicine at the University of Vermont in Burlington. A suitable match for both Clarissa and William.

"Stewart-Arnold Nuptials: William Becker Stewart, eldest son of Hon. and Mrs. James Stewart, of Oneonta, and Miss Clarissa Sands Arnold, daughter of the late Senator Frank B. Arnold, of Unadilla, were quietly married at St. Matthew's Episcopal Church at Unadilla, at 4 o'clock yesterday afternoon…The wedding was witnessed only by the near relatives of the bride and groom and was entirely free from ostentation and display. The couple was unattended. The bride was attired in her traveling gown.

After the ceremony... the party retired to the home of the bride, where a wedding luncheon was served. Mr. and Mrs. Stewart will arrive in Oneonta today and be the guests of Mr. and Mrs. James Stewart for a brief stay. The groom will proceed to Burlington, Vt., on Friday, to continue his medical studies at the University of Vermont. Mrs. Stewart will, as soon as she can, close her residence at Unadilla, go to Burlington and pass the winter with her husband there.

The wedding is one that interests elite circles of the two villages, uniting as it does members of representative and honored families of Oneonta and Unadilla and is but the natural outcome of the strong attachment which has formed between the young people. Mr. Stewart is a young man favored by birth and attainments... Possessed of an attractive personality and a musical voice, he has won the affections of a charming young woman...That happiness unalloyed and prosperity abundant may be theirs will be the sincere wish of all friends."

The Daily Star, Oneonta, NY, Jan. 1, 1903. Clipping from Clarissa's Scrapbook.

*

Clarissa and William lived in Burlington until William graduated in 1904. In 1905, they moved to Bennington, Vermont, where William began his medical practice. Two children were born; James William Stewart, 1904, and Clara Sands Stewart, 1906.

Clarissa, William and James with the Stewart Family, 1904 [1]

While in Bennington, William's health began to deteriorate and he was diagnosed with Bright's Disease (Nephritis). The disease would eventually lead to their return to Unadilla in 1909, and Clarissa's home. William died on August 21st, 1910, leaving Clarissa a widow at thirty-three with their two young children to raise on her own.

Clarissa with James and Clara

In 1915, Clarissa married her old friend, Harrison L. Beatty, of Bainbridge, NY, and she and her family went to live with him in Bainbridge until his death in 1919, when she and her children returned to Unadilla.

Clarissa's Scrapbook contains many saved art projects and mementos from her son, James, and a few from Clara. When Clara was a child, she had an operation to remove a cyst from her brain, and the damage, caused either by the cyst or the operation, led to seizures and uncontrollable outbursts of temper. She was eventually institutionalized in the 1920's and spent most of her adult life in confinement. In the 1970's, with the availability of new medications, she was released and lived quietly with a companion until her death in 1979.

In the 1920's, Clarissa became interested in investing in Florida real estate and spent the last few years of her life dividing her time between her home in Unadilla and Florida. In 1925, James married Helen Vaughn Morris of Milford Center, New York, and they were also living in Florida part of the year. On one of Clarissa's return trips to Unadilla, she was involved in an automobile accident and the injuries she sustained resulted in her death on October 1, 1926. James and Helen returned to Unadilla and the house that had been his mother's family home.

Clarissa Sands Arnold Stewart Beatty, 1877-1926

James and Helen continued to live in the family home in Unadilla and their sons, William Morris Stewart and David Arnold Stewart, were born while living in the gray stone house. In 1936, the house was sold and the family moved to Oneonta so James could pursue other business interests.

An extensive library, mostly collected by Clarissa's father, Frank Arnold, had been left with the house at the time of the sale. Years later, the new owners of the stone house contacted David Stewart, younger son of James and Helen, asking if there was any interest in some of the books of family association that had been left with the house. If so, they were being kept in the garden house at the rear of the property. Among those books were Clarissa's Diary, Scrapbook and Photo Album, along with her personal copy of Karl Baedeker's, *Italy, Handbook for Travelers. First Part: Northern Italy*... all from her European Tour.

*

The Endnotes

Part I * England

1. Financing the trip was managed with "Letters of Credit" issued on funds deposited with the traveler's bank in the USA. These "Letters" were "drawn" upon to obtain cash, which was then subtracted from the value on the note until the Letter was depleted. Karl Baedeker's guidebooks recommend this means as the safest and most expedient way of funding such an extensive journey in 1900.

2. Cars; Clarissa is referring to a tramway system. They were in London in 1900, but not apparently in the city center. "About 130 miles of tramways, with over 1000 cars, and carrying 150 million passengers annually, are in operation, and are convenient for visiting the outlying districts of London." *London*, 34.

3. "Among the characteristic sights of London is the Lord Mayor's Show (9th Nov.), or the procession in which – maintaining an ancient and picturesque, though useless custom – the newly elected Lord Mayor moves, amid great pomp and ceremony, through the streets from the City to the Courts of Justice, in order to take the oath of office." *London*, 98.

4. P.T. Barnum's Great Traveling Museum, Menagerie, Caravan & Hippodrome, which eventually became the Ringling Brothers & Barnum & Bailey Circus in 1907.

5. Stephanus Johannes Paulus Kruger, 1825-1904; South African Transvaal statesman, who became known as Om Paul. President for many years, he was in Paris in 1900 seeking European support for his countrymen's unsuccessful war against the British Empire in The Second Boer War, 1899-190Encyclopedia Britannica. "Paul Kruger". http://www.britannica.com/EBchecked/topic/323870/Paul-Kruger.

Part II * Paris

1. The 800 Swiss Guards were killed defending the King and Queen of France, Louis XVI and Marie Antoinette, from the Tribunes of the French Revolution on August 10, 1792. Wikipedia. "Swiss Guards: Swiss Guards in France." http://en.wikipedia.org/wiki/Swiss_Guard

2. Exposition Universelle in Paris; 14 April 1900 - 10 Nov. 1900; A World's Fair, attended by 50 million people. Wikipedia. "Exposition Universelle (1900)". http://en.wikipedia.org/wiki/Exposition_Universelle_(1900)

Part III * Italy

1. The "... celebrated Iron Crown, with which the German Emperors were crowned as Kings of Lombardy... used at the coronation of the Emp. Charles V (King of France) in 1530, of Napoleon in 1805... said to have been made from a nail of the true Cross." Actually, it is in the Cathedral S. Giovanni in the town of Monza, 8 miles from Milan. *Northern Italy*, 137.

2. " 'Tempio di Cremazione', for the burning of dead bodies. Presented to the town in 1876 by a Swiss resident and greatly enlarged in 1896 (inspection permitted). The process of cremation occupies less than 1 hr. and the cost is 40 Fr. Paupers are cremated without charge." *Northern Italy*, 133.

3. "Hotel Molaro, 56, Via Gregoriano. Healthiest Situation in Town, and very Central. Old Reputation for its Comfort and Moderate Charges." Murray, John (Firm). *A Handbook of Rome and the Campagne*. J Murray, 1899. Digitized May 20, 2008. 34, Back of text; Handbook Advertiser. http://books.google.com/books?id=XhEbAAAAYAAJ

4. The year 1900, had been proclaimed a Jubilee Year by Pope Leo XIII, the first in the 19th century. The tradition was started in 1300, by Pope Boniface VIII, as a year of remission of sins and pardon and was to be celebrated every 50 years. On December 24th, 1899, the Holy Door in St. Peter's, the Porta Santa, was opened by the Pope, marking the start of the Jubilee Year. This service on Dec. 24th, 1900, marked the end. www.aquinasandmore.com/index.cfm/title/What-is-a-Jubilee-Year/

5. Pope's Angels; Boys who were castrated to retain their full soprano voices. When grown, some became the most celebrated operatic stars in Italy. The practice became illegal after 1870 and Pope Leo XIII prohibited the hiring of new Castrati to sing in the churches. In 1900, there were still

a few Castrati singing in the Sistine Chapel and some of the Basilicas. Wikipedia. http://en.wikipedia.org/wiki/Castrato

6. "Babington's Tea Rooms; Confectioners, Tea Rooms: Piazza de Spagna 23." *Central Italy*, 129. "Good for a very pricey spot of tea and other dainty British edibles. Opened in 1893 by a Derbyshire lady, it was the ex-pat hub of the later Grand Tour." Bramblett. *Rome*, 116.

7. The Colosseum; "... originally called the Amphitheatrum Flavium, the largest theatre, and one of the most imposing structures in the world, completed by Titus in AD 80. It was inaugurated by gladiatorial combats, continued during 100 days, in which 5000 wild animals were killed, and naval contests were exhibited." *Central Italy*, 255.

8. The Catacombs; "... the Burial places of the early Christians... The Roman law prohibiting the interment of the dead, or even their ashes, within the precincts of the city, was of course binding on the Christians also. We accordingly find their burying-places situated outside the gates, on the great highroads." *Central Italy*, 384.

9. Ancient town west of Naples located on Golfo di Pozzuoli..."On the S. side of the Lake (Lago Lucrino), are grottoes and cuttings, hewn in the tufa rock... The grotto is 280 paces in length, and blackened with the smoke of torches. The visit on the whole is scarcely worth the trouble, and the demands of the guides should be beaten down." *Southern Italy*, 99.

10. Bathing; "Baths of every kind (floating baths) at the entrance to the Grand Canal, but muddy at high tide. The excellent Lido Sea Baths are much pleasanter (season from June to Sept.; temperature of the water 70-80F.). In summer a steamboat plies every hour in the morning and every half hour in the afternoon... A gondola takes at least ½ hr., two gondoliers desirable or, in wind, necessary." *Northern Italy*, 245, 300.

Part IV * Germany, The Netherlands & Belgium

1. The Royal Order of Saint George for the Defense of the Faith and the Immaculate Conception; founded in Germany by Maximillian II in 1726. A Catholic Order, "... transformed from a Crusading Order to an exclusive religious institution of the nobility." The current Grand Master (2009) is Franz, Duke of Bavaria. Wikipedia. "Franz, Duke of Bavaria". http://en.wikipedia.org/wiki/Royal_Order_of_Saint_George/

2. "The Peterkins" is a reference to a collection of stories written by Lucretia Peobody Hale, 1820-1900, concerning the family, Peterkin, and their (mis) adventures. The stories were published as *The Peterkin Papers* in 1886. The four girls girls begin referring to themselves as "The Peterkins" in Munich, and seem delighted by the comparison.

3. Neues Hof-Theatre; Built in 1841, by Gottfried Semper. Known (2009) as The Semper Opera House, one of the most famous in the world.

4. Life Magazine; Published from 1883-1936, as a humor and general light-entertainment magazine. In 1936, it became the 1st US all-photography news magazine, ceasing publication in 2007.

5. A false report; Ida Saxton McKinley, First Lady of the United States, had been an invalid since 1873, following the illness and death of a child. She was to outlive her husband, dying in 1907.

6. "The Linden, a street 196 ft. in width, deriving its name from the avenues of lime-trees interspersed with chestnuts with which it is planted, resembles the boulevards of Paris... and is flanked with handsome palaces, spacious hotels and attractive shops..." *Northern Germany*, 24.

7. Heinrich Schliemann, 1822-1890; German treasure hunter and excavator of the ancient cities of Troy and Mycenae. Many of the treasures were "... presented to the German Empire by the distinguished discoverer." *Northern Germany*, 61.

8. The Portrait of Elisabeth Bas was willed to the Rijksmuseum in 1880. In 1911, it was proclaimed to not be painted by Rembrandt, but by Ferdinand Bol. Still controversial (2009).

9. The International Peace Conference of 1899; attended by twenty-six world powers and reaching an agreement to ban certain types of modern technology in future wars; Bombing from the Air, The Use of Chemical Weapons, and Hollow Pointed Bullets. Wikipedia. "Hague Conventions (1899 and 1907)." http://en.wikipedia.org/wiki/Hague_Conventions_(1899_and_1907)

10. "The Regent and Doelen picture are among the most conspicuous creations of the Dutch School of painters. It was the custom for the Presidents (Regents) of the various corporations and charitable institutions to place in the guild-halls and shooting galleries (Doelen) portraits of groups of members of the various guilds." *Belgium and Holland*, lvi.

11. The Inquisition flared up during the occupation of Belgium and the Netherlands by Spain in the 16th c. condemning thousands to death. "Council of Troubles". http://www.britannica.com/EBchecked/topic/606789/Council-of-Troubles#

12. German Epic Poem, "The Nibelungenlied", written c. 1180-1210, is the story of a treasure, known to be an inexhaustible source of power for its holders, that was thrown into The Rhine near the city of Worms. The story is the basis for, The Ring Cycle Opera, by Richard Wagner. "Nibelunglied". http://en.wikipedia.org/wiki/Nibelunglied

Part V * Switzerland

1. In 1893, a cog-rail line began service connecting Grindelwald, over the Kleine Scheidegg, to the village of Lauterbrunnen in the next valley, both directions. Clarissa and Party use this train to return to Grindelwald.

Part VI * Return to Paris & Home

1. "The most fashionable shops are to found in the neighborhood of the Opéra; Rue de la Paix, Rue Taitbout, Rue Louis-le-Grand, Rue du Quatre Septembre, and the adjoining Boulevards. At these a simple walking-dress is said to cost not less than 400 fr., while an evening costume may amount to 1500 fr... It is generally possible to reduce the prices by a little bargaining." Baedeker, *Paris and Environs*, 42.

2. The *SS Zeeland*... "launched on 24 November 1900, *Zeeland* made her maiden voyage from Antwerp to New York on 13 April 1901, sailing under the British flag." "*SS Zeeland*". http://en.wikipedia.org/wiki/SS_Zeeland_(1901)

3. President William McKinley, Jr., was shot September 5, 1901, while visiting the Pan American Exposition in Buffalo, NY, with Mrs. McKinley. He died September 14, 1901. "William McKinley". http://en,wikipedia.org/wiki/William_McKinley

A Brief Biography * Clarissa Sands Arnold

1. Four Generations, from left to right:

   Back Row: Alice Graves Stewart & her husband, Hugh Ford Stewart 1879-1940 (Will Stewart's brother); Baby, James William Stewart 1904-

1958; William Becker Stewart 1877-1910 & Clarissa Sands Arnold Stewart 1877-1926

Front Row: Harriet Ford Stewart 1853-1927 (Will Stewart's mother); Harriet's father & mother, Dewitt Ford 1826-1909 & Caroline Fairchild Ford 1825-1910; James Stewart 1840-1911 (Will Stewart's father)

Center Front: Caroline Fairchild Stewart 1896-1970 (younger sister of William & Hugh)

Works Cited

Baedeker, Karl. *Belgium and Holland, Including the Grand-Duchy of Luxembourg.* Leipsic: Karl Baedeker, 1901.

Baedeker, Karl. *Great Britain, Handbook for Travelers.* Leipsic: Karl Baedeker, 1897.

Baedeker, Karl. *Italy, Handbook for Travelers. First Part: Northern Italy Including Leghorn, Florence, Ravenna and Routes Through Switzerland and Austria.* Leipsic: Karl Baedeker, 1899. [Purchased in Florence, Italy, March 5, 1901 by Clarissa S. Arnold. The book has numerous notations by Clarissa while in Florence and is protected by a leather cover.]

Baedeker, Karl. *Italy, Handbook for Travelers. Second Part: Central Italy and Rome.* Leipsic: Karl Baedeker, 1900.

Baedeker, Karl. *Italy, Handbook for Travelers. Third Part: Southern Italy and Sicily.* Leipsic: Karl Baedeker, 1900.

Baedeker, Karl. *London and its Environs.* Leipsic: Karl Baedeker, 1898.

Baedeker, Karl. *Northern Germany as Far as the Bavarian and Austrian Frontiers.* Leipsic: Karl Baedeker, 1897.

Baedeker, Karl. *Paris and Environs with Routes from London to Paris.* Leipsic: Karl Baedeker, 1900.

Baedeker, Karl. *The Rhine from Rotterdam to Constance.* Leipsic: Karl Baedeker, 1900.

Baedeker, Karl. *Southern Germany Including Wurtemberg and Bavaria.* Leipsic: Karl Baedeker, 1895.

Baedeker, Karl. *Switzerland and the Adjacent Portions of Italy, Savoy, and Tyrol.* Leipsic: Karl Baedeker, 1899.

Bramblett, Reid, and Jeffrey Kennedy. *DK Eyewitness Top 10 Travel Guides, Rome.* New York: DK Publishing, 2002.

Stowe, William. *Going Abroad, European Travel in Nineteenth-Century American Culture.* Princeton: Princeton University Press, 1994.

Deborah Stewart Weber, editor of Clarissa's Diary, is a great-granddaughter. Born in Cooperstown, New York, not far from Unadilla, she now lives in Sioux Falls, South Dakota, with husband Gary, and Maggie, their small black dog.

LaVergne, TN USA
10 February 2010
172633LV00004B/4/P